Informal Venture Capital

Informal Venture Capital

Evaluating the impact of
business introduction services

Edited by
Richard T. Harrison
University of Ulster at Jordanstown

Colin M. Mason
University of Southampton

 PRENTICE HALL
WOODHEAD-FAULKNER

London   New York   Toronto   Sydney   Tokyo   Singapore
Madrid   Mexico City   Munich

First published 1996 by
Woodhead-Faulkner (Publishers) Limited
Campus 400, Maylands Avenue
Hemel Hempstead
Hertfordshire, HP2 7EZ
A division of
Simon & Schuster International Group

Typeset in 10/12pt Plantin
by Hands Fotoset, Leicester

Printed and bound in Great Britain by
Hartnolls Ltd, Bodmin, Cornwall

British Library Cataloguing in Publication Data

A catalogue record for this book is available from
the British Library

ISBN 0-13-355660-3

1 2 3 4 5   00 99 98 97 96

Contents

Figures

Tables

Contributors

ANDREW BLAIR is founder of the Enterprise Research Foundation for Small Business Studies, 15 Redington Gardens, London NW3 7SA.

RENA BLATT is with Small Business Ontario, Ministry of Industry, Trade and Technology, Government of Ontario, 7th Floor, Hearst Block, 900 Bay Street, Toronto M7A 2E1, Canada.

DONALD J. BROWN holds the McAdams-Frierson Chair of Bank Management in the College of Business at Arkansas State University, PO Box 609, Arkansas 72467, USA.

LUCIUS CARY is founder and managing director of Venture Capital Report Ltd, Boston Road, Henley-on-Thames, Oxfordshire RG9 1DY.

RICHARD COON was a partner in Blackstone Franks Chartered Accountants, Barbican House, 26–34 Old Street, London EC1V 9HL when he wrote the chapter for this book.

JOHN FREEAR is Associate Dean of the Whittemore School of Business and Economics, University of New Hampshire, Durham, New Hampshire 03824-3593, USA.

JIM CLARKE is Assistant Director, Authorisation, Compliance and Enforcement Division, Securities and Investment Board, Gavrelle House, 2–14 Burnhill Row, London EC1Y 8RA.

RICHARD T. HARRISON is Professor of Management Development in the Centre for Executive Development, University of Ulster at Jordanstown, Co. Antrim, Northern Ireland BT37 0QB.

EDWARD KNIGHTON is a director of Priory Investments Ltd, Third Floor, 1–11 Hay Hill, London W1X 7LF.

PETER KOPPEL is with the Danish Technological Institute, Gregersensvej, PO Box 141, DK-2630 Taastrup, Denmark.

HANS LANDSTRÖM is associate professor of industrial management and research coordinator of the Scandinavian Institute for Research in Entrepreneurship, Halmstad University, S-301 18 Halmstad, Sweden.

COLIN MASON is Reader in Economic Geography at the University of Southampton, Southampton SO17 1BJ.

CHRISTER OLOFSSON is Professor in the Department of Economics, The Swedish University of Agricultural Sciences, Box 7013, S-750 07 Uppsala, Sweden.

MARY KAY SULLIVAN is an Assistant Professor of Management at Maryville College, PO Box 2813, Maryville, Tennessee 37801, USA.

ALLAN RIDING is Professor of Finance in the School of Business, Carleton University, 1125 Colonel By Drive, Ottawa K1S 5B6, Canada.

SIMON M. SHORTER's chapter is based on work that he undertook as part of his MBA degree at Manchester Business School, Booth Street West, Manchester M15 6PB.

CHARLES R. B. STOWE is Professor in the Department of General Business and Finance at Sam Houston State University, Huntsville, Texas 77341, USA.

WILLIAM E. WETZEL JR is Director Emeritus of the Center for Venture Research at the Whittemore School of Business and Economics, University of New Hampshire, Durham, New Hampshire 03824-3593, USA.

Preface

The existence of a continuing finance gap for small firms has been the subject of on-going debate in many countries. This gap is particularly identified with a shortage of equity capital, and is experienced most sharply by certain types of firm (notably high-tech ventures) at particular stages of development (especially those looking for seed and start-up capital) and in specific regions (outside the major national financial centres). By the late 1980s the deteriorating availability of finance for small firms reflected two factors. First, the recession had begun and the banks were beginning to experience mounting losses on their small business loan portfolio, with the result that they were becoming more cautious in making further loans to small business – increasingly, concern about the implications of this 'credit crunch' has emerged on an international scale, and is not restricted to the experience of the UK or the USA alone. Second, the venture capital industry, which had already shifted its investment focus away from early stage investments (in both North America and Europe, although to a greater extent in Europe), was encountering increasing difficulties in raising new funds from the institutions.

Although a number of studies undertaken during the 1980s in the USA had demonstrated that the informal venture capital market (that is, the provision of new equity capital by private individuals direct to unquoted businesses in which they have no prior interest) played a major role in the financing of entrepreneurial businesses, this work had not penetrated the UK or the rest of Europe. Following the completion of a study of the Business Expansion Scheme – a UK initiative which attempted, largely unsuccessfully, to encourage private investment in unquoted companies – we embarked on a study in 1990, funded under the ESRC's Small Business Research Initiative, to replicate the US research on informal venture capital in order to discover whether there was an informal venture capital market in the UK. Towards the end of 1990 we presented some preliminary findings from our research at a number of academic and practitioner-oriented conferences. We confirmed that an informal venture capital market did exist in the UK and that it was playing a significant role in channelling risk finance to the SME sector (small and medium-sized enterprises). We also drew attention to a feature of this market, noted in the US research some ten years earlier by Professor William Wetzel, that business angels could not find enough investment opportunities, while entrepreneurs found it difficult to identify and locate business angels because of their passion for anonymity. We concluded, as did Wetzel earlier in the USA, that there is a need for a mechanism which would provide a channel of communication between angels and entrepreneurs to improve the efficiency of the informal venture capital market.

The Small Firms Policy Branch of the UK Employment Department – one of the sponsors of the ESRC research programme – was impressed both at the role played by business angels in financing small firms and by the untapped potential of the informal venture capital market. Towards the end of 1990, Eric Forth MP, the Small Firms Minister at the time, suggested that the government might back the creation of a marriage-broking service for investors and entrepreneurs in an attempt to stimulate informal investment in small businesses. We were subsequently invited to discuss our ideas in more detail with his civil servants in the Small Firms Policy Branch. In the spring of 1991 the Minister visited the USA where he examined some 'match-making' organisations in detail. In the early summer of that year it was announced that the Department of Trade and Industry (which had resumed responsibility for small firms policy) would provide pump-priming finance to support the establishment of a small number of locally or regionally based informal investment demonstration projects. These would test the proposition that bringing together informal investors and small businesses seeking finance by means of a business introduction service does satisfy a genuine market need and offers a potentially worthwhile way of channelling new resources into the small firm sector. The government saw the Training and Enterprise Councils (TECs) – key players in the local enterprise scene – as the most appropriate organisations to operate services of this type, and bids were therefore invited from TECs in England and Wales to operate a small number of pilot business introduction services. In the autumn of 1991 five TECs were selected to run the demonstration projects.

This book reflects the interpenetration of academic research and policy formulation which has characterised this research project, and its publication is testament to the ability of academic research to shape and influence the direction and outcome of public policy. In particular, this book has its origins in a seminar that we organised in January 1992 at Knutsford, Cheshire, on behalf of the Small Firms Policy Branch of the DTI for staff of the five TECs and their partner organisations which were to be involved in managing the business introduction services. The objective was to highlight through research and case studies some of the operational considerations involved in the successful operation of a business introduction service. Earlier versions of the chapters by William Wetzel and John Freear on the Venture Capital Network in the USA (perhaps the best-known business introduction service), Lucius Cary on *Venture Capital Report* (perhaps the longest-established business introduction service), Andrew Blair on a private investor syndicate, Richard Coon on a business introduction service operated by an accountancy firm, Jim Clarke on the implications of the Financial Services Act as well as our overview (Chapter 2) were all presented at the seminar.

These chapters have been supplemented by a number of additional chapters that have been specially commissioned for the book. In addition to our introductory overview of the role and nature of informal venture capital in North America and Europe, we have contributed a further two chapters – an evaluation of LINC, a prominent UK business introduction service, and an interim evaluation of the five TEC informal investment demonstration projects which we were commissioned by the DTI to undertake. A further chapter by Simon Shorter examines the background to the establishment of one of these projects. We invited further chapters by Mary Kay Sullivan and by Donald Brown and Charles Stowe on US developments, and a chapter by Rena Blatt and Allan Riding on COIN, a Canadian business introduction service. Finally, to reflect growing interest in informal venture capital elsewhere in Europe, we invited Hans Landström and Christer Oloffson to contribute a chapter on developments in informal venture capital networks in Sweden, and Peter Koppel to provide an account of developments in Denmark, which have drawn on the experience to date of the USA and the UK.

This book is the first formal output of the International Informal Venture Capital Research Network, an informal (it could hardly be otherwise!) grouping of researchers in North America and Europe involved in informal venture capital research, which was established at the Babson Entrepreneurship Research Conference at the University of Pittsburgh in 1991.

We are grateful to Patrick Taylor-Martin, Mike Yates and Sandra Newton of the Small Firms Policy Branch of the Department of Trade and Industry for involving us in policy developments in this field. It has been exciting to move from 'chalk-face' to 'coal-face'. We are particularly grateful to them for their role in obtaining permission from HMSO to publish a revised version of our interim assessment of the informal investment demonstration projects as a chapter in this book. We are also grateful to all of the contributors for agreeing so readily to participate in this project. Last, but by no means least, we wish to record our thanks to the following who contributed in various ways to the production of this book: Ivor Butcher, for his initial enthusiasm for our proposal, Hazel Cameron, Dr Jim Milne, and Alan Burn and his colleagues in the University of Southampton Cartographic Unit.

Richard Harrison
Belfast, Northern Ireland

Colin Mason
Hedge End, Hampshire

PART I

Informal venture capital and business introduction services

CHAPTER 1

Informal venture capital

Richard T. Harrison and Colin M. Mason

The funding crisis

Despite major changes in the number and range of sources of finance for new and small ventures in recent years, the availability and cost of finance, especially long-term investment capital, is one of the most important constraints on the formation and development of small and medium-sized enterprises (SMEs) (NEDC, 1986; Monck *et al.*, 1988; Mason *et al.*, 1988; ACOST, 1990; Binks *et al.*, 1992; CBI, 1993; EVCA, 1993a; Landström, 1993). Obtaining finance is particularly difficult for new and recently established firms, fast-growing businesses and technology-based businesses. Access to public stock markets is precluded to the vast majority of small businesses because of the high fixed costs involved (Buckland and Davis 1989), while reliance on debt finance leads to dangers of undercapitalisation, which is the most frequent cause of business failure.

In terms of debt finance, banks have curtailed corporate lending as a result of substantial losses arising from Third World debts, international property debts and, increasingly, contemporary corporate failures in both the corporate and SME sectors. The potential for banking practice to constrain entrepreneurial performance is particularly acute during recessionary periods when the inherent conservatism of the banks becomes more visible (Ennew and Binks, 1993), and the current position has led to accusations that, from the SME perspective and from that of other financial institutions in the sector, 'the banks are on strike' (Murray, 1991a: 74).

In the United Kingdom four key areas of difficulty in bank–SME relationships have been identified. First, banks have become more circumspect in their lending by seeking greater security for loans and placing greater importance on the level of gearing, which, in turn, increases the need for firms to raise additional equity finance, in many cases beyond that which can be raised from personal resources (Deakins and Hussain, 1991). No longer can businesses expect to obtain what is in effect equity finance but at overdraft rates of interest (Batchelor, 1991). One significant effect of the recent fall in house prices in the United Kingdom, for example, has been a reduction in the ability of new firm founders to raise loan finance by offering their house as security against a loan or by taking out a second mortgage. The fixation of banks with security is a particular problem for service sector businesses: banks tend to emphasise tangible assets and are uncomfortable with businesses whose key assets take the form of human resources.

Second, banks are giving greater recognition to risk in the financing of loans. Indeed, business size itself, and the associated perception of risk and security, is an important determinant of bank attitudes in its own right, with bank managers regarding the bigger businesses as better than the smaller ones (Vyakarnam and Jacobs, 1991). Third, the cost of bank services, such as cheque clearing, has risen, small firms' access to overdraft facilities has been limited because of the difficulties in recovering much of the credit boom lending of the late 1980s, and there continue to be claims that the margins on loans have widened. It is, in any case, clear that in the United Kingdom at least, heavy reliance on short-term debt finance imposes significant costs on existing and small and medium-sized businesses, and constrains the establishment of new businesses: one recent study, for example, concluded that SMEs were paying between 1.9 per cent above base (the average of the lowest interest rates charged) and 4.5 per cent above base (the average of the highest interest rates charged) for loans and, equivalently, between 2 and 6 per cent for overdrafts, although some loans were made at 7 and 8 per cent above base rate (Scottish Enterprise, 1993: 38). These loadings serve to emphasise the already high real interest rates being experienced in the United Kingdom (Table 1.1).

Finally, in recognition of some of these problems in the lending relationship, and in particular having recognised the need for greater information on how loans to SMEs are to be used and to monitor loans, banks are now undertaking much more detailed investigations of their clients. Ironically, however, the need for more detailed information necessary for an improvement in bank–SME relationships will result in a further increase in the cost of bank-provided finance, and a further stimulus to the deterioration of the relationship on cost, not relationship, grounds (Ennew and Binks, 1993). Greater scrutiny will also mean that it will be much harder for SMEs to use overdrafts and loans as a substitute

Table 1.1 International real interest rates

	1989	1990	1991	1992
Germany	1.90	5.60	5.85	5.43
United States	4.40	2.76	2.97	0.95
Japan	1.94	2.93	4.33	2.98
UK	5.32	5.66	7.41	6.65

Source: Scottish Enterprise (1993: 33).

for equity capital. As a result, the consequence of this new attitude among banks towards lending 'could force small businesses to seek alternative funds from venture capital funds' (*Financial Times*, 1993: 5). Indeed, by the early 1990s a Forum for Private Business survey in the United Kingdom reported that 15 per cent of small business owners were considering raising equity capital (quoted in McMeekin, 1991). The need for the SME sector to diversify its sources of finance is also being recognised by the banking industry. In the UK, for example, the Midland Bank (1992) has highlighted the position of SMEs – with already high levels of gearing built up in the late 1980s, and weak profitability caused by the recession – which will have particular problems in raising finance as the economy picks up. The difficulty of businesses with insufficient collateral to support new borrowings has been exacerbated by the sharp drop in asset values in recent years. Without an increase in working capital, many companies will be at risk from overtrading to meet increased sales during economic recovery: the overhang of existing debt, combined with changes in bank lending practices, has made some businesses reluctant to borrow, increasing the significance of the availability of alternative sources of long-term finance, particularly in the form of equity.

These trends in the availability of loan finance for SMEs are by no means unique to the UK. In the USA, for example, there is much talk of a 'credit crunch' for smaller businesses that do not have access to public markets (Peek and Rosengren, 1992). Losses on real estate following the bursting of the real estate bubble have significantly eroded the capital of banks precisely at the time when regulations concerning their capital requirements had been introduced. In order to conform to regulatory requirements concerning capital-to-asset ratios at a time when their capital has been declining, banks have had to reduce lending. As a consequence, they have not been able to meet the credit needs of SMEs, most of whom are dependent on banks for finance. Goodman and Allen (1992) note that many entrepreneurial firms in the USA are finding it harder to acquire new loans, and are encountering more difficulties in the application/review process, reporting requirements and collateral requirements. Their findings therefore clearly indicate that banks are revoking credit lines on small but creditworthy mid-market companies. The primary strategy being used by SMEs to cope with this credit tightening is short-term cash flow improvement through techniques such as receivables financing, personal refinancing from savings or refinancing home mortgages, and company retrenchment through downsizing, layoffs and salary reductions (Allen and Goodman, 1993). However, as the economy rebounds these 'band-aid' solutions will significantly constrain the ability of SMEs to respond and grow.

At the very time that demand for equity finance is increasing among SMEs, the supply of venture capital – the main institutional source of equity capital – is diminishing. The expansion of venture capital activity in most developed countries during the past ten to fifteen years has provided a new source of long-term investment capital. Venture capital activity originated in the USA immediately after World War II, but expanded enormously during the 1980s as a result of changes in tax and securities legislation. In 1979 there were about 225 venture capital firms, which invested $460 million in 375 companies. At its peak in 1987, over 700 venture capital firms invested $3.94 billion in over 1,700 companies. By the end of the decade this level of activity had fallen back a little, with over $3 billion invested in over 1,300 companies (Bygrave and Timmons, 1992). A similar expansion in venture capital activity occurred during the 1980s in a number of other countries which had little or no prior experience of this form of financial activity. In Canada, the venture capital industry expanded between 1980 and 1990 from 20 firms with a pool of $350 million to about 75 firms and a pool of $3.3 billion (MacDonald, 1991). In the UK prior to 1979, there were about 20 venture capital companies with a total investment of £20 million. By 1993 there were well over 100 venture capital firms which invested £1.23 billion in 1,066 companies (plus a further £191 million in 136 companies in other countries) (BVCA, 1994a). There has also been an increase in venture capital activity in other European countries (EVCA, 1993b). Indeed, Europe has overtaken the USA in terms of venture capital investments (EVCA, 1993a), with a total of 4.7 billion ecu ($1 = 1.13 ecu) invested in 6,197 companies in 1992 (EVCA, 1993b).

The venture capital industry has had a catalytic role in the entrepreneurial process by identifying, financially supporting and nurturing growth-minded businesses with entrepreneurial talent to start up and grow. The evidence for this is most clear cut in the USA. Bygrave and Timmons (1992) note that venture-capital-backed companies have added value through technological and market innovations, while their economic contributions have included significant job creation, new R & D expenditures, export sales and payment of taxes. World-class technology companies such as Digital Equipment Corporation, Apple Computer, Sun Microsystems, Lotus, Compaq and Prime Computer, as well as market innovators such as Federal Express and Staples Inc., were backed by venture capitalists at their start-up. In Europe too, venture-capital-backed companies have, in aggregate, experienced above average rates of employment growth, with the EVCA describing such companies as 'engines for our economies' (EVCA, 1993a: 4). At a subnational level, an active local venture capital industry has played a critical role in the development of 'high-tech' clusters such as Silicon Valley and Route 128 (Florida and Kenney, 1988; Bygrave and Timmons, 1992).

However, the venture capital industry is in a process of change throughout the developed world. Venture capital funds have shifted away from early stage investments in favour of providing development capital and financing management buyouts and buyins (MBOs/MBIs). In the UK, the proportion of total venture capital investment accounted for by start-up and early stage finance was 27 per cent by value and 34 per cent by number of financings in 1984. As Table 1.2 makes clear, however, the proportion of finance (and the amount) being invested in start-up and early stage ventures by the formal venture capital industry has fallen sharply (to 6 per cent in 1993), and the overall average investment per start-up and early stage venture has remained above £300,000 in

Table 1.2 Institutional venture capital in the UK in start-up and early stage companies

	£ million	Number of companies	% of venture capital investment	Average investment (£000)
1989	215	521	15	413
1990	128	340	12	376
1991	58	273	6	212
1992	82	222	7	369
1993	69	236	6	294

Source: BVCA.

the 1990s. One explanation for this shift away from early stage investments in the UK is the significant fixed costs represented by evaluation and monitoring activity preceding and accompanying venture capital investments: for example, initial accountancy and legal fees are unlikely to be less than £50,000, making it uneconomic for a venture capital fund to consider investments below £250,000 (Batchelor, 1993).

There has also been a shift in the focus of the US venture capital industry away from its traditional concern with financing early stage investments in favour of expansions and management buyouts. This trend is attributed by Bygrave and Timmons (1992) to the displacement of 'classic' venture capital by 'merchant capital' funds. Classic venture capital is concerned with early stage investments and involves skills that add value in company forming, building and harvesting; merchant capital funds, on the other hand, are almost entirely dependent upon institutional investors, emphasise financial engineering know-how, transaction crafting and closing and fee generation, and are obsessed with short-term gains. Nevertheless, although the USA has experienced a decline in venture capital investments in start-ups it still accounted for 25 per cent of total financings in 1992 (Gupta, 1993).

A final factor in the decline in the availability of venture capital in the UK is the increasing difficulties experienced by funds in raising additional capital from institutional investors, particularly since 1989, as a result of the increasing ambivalence of institutional investors to venture capital activity, and venture capital fund managers report profound concern over the longer-term availability of funds (Murray, 1991a, 1991b): the supply of new venture capital funds in the United Kingdom fell by 70 per cent between 1989 and 1992 (Murray, 1991b, 1993). The US venture capital industry has also encountered difficulties in raising new funds and is therefore hoarding what finance it has (*Economist*, 1991).

These trends are being viewed with disquiet in both the UK and the USA. In both countries there is growing concern that these changes in the availability of loan and equity finance will adversely affect both the rate of new business formation and the growth of established firms, thereby impairing the ability of the economy to recover from recession (Binks, 1993; Allen and Goodman, 1993). Many SMEs will require additional finance to cope with increased sales, inventory replacement, plant expansion, equipment purchase and R & D investment as the economy recovers, but their ability to raise external finance has been reduced and SMEs' awareness of the various options open to them outside the traditional banking industry (e.g. asset-based financing, private placement, informal investment and strategic alliances) is very limited (Allen and Goodman, 1993).

The role of informal venture capital

There is a widespread recognition, in the context of the emergence of this finance gap, that the reliance of SMEs on debt finance must be reduced and that sources of equity finance need to be increased (Mason and Harrison, 1992). This is not, however, necessarily an appropriate role for the banks themselves to play: the majority of banks (at least in the UK) feel that the culture of the risks inherent in equity investment make it inappropriate for direct provision by themselves (Bank of England, 1995), and their various attempts to operate small-scale venture capital funds have been unsuccessful (Bank of England, 1994). In the USA, a series of studies throughout the 1980s established that a well-developed informal venture capital market plays a major role in meeting the financing needs of smaller companies (Wetzel, 1981, 1986a, 1986b, 1987; Gaston, 1989a, 1989b; Aram, 1989; Neiswander, 1985). The informal venture capital market comprises private individuals – commonly referred to as informal investors, business angels (by analogy with the traditional finances of theatrical productions) or independent investors – who provide risk capital directly to new and growing businesses in which they have no prior connection. According to Wetzel (1986a: 121), angels 'represent the largest pool of risk capital in the US' and 'finance as many as twenty times the number of firms financed by institutional venture capitalists', while 'the aggregate amount they invest is perhaps twice as big' (Wetzel, 1986b: 88). Gaston (1989a) similarly concludes that informal venture capital is the single largest source of external equity capital for small businesses in the United States, almost exceeding all other sources combined. In terms of the value of the investments made, informal investment is almost twice as large as private placements and is eight times larger than institutional venture capital investments (see Chapter 6). Informal investors are particularly important in providing seed and start-up financing; according to Freear and Wetzel (1988: 353), 'private individuals are dominant where relatively small amounts are involved, and in those later stage financings involving under $1 million'. Informal risk capital is also a significant source of external equity capital for small businesses in Canada (Riding and Short, 1987a, 1987b; Short and Riding, 1989; Government of Ontario, 1990).

On the basis of this evidence, the report of the Advisory Committee on Science and Technology (ACOST) in the UK concluded that 'an active informal venture capital market is a pre-requisite for a vigorous enterprise economy' (ACOST, 1990: 41). However, there has been, until recently, no equivalent information to that in the USA on the size of the informal risk capital pool in the UK and the rest of Europe, and its significance as a source of equity capital for SMEs. Many overviews of the availability of finance for small firms have ignored the role – actual or potential – of business angels in the UK (NEDC, 1986; Burns, 1987; Boocock, 1990). The ACOST study observed that 'we do not know of any study which documents its size' (ACOST, 1990: 39), although it suggested that informal investment in the UK remained 'underdeveloped' by comparison with its US equivalent (ACOST, 1990: 41). However, there is evidence that private individuals emerged during the 1980s 'as an alternative source of finance in Britain for the small company which is unable to raise money from more conventional sources' (Batchelor, 1988: 9), and similar trends are reported for Scandinavia (see Chapters 15 and 16 below; Landström, 1993).

This increase in informal investment activity in the UK seems likely to reflect the greater opportunities for wealth accumulation by entrepreneurs and senior managers in industry and commerce, for whom an informal investment may be an attractive speculative investment. Until recently, high rates of taxation made it difficult for such people to accumulate sufficient amounts of disposable capital; most was either tied up in their own businesses or saved through tax-efficient institutional channels (ACOST, 1990). However, the tendency for salaries of senior employees to increase disproportionately, the increasing use of stock options offering the prospect of capital gain, cuts in the top rate of income tax, 'golden handshakes', generous early retirement incentives to senior managers made redundant, high levels of acquisition of small owner-managed companies by the corporate sector, and the creation of the Unlisted Securities Market (USM) and Third Markets to enable entrepreneurs to sell stakes in their companies have all contributed to an increase in the number of business people with disposable wealth. Indeed, a prime source of business angels, as in the USA (Conlin, 1989), is cashed-out entrepreneurs. Anecdotal evidence suggests that the small business sector is often viewed as an attractive 'alternative' investment for some of this newly acquired capital (Batchelor, 1989; Cary, 1993).

The importance of informal venture capital as a source of equity finance for SMEs in the United Kingdom has now been clearly established (Harrison and Mason, 1992a, 1993; Mason and Harrison, 1994). Further evidence from surveys of sources of finance used by small business indicates that private individuals are the most important source of *external* equity capital after family and relatives (Mason and Harrison, 1993; Small Business Research Trust, 1991). Extrapolation of these findings suggests that the size of the UK's informal risk capital pool is in the £2 billion to £4 billion range. To put this figure into some kind of context, the formal venture capital industry has invested about £1 billion per annum in the UK in recent years. However, well over half of this amount was invested in management buyouts, buyins, acquisitions and secondary purchases. Moreover, the average size of informal investments is substantially lower than that made by venture capital funds, so the number of businesses which have raised finance from informal venture capital sources will substantially exceed the number of financings by venture capital funds (1215 in 1993, of which over one-quarter were MBOs/MBIs and secondary purchases) (BVCA, 1994a). Overall, it has been estimated that total institutional venture capital invested in the small business sector in the UK, which is that sector most likely to use informal sources of capital, is around £1.25 billion (Bannock, 1991). In other words, informal venture capital is at least twice as important to the entrepreneurial small venture sector as formal venture capital (Harrison and Mason, 1993).

In this introductory chapter (and in Chapter 14 below), we argue that SMEs are facing a renewed finance gap caused both by recent developments in the banking and venture capital sectors, which are leading to a tightening in the availability of both loan and equity finance, and by inefficiencies in the flow of capital in the market, due to incomplete information on capital sources and investment opportunities. An expansion of the informal venture capital market is, therefore, essential if new and growing businesses are not to be starved of capital. However, the informal venture capital market is disorganised and fragmented, limiting its ability to assume a significantly greater role in the financing of SMEs. Providers of finance experience a shortage of investment opportunities, while, at the same time, businesses seeking finance are unable to identify business angels. The establishment of a network of business introduction services to provide a channel of information between investors and businesses offers a means of overcoming these difficulties and improving market efficiency (see Chapter 4). This concept is attracting growing interest from national and local governments and from organisations responsible for local or regional economic development as well as from the private sector. Many of these initiatives are reviewed in subsequent chapters in this volume. Our objective in the remainder of this chapter is to review the nature of the informal venture capital market and identify alternative mechanisms for closing the information gap which prevents the effective flow of investment capital.

Informal venture capital: an overview

Informal investors are a heterogeneous group, comprising at one extreme someone who may make one such investment in a lifetime, perhaps to help a friend set up in business, and at the other extreme someone who is continuously on the lookout for investment opportunities and makes frequent investments. Based on UK evidence, the 'typical' business angel is a relatively infrequent investor (Mason and Harrison, 1994): most make no more than one investment per year, although there is a small minority of more active investors. On average, they invest in around 8 per cent of the investment opportunities that they identify. They learn of investment opportunities primarily from friends and business associates. The key factors in their decision whether or not to invest are the quality of management and the growth potential of the business. They seek a financial return on their investments in the form of capital appreciation, although many informal investors are also motivated, in part, by non-financial considerations.

Informal investors generally inject very small amounts of capital into the firms in which they invest, typically in the range £10,000 to £30,000. Only a minority of angels commit more than £50,000 to a single investment (Table 1.3). Investments that are syndicated between a number of informal investors involve larger amounts. Informal investments include direct equity as well as loans and loan guarantees (Mason and Harrison, 1994). However, our survey of LINC members indicates that they invest much larger amounts (Mason *et al.*, 1991; see also Chapter 7), which in turn suggests that informal investors who participate in financial match-making services are biased towards the more active end of the spectrum.[1] Their lower investment frequency reflects the greater amount of information on investment opportunities that they receive as a result of their membership of a match-making organisation. Informal investors make investments in virtually all industrial sectors and at all stages of company development, although with a bias towards early stage ventures. However, they have a strong preference for investing in companies that are located fairly close to where they live and work (typically within 100 miles). This geographic pattern of investment partly reflects the localised nature of the referral sources used by informal investors in generating deal flow. However, it also reflects the desire of most informal investors to play an active 'hands on' role in the businesses in which they invest. Thus, by raising finance from business angels, small firms can benefit from the substantial commercial skills and entrepreneurial experience of their investors. Informal investors, therefore, contribute to closing both the equity gap and the people/experience gap which constrain the development of SMEs. Most

Table 1.3 Some dimensions of informal investment activity in the UK

	Informal investors survey	LINC investors survey
Size of sample	86	53
Number (percentage) of respondents who had made informal investments in the previous three years	60 (70%)	33 (62%)
Percentage of investment opportunities seriously considered	17	10
Total number of investments made in previous three years	172	76
Deal acceptance rate	8%	2%
Median amount invested per investor in the past three years (loans and equity)	£22,000	£100,000
Median amount invested per firm	<£10,000	£30,000
Proportion of syndicated deals	36%	42%

Sources: Mason and Harrison (1994); Mason *et al.* (1991).

small business owners who have raised finance from informal investors report that their role as a sounding board is particularly valuable (Harrison and Mason, 1992b). Finally, they usually accept a minority equity position and are often prepared to take a relatively long-term view of the investment.

In general, this profile of the attitudes, behaviours and characteristics of UK informal investors closely parallels that for other countries, including Sweden, the United States and Canada (see Tables 1.4 and 1.5): as has been pointed out elsewhere (Harrison and Mason, 1992a) there are few statistically significant differences in investor characteristics. However, as Table 1.3 above suggests for the UK, and as Gaston (1989b) has suggested for the USA, the population of informal investors is heterogeneous. Accordingly, as subsequent chapters in this volume make clear, different types of business introduction service are appropriate for different types of investor. Furthermore, despite their broad similarity in characteristics, the significance of informal investment in the UK is generally regarded as small when compared with the situation in the USA (ACOST, 1990; Bannock, 1991).

Despite the declining availability of alternative sources of loan and equity finance, the informal venture capital market remains largely underutilised by small businesses. Most informal investors want to invest more, but cannot find sufficient investment opportunities that meet their investment criteria. For example, in the UK between seven and nine out of every ten informal investors would have invested more if they had come across a greater number of suitable investment opportunities. As a result, many informal investors have substantial uncommitted funds available, equivalent to up to three times the total amount that they had invested during the previous three years (Table 1.6).[2]

This reflects the nature of the informal risk capital market, which a leading US authority has described as 'a giant game of hide-and-seek with everyone blindfolded' (Gaston, 1989b: 4). Informal investors have a preference for anonymity (for obvious reasons) and so are largely invisible. Unlike venture capital funds, they are not listed in any directories. As a result, the search by an

Table 1.4 Informal investor characteristics: international comparisons

	United Kingdom	Sweden	USA	Canada
Age (years)	53	54	47	47
Sex	99% male	–	95% male	98% male
Annual family income	£46,000	60% > 500,000 SEK	$90,000	$176,800 (Cdn)
Net worth	£312,000	57% > 5m SEK	$750,000	$1.36m (Cdn)
Previous entrepreneurial experience	57%	96%	83%	75%

Sources: UK: Mason and Harrison (1994); Harrison and Mason (1992a);
Sweden: Landström (1993); USA: Gaston (1989b); Canada: Riding *et al.* (1993);
Venture Economics (1990).

Table 1.5 Informal investor investment behaviour: international comparisons

	United Kingdom	Sweden	USA	Canada
Number of investments	2 every 3 years	1 a year	2 every 3 years	1 a year
Rejection rate	7 out of 8	7 out of 10	7 out of 9	9 out of 10
Average size of investment	£10,000	500,000 SEK	$58,900	$207,000 (Cdn)
% of net worth accounted for by informal investments	53% < 10%	33% < 10% 33% 10–24% 33% > 24%	–	40% < 10%
Primary sources of information on investment opportunities	Business associates; friends		Friends; business associates	Knew the entrepreneur; friends; business associates
Main sectors	Retail/wholesale; consumer services; high-tech manufacturing	Finance/real estate; manufacturing industrial products	Retail/wholesale; finance/ real estate; services; high-tech manufacturing	natural resources; manufacturing – industrial and commercial; real estate
Main stage of business development	Young firms (34%) Start-ups (30%) Established firms (18%)	Infant/young firms (43%) Established firms (31%) Start-ups (27%)	Start-ups (56%) Infant/young firms (24%) Established firms (20%)	Seed and start-up (30%) 1st stage (15%) Expansion (43%)
Location of investments (distance from home)	67% < 100 miles 54% < 50 miles		72% < 50 miles	53% < 50 miles
Involvement with investee business	69%	93%	83%	85%
Most common types of involvement	Board of directors; consulting	Board of directors; consulting	Consulting; working part-time	Board of directors; consulting
Minority voting control	81%	65%	56%	(10% majority ownership)
Proportion of those who wish to make more investments	75%	75%	54%	–
Amount available for investment	£50,000	1.5m SEK	–	–

Source: As for Table 1.4.

Table 1.6 Availability of informal risk capital

	Informal investors survey	LINC investors survey
Proportion of investors who want to invest more	70%	86%
Median amount available for investment	£50,000	£100,000
Ratio of amount available for investment to the amount invested in the previous three years	3:1	1.4:1

Sources: As for Table 1.3.

entrepreneur for private sources of venture capital is often unsuccessful. The search by informal investors for investment opportunities is also frequently unsuccessful. Because of the considerable time required to search for and appraise investment opportunities, and the fact that for most investors it is not a full-time occupation, they generally adopt an *ad hoc*, unscientific and passive approach, placing considerable reliance on friends and business associates for referrals. Thus, serendipity largely determines the number and quality of investment opportunities that come to an investor's attention. Not surprisingly, the proportion of informal investors in our survey, most of whom were not members of any business introduction service, who were dissatisfied with existing channels of communication with businesses seeking finance exceeded those who thought that such channels were satisfactory (Figure 1.1). Dissatisfaction with

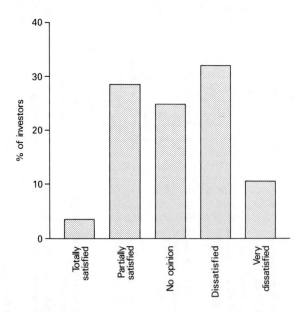

Figure 1.1 Investor satisfaction with existing channels of communication with businesses seeking finance.

existing channels of communication with businesses seeking finance was greatest in the Midlands and North (including Scotland and Wales): 75 per cent of investors in these regions were dissatisfied or very dissatisfied with existing channels of communication with businesses seeking finance, compared with only 30 per cent of investors in London and the South East, East Anglia and the South West.[3] It can be inferred from this evidence that many informal investors – particularly in the 'provinces' – believe that there is a need for better information sources on informal investment opportunities.

Improving information channels in the informal risk capital market: the role of business introduction services

Various economic development bodies and private sector organisations have responded to this evidence of market inefficiency by establishing business introduction services – alternatively termed financial marriage bureaux, financial match-making services or business referral services. These services seek to overcome the two major sources of inefficiency in the informal venture capital market, namely the invisibility of business angels and the high search costs of angels for businesses and businesses for angels, by enabling entrepreneurs to locate private investors and providing investors with a means of identifying and examining investment proposals.

Most of the business introduction services in North America are based on providing a computer matching service (Texas Capital Network, 1994). The first of these services – the Venture Capital Network (VCN) – was established at the University of New Hampshire in 1984, primarily to serve investors and businesses in New England (Wetzel, 1984, 1986a, 1986b, 1987; Foss, 1985). It is now operated as the Technology Capital Network by the MIT Enterprise Forum Inc. of Cambridge, Mass. VCN has made its copyrighted materials and software available for purchase and provides a training course, enabling the system to be replicated by 21 other organisations in 19 other states in the USA and also in Canada, although not always successfully (Table 1.7) (see also Chapters 3 and 6).

Computerised matching services all work in essentially the same manner. Investors complete a short questionnaire (about four pages) which provides details of the types of investment opportunity that are of interest to them. Entrepreneurs also complete a short questionnaire which provides information on the characteristics of the business venture and enclose an executive summary of their business plan. Once the questionnaires are computerised, a three-stage matching process takes place. The computer first searches among its investor subscribers for angels whose investment preferences match the characteristics of the business seeking finance. Then, when matches are found, the entrepreneur's application, which provides a description of the investment opportunity, is sent to the matched-up angel. If the investor is interested, further information can be

Table 1.7 Computer match-making services in the USA and Canada

Network name	Location	Area served	Registration fees	
			Companies	Investors[a]
Venture Capital Network	Cambridge, MA	Mostly North East	$250 p.a.	$250 p.a.
Georgia Capital Network	Atlanta, GA	Georgia	$75 p.a.	None
Kentucky Investment Capital Network	Frankfort, KY	Kentucky	None	None
Mid-Atlantic Investment Network	College Park, MD	Mostly mid-Atlantic	$35 p.a.	$300 p.a.
Northwest Capital Network	Portland, OR	Oregon	$100 p.a.	$225 p.a.
Pacific Venture Capital Network	Irvine, CA	Mostly California	$200 6 mths	$200 p.a.
Private Investor Network	Aitken, SC	South Carolina	$100 p.a.	$200
Tennessee Venture Capital Network	Murfreesboro, TN	Tennessee	$100 6 mths	None
Texas Capital Network	Austin, TX	Texas	$100 6 mths	$200 p.a.
Venture Capital Network of Minnesota	St Paul, MN	Mostly Minnesota	$100 6 mths	$100 6 mths
Washington Investment Network	Seattle, WA	Washington	None	None
Venture Capital Exchange	Tulsa, OK	Mostly Oklahoma and adjacent states	$100 p.a.	$100 p.a.
Canada Opportunities Investment Network (COIN)	Toronto, Ont.	Throughout Canada	$195 Cdn/ $295 Cdn p.a.[b]	$295 Cdn p.a.

[a] Individual subscription rate: many organisations have a higher subscription for organisations.
[b] Individual and corporate rates respectively.
Source: INC (1991: 166), with additions.

requested in the form of an executive summary of the entrepreneur's business plan. Up to this stage, names are not disclosed to either party. However, if the investor wishes to go further, the matching service will provide an exchange of names and telephone numbers so that both parties can meet. Because of the operation of Securities and Exchange Commission guidelines, the involvement of the matching service ends at this point. What happens after direct contact is made is strictly a matter for the angels and entrepreneur (Gaston, 1989b).

An alternative approach is to provide a forum at which selected entrepreneurs can present their business plans to a group of selected investors. The Enterprise Corporation of Pittsburgh, for example, organises regular meetings at which entrepreneurial businesses are introduced to private investors in this way. It also organises a 'Venture Capital Fair' at which emerging high-growth-potential businesses make presentations to venture capitalists and merchant bankers. Both activities are just part of a much broader range of initiatives, all of which are designed 'to assist entrepreneurs in developing new businesses with significant employment potential in the Pittsburgh area'. The latter event is similar to the 'Growth Capital Symposium', which the University of Michigan has organised since 1979 to give owner-managers of selected emerging growth companies the opportunity to present their companies and management teams to a range of investor types, including venture capitalists, larger companies seeking strategic partners, investment bankers, private investors and professional service firms, and to demonstrate their products or services (Brophy and Chalmers, 1991). A number of comparable programmes have been developed elsewhere in the USA, including the Pennsylvania Private Investors Group, established in 1991 to provide seed funds to start-ups. This group of 30 successful entrepreneurs and chief executives has since provided more than $2 million to eight ventures (Gupta, 1993).

A third approach to match making is by means of some kind of publication, which provides a listing of businesses seeking finance that is circulated either to subscribers or to targeted potential investors. This may be either a stand-alone activity or undertaken in conjunction with other forms of matching system. For example, the Investment Matching Service of Alberta, an initiative of the government of Alberta, publishes a catalogue giving brief details of companies seeking finance to support a computer-matching referral system.

For the most part, business introduction services in the USA and Canada are operated by not-for-profit organisations such as universities and chambers of commerce. Most are funded through a combination of subscriptions and state/provincial and national government programmes, charitable foundations and sponsorship from banks, public utility companies, CPA firms and other firms having an interest in local economic growth. For example, seed capital for VCN was provided by the Business and Industry Association of New Hampshire in the form of an interest-free loan. Subsequent funding was obtained from the US Economic Development Administration, corporate sponsors (three international accounting firms, a firm of attorneys, and a computer company) a charitable foundation and the University of New Hampshire (which also provided office space and all utilities except telephones) (see Chapter 3). Venture Capital Exchange is funded by a charitable foundation (Hisrich, 1988). The Enterprise Corporation of Pittsburgh is financed by various corporate, community and family foundations in the Pittsburgh area and through grants from the Ben Frankin Partnership. COIN is an initiative of the Ontario Chamber of Commerce, but has also received provincial and federal funding and some corporate sponsorship (see Chapter 4). Finally, the Investment Matching Service of Alberta is entirely funded by the government of Alberta.

The situation in the United Kingdom is much more diverse. A threefold typology can be identified. The first category comprises commercial *private sector, for-profit match-making initiatives*. These, in turn, can be subdivided into two categories. The first group are stand-alone activities. The most prominent example is *Venture Capital Report*, which was founded in 1978 (see Chapter 8).

It publishes a monthly investment bulletin containing between five and ten articles on entrepreneurs seeking to raise risk capital. These articles, which are researched and written by VCR staff on the basis of information supplied by the entrepreneur in a questionnaire and subsequent meeting, provide a detailed account of both the strengths of the project and any missing ingredients, both financial and non-financial. Subscribers can make contact directly with any of the businesses in which they are interested (Cary, 1991).

A number of other national business introduction services, operated on a commercial basis, have recently been established in the UK. Capital Exchange, which was formed in 1992, publishes a national listing of businesses seeking finance. VentureNet, which was launched in mid-1994, and is a subsidiary of the Enterprise Support Group, a private sector business consulting firm which came into existence following an MBO from 3i, provides a computerised database of investment opportunities which private investors can have access to in order to perform their own searches using their own investment criteria. Most recently, National Westminster Bank has launched its NatWest Angels Service (in November 1994), initially on a pilot basis for six months following a study which identified the need for a national business angels introduction service provided by an organisation with credibility in the area of finance (Innovation Partnership, 1993). The rationale for this initiative was set out as follows: 'as part of the total debt/equity funding package, business angels can play a major role in helping . . . firms develop into strong, truly competitive businesses with a real opportunity to achieve their full potential' through the provision of both finance and value-added skills (*Innovation Business*, 1994).

A number of other free-standing, for-profit business introduction services have also been launched over the years. However, most have disappeared, suggesting that they have been unable to operate at a profit. One example is Venture Associates, which was established by an ex-Lloyds' broker. He encountered problems in developing a client base of businesses and investors. In addition, his professional advisers warned him that he was technically in breach of the Financial Services Act. As a result, he wound up Venture Associates after less than a year. Nevertheless, such experiences do not appear to deter others from attempting to develop such ventures on a for-profit basis.

The second category of private, for-profit business introduction services are those which have been established by accountancy firms as an adjunct to their main activities. These have generally been established by smaller, local accountancy practices (the business introduction services of the large accountancy firms tending to be targeted at businesses for sale). Such services are typically small-scale, low-profile and locally focused, and identify matches in a highly personalised way. One example is Saxon, Todd and Co., a Cheshire-based firm of accountants with 37 investors on its books (*Manchester Evening News*, 18 October 1991). However, there are exceptions. For example, Blackstone Franks, a London-based firm of accountants, has recently formed a business introduction service as part of its corporate finance division (see Chapter 11). Blackstone

Franks publishes a regular investment opportunities bulletin, although most of the matching is undertaken through a personalised approach.

The second main category comprises *local enterprise agencies*. LINC, the Local Investment Networking Company, was established in 1987 to integrate the financial marriage bureaux of various local enterprise agencies into a nationwide business introduction service (see Chapter 7). A number of the founding enterprise agencies have subsequently dropped out. Currently LINC has 12 active member agencies. Following its own commissioned research into informal investment in Scotland (KPMG, 1992), Scottish Enterprise has provided funding to enable LINC to operate throughout Scotland. LINC publishes a monthly investment bulletin that provides a 60-word description of businesses seeking finance, which is circulated to subscribers. Investors wishing further particulars on any of the investment opportunities appearing in the bulletin can request a business plan summary. It also has a computer database to match each business with the most suitable investor. Some of the member agencies also organise investors' meetings at which entrepreneurs present their business plans to an audience of potential investors. A related scheme – BP Innovation LINC – was launched to operate alongside LINC, to introduce inventors with marketable ideas to private investors who are interested in funding technical businesses. At its peak this scheme was administered by 22 enterprise agencies; it has now effectively ceased operation and its activities have been subsumed under those of LINC itself (Figure 1.2).

The third category comprises *public sector business introduction services*. Some local authorities have established 'marriage bureaux', although with varying degrees of success. One of the most successful has been *Cheshire Contacts*, a quarterly bulletin published by Cheshire County Council. This provides both a confidential business investment introduction service, listing businesses seeking finance and individuals and organisations looking for investment, and also business-to-business advertising for a range of business opportunities either available or wanted (e.g. technical, business and consultancy services). The publication also lists executives available and wanted. The *Cheshire Contacts* experience has subsequently formed the basis for the development of one of the recent DTI TEC-based demonstration projects (Chapter 14). A number of other public sector organisations have also been involved in establishing business introduction services, although generally with limited success. For example, the Rural Development Commission set up 'Investorlink' in Wiltshire, but this initiative did not survive the loss of its founder when he moved to another post within the RDC. The range of organisations operating business introduction services has recently been expanded as a result of government interest in promoting informal investment activity. The Department of Trade and Industry has provided £20,000 per annum for three years to support the establishment of five projects selected from a total of 19 bids (see Chapter 14). A number of other TECs, including some that were unsuccessful in their bids to be selected as one of the pilot projects, have also established their own business introduction

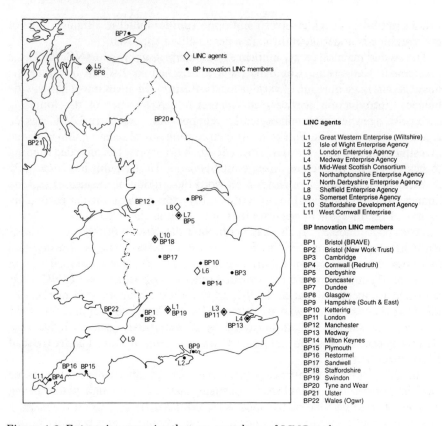

LINC agents

L1   Great Western Enterprise (Wiltshire)
L2   Isle of Wight Enterprise Agency
L3   London Enterprise Agency
L4   Medway Enterprise Agency
L5   Mid-West Scottish Consortium
L6   Northamptonshire Enterprise Agency
L7   North Derbyshire Enterprise Agency
L8   Sheffield Enterprise Agency
L9   Somerset Enterprise Agency
L10 Staffordshire Development Agency
L11 West Cornwall Enterprise

BP Innovation LINC members

BP1   Bristol (BRAVE)
BP2   Bristol (New Work Trust)
BP3   Cambridge
BP4   Cornwall (Redruth)
BP5   Derbyshire
BP6   Doncaster
BP7   Dundee
BP8   Glasgow
BP9   Hampshire (South & East)
BP10 Kettering
BP11 London
BP12 Manchester
BP13 Medway
BP14 Milton Keynes
BP15 Plymouth
BP16 Restormel
BP17 Sandwell
BP18 Staffordshire
BP19 Swindon
BP20 Tyne and Wear
BP21 Ulster
BP22 Wales (Ogwr)

Figure 1.2 Enterprise agencies that are members of LINC and
BP Innovation LINC.

services (BVCA, 1993; 1994b). In addition to LINC, which operates across the
country with 12 local participating agencies (including Scotland), there are now
at least 13 locally operating public not-for-profit business introduction services
in the UK (BVCA, 1994b).

As is the case with venture capital, the UK leads the rest of Europe in the
promotion of informal risk capital. Our knowledge is patchy, although our
impression is that activity is limited. However, the existence of informal
investment activity is confirmed in a number of European countries, including
the Netherlands (van Peer, 1988), Sweden (Landström, 1991 and Chapter 15),
Denmark (Chapter 16) and France, where Welles (1991: 106) comments that 'yet
a new phenomenon is arising in the provinces: entrepreneurs who have built
companies are now turning to finance new ones'.

Conclusion

The informal venture capital market plays a major role in the development of entrepreneurial companies, and, in the UK context, the underdevelopment of this market is 'a major gap in the spectrum of funds for smaller companies and a major contribution to barriers to growth' (ACOST, 1990: 39). A significant element in the underdevelopment of this market is the existence of inefficiencies which limit its potential role in financing SMEs. Most informal investors want to invest more, but cannot find sufficient investment opportunities which meet their investment criteria; entrepreneurs seeking capital also experience difficulty in identifying potential informal investors. In the absence of effective channels for investors and entrepreneurs to make contact with each other, and in view of the considerable time to search for and appraise investment opportunities, combined with the fact that for most investors it is a spare-time activity, investors generally adopt an *ad hoc*, unscientific and passive approach, relying heavily on friends and business associates for referrals. Equally, informal investors comprise an unorganised, fragmented and, because of their desire for anonymity, largely invisible market which makes them very difficult to identify by entrepreneurs seeking private sources of venture capital.

Although market inefficiency is characteristic of all countries, as many of the following chapters demonstrate, there is evidence to suggest that its severity is even greater outside the USA. A comparison of the informal venture capital market in the USA and the UK (Harrison and Mason, 1992a) indicates that the inefficiencies which characterise the market in the UK are compounded as a result of three factors: first, less effective information networks leading to lower-quality information on investment opportunities and more redundant information; second, generally less experienced and less sophisticated investors; and third, the limited involvement of UK informal investors in investment syndicates. These three factors are in turn reflected in the significantly higher deal flow received by UK informal investors and their lower investment rate compared to their US equivalents, and the higher proportions of UK informal investors who are unable to find enough deals and are dissatisfied with existing channels of communication with businesses seeking finance.

The establishment of business introduction services, to provide such channels of communication, represents one effective way of overcoming the sources of inefficiency in the informal venture market represented by the invisibility of informal investors, the fragmented nature of the market and the high search costs for businesses seeking investors and investors seeking investment opportunities. Such services enable entrepreneurs to bring their investment proposals to the attention of a number of private investors simultaneously, and provides investors with a convenient means of identifying and examining a range of investment proposals while retaining their anonymity until they are ready to enter negotiations with an entrepreneur.

As the case study evidence from the USA, Canada, the UK and Scandinavia presented in this volume makes clear, the establishment of business introduction services is not, of itself, a panacea for the equity gap. However, five groups of economic benefits arising from the establishment of effective well-resourced business introduction services can be identified. First, these services facilitate introductions and matches between investors and entrepreneurs which raise the overall level of informal investment activity. Second, these services provide firms, and to a lesser extent investors, with business advice, counselling and signposting services which are of value in their own right, even where investments are not made. Third, as most informal investors are hands-on investors, investments facilitated by these services bring access to a potentially wide range of other investor inputs such as know-how, contacts, advice and consultancy. Fourth, the secondary effects, or collateral benefits, of investments facilitated by business introduction services including the firm's ability to raise additional equity or loan finance on the strength of the initial investment, may be significant, and in many cases may outweigh the direct investment. Fifth, the operation of a business introduction service, by mobilising what would otherwise be fragmented and invisible sources of risk capital to make them accessible to small businesses, contributes to awareness raising amongst investors, businesses and professional and support networks of informal venture capital issues. Taking all of these value-added impacts into account, the evidence collected in this volume confirms that business introduction services are a worthwhile and beneficial experiment. As we suggest in the next chapter, however, they remain at the trial and error stage. Accordingly, the prospects for new initiatives will be enhanced if they seek to learn from the pioneering schemes and recognise the diversity of the informal investor population.

Notes

1. Further support for this conclusion is provided by Blackstone Franks' business introduction service, in which investors typically have in excess of £100,000 available for investment and are looking to put £50,000 to £250,000 in a single investment (Chapter 11).
2. However, it is not known how liquid these funds are. Some evidence from COIN in Canada suggests that the amount which investors state they have available for investment is likely to be an underestimate, and they may be willing to invest more in practice at the deal stage, or will bring in friends/associates to provide additional finance (see Chapter 4 for a further discussion of COIN).
3. However, this conclusion should be treated with some caution in view of the small number of respondents ($N = 28$) to this question.

References

Advisory Council on Science and Technology (ACOST) (1990) *The Enterprise Challenge: Overcoming barriers to growth in small firms*, London: HMSO.

Allen, K. R. and J. Goodman (1993) 'The working capital crisis: how rapidly growing firms are coping', paper presented at the 13th Babson Entrepreneurship Research Conference, University of Houston.

Aram, J. (1989) 'Attitudes and behaviours of informal investors toward early-stage investments, technology-based ventures and co-investors', *Journal of Business Venturing*, **4**, pp. 333–47.

Bank of England (1994) *Finance for Small Firms*, London: Bank of England.

Bank of England (1995) *Finance for Small Firms: A second report*, London: Bank of England.

Bannock, Graham and Partners Ltd (1991) *Venture Capital and the Equity Gap*, London: Graham Bannock and Partners Ltd on behalf of the National Westminster Bank plc.

Batchelor, C. (1988) 'Private financing: money and time to offer', *Financial Times*, 19 July, p. 9.

Batchelor, C. (1989) 'Business angels: an investment of time and money', *Financial Times*, 21 November, p. 21.

Batchelor, C. (1991) 'Venturing into fresh fields to find finance', *Financial Times*, 17 September, p. 14.

Batchelor, C. (1993) 'From lender to investor', *Financial Times*, 23 March, p. 15.

Binks, M. (1993) 'Sources of finance for small and medium-sized enterprises in the UK: the banks', paper presented at a CBI Workshop on Finance for SMEs.

Binks, M. R., C. T. Ennew and C. V. Reed (1992) 'Information asymmetries and the provision of finance to small firms', *International Small Business Journal*, **11**(1), pp. 35–46.

Boocock, J. G. (1990) 'An examination of non-bank funding for small and medium-sized enterprises in the UK', *Service Industries Journal*, **10**, pp. 124–46.

British Venture Capital Association (1993) *A Guide to Business Introduction Services*, London: BVCA.

British Venture Capital Association (BVCA) (1994a) *1993 Report on Investment Activity*, London: BVCA.

British Venture Capital Association (BVCA) (1994b) *Sources of Business Angel Capital 1994/95*, London: BVCA.

Brophy, D. J. and B. R. Chalmers (1991) 'The growth capital symposium: an intervention into the market for venture capital', paper presented at the 11th Babson Entrepreneurship Research Conference, University of Pittsburgh.

Buckland, R. and E. W. Davies (1989) *The Unlisted Securities Market*, Oxford: Clarendon Press.

Burns, P. (1987) 'Financing the growing firm', *Proceedings of the 10th National Small Firms Policy and Research Conference*, Cranfield School of Management, Cranfield Institute of Technology.

Bygrave, W. D. and J. A. Timmons (1992) *Venture Capital at the Crossroads*, Boston, MA: Harvard Business School Press.

Cary, L. (1991) *The Venture Capital Report Guide to Venture Capital in Europe*, 5th edn, London: Pitman.

Cary, L. (1993) *The Venture Capital Report Guide to Venture Capital in Europe*, 6th edn, London: Pitman.

Confederation of British Industry (CBI) (1993) *Finance for Growth: Meeting the needs of small and medium enterprises*, London: CBI.

Conlin, E. (1989) 'Adventure capital', *INC Magazine*, September, pp. 32–48.

Deakins, D. and G. Hussain (1991) *Risk Assessment by Bank Managers*, Birmingham: Department of Financial Services, Birmingham Polytechnic Business School.

Economist (1991) 'Venture capital: plenty to gain?', 7 December, p. 126.

Ennew, C. and M. R. Binks (1993) 'Financing entrepreneurship in recession: does the banking relationship constrain performance?', paper presented at the 13th Babson Entrepreneurship Research Conference, University of Houston.

European Venture Capital Association (EVCA) (1993a) 'Venture capital in Europe: its role and development', *Venture Capital Policy Paper*, Zaventem, Belgium: EVCA.

European Venture Capital Association (EVCA) (1993b) *EVCA Yearbook*, London and Zaventem, Belgium: KPMG and EVCA.

Financial Times (1993) 'Business adjusts to tighter credit', 27 February, p. 5.

Florida, R. L. and M. Kenney (1988) 'Venture capital and high technology entrepreneurship', *Journal of Business Venturing*, 3, pp. 301–19.

Foss, D. C. (1985) 'Venture Capital Network: the first six months of an experiment', in J. A. Hornaday, E. Shils, J. A. Timmons and K. H. Vesper (eds.), *Frontiers of Entrepreneurship Research 1985*, Wellesley, MA: Babson College, pp. 314–24.

Freear, J. and W. Wetzel (1988) 'Equity financing for new technology-based firms', in B. A. Kirchhoff, W. A. Long, W. E. McMullen, K. H. Vesper and W. E. Wetzel (eds.), *Frontiers of Entrepreneurship Research 1988*, Wellesley, MA: Babson College, pp. 347–67.

Gaston, R. J. (1989a) 'The scale of informal capital markets', *Small Business Economics*, 1, pp. 223–30.

Gaston, R. J. (1989b) *Finding Private Venture Capital for your Firm: A complete guide*, New York: Wiley.

Goodman, J. P. and K. R. Allen (1992) 'The credit crunch: are Federal policies putting entrepreneurial firms on a debt diet?', paper presented at the 12th Babson Entrepreneurship Research Conference, INSEAD, Fontainebleau.

Government of Ontario (1986) *The Ontario Investment Network*, Small Business Advocacy Report No. 9, Toronto: Small Business Branch, Ministry of Industry, Trade and Technology.

Government of Ontario (1990) *The State of Small Business: 1990 annual report on small business in Ontario*, Small Business Ontario, Ministry of Industry, Trade and Technology, Toronto.

Gupta, U. (1993) 'The flow of venture capital to small companies nearly doubled in 1992', *Wall Street Journal*, 1 June, p. 132.

Harrison, R. T. and C. M. Mason (1992a) 'International perspectives on the supply of informal venture capital', *Journal of Business Venturing*, 7, pp. 459–75.

Harrison, R. T. and C. M. Mason (1992b) 'The roles of investors in entrepreneurial companies: a comparison of informal investors and venture capitalists', Venture Finance Research Project, Working Paper No. 5, Southampton: Urban Policy Research Unit, University of Southampton.

Harrison, R. T. and C. M. Mason (1993) 'Finance for the growing business: the role of informal investment', *National Westminster Bank Quarterly Review*, May, pp. 17–29.

Hisrich, R. D. (1988) 'New business formation through the Enterprise Development Centre: a model for new venture creation', *IEEE Transactions on Engineering Management*, 35, pp. 221–31.

Innovation Business (1994) 'Business angels: NatWest to launch service for private investors', no. 7, p. 2.

Innovation Partnership (1993) Extracts from a study into Private Investor Networks commissioned by National Westminster Bank plc Technology Unit, The Innovation Partnership Ltd, Manchester.

KPMG Management Consulting (1992) *Investment Networking*, Glasgow: Scottish Enterprise.

Landström, H. (1991) 'Private investors in Sweden: an agency theory approach', paper to the RENT V Research in Entrepreneurship 5th Workshop, Vaxjo University.

Landström, H. (1993) 'Informal risk capital in Sweden and some international comparisons', *Journal of Business Venturing*, 8, pp. 525–40.

MacDonald, M. (1991) *Creating Threshold Technology Companies in Canada: The role for venture capital*, Ottawa: Science Council of Canada.

Mason C. M., J. Harrison and R. T. Harrison (1988) *Closing the Equity Gap? An assessment of the business expansion scheme*, London: Small Business Research Trust.

Mason, C. M. and R. T. Harrison (1992) 'The supply of equity finance in the UK: a strategy for closing the equity gap', *Entrepreneurship and Regional Development*, 4, pp. 357–80.

Mason, C. M. and R. T. Harrison (1993) 'Informal risk capital: a review of US and UK evidence', in R. Atkins, E. Chell and C. Mason (eds.), *New Directions in Small Business Research*, Aldershot: Avebury, pp. 155–76.

Mason, C. M. and R. T. Harrison (1994) 'The informal venture capital market in the UK', in A. Hughes and D. J. Storey (eds.), *Financing Small Firms*, London: Routledge, pp. 64–111.

Mason C. M., R. T. Harrison and J. Chaloner (1991) *The Operation and Effectiveness of LINC. Part 1: Survey of investors*, Southampton: Urban Policy Research Unit, University of Southampton.

McMeekin, D. (1991) 'Finance for enterprise: closing the equity gap', paper to the 14th Small Firms Policy and Research Conference, Lancashire Enterprises Ltd/ Manchester Business School.

Midland Bank (1992) *The Changing Financial Requirements of Smaller Companies*, London: Midland Bank Business Economics Unit.

Monck, C. P. S., R. B. Porter, P. R. Quintas, D. J. Storey and P. Wynarczyk (1988) *Science Parks and the Growth of High Technology Firms*, Beckenham, Kent: Croom Helm.

Murray, G. (1991a) 'The changing nature of competition in the UK venture capital industry', *National Westminster Bank Quarterly Review*, November, pp. 65–80.

Murray G. (1991b) *Change and Maturity in the UK Venture Capital Industry 1991–95*, Coventry: Warwick Business School.

Murray, G. (1993) 'Venture capital', paper presented at a CBI Workshop on Finance for SMEs.

NEDC (1986) *External Capital for Small Firms*, London: National Economic Development Office.

Neiswander, D. K. (1985) 'Informal seed stage investors', in J. A. Hornaday, E. B. Shils, J. A. Timmons and K. H. Vesper (eds.), *Frontiers of Entrepreneurship Research 1985*, Wellesley, MA: Babson College, pp. 142–54.

Peek, J. and E. S. Rosengren (1992) 'The capital crunch in New England', *New England Economic Review*, May/June, pp. 21–31.

Riding, A. L. and D. M. Short (1987a) 'Some investor and entrepreneur perspectives on the informal market for risk capital', *Journal of Small Business and Entrepreneurship*, 5(2), pp. 19–30.

Riding, A. L. and D. M. Short (1987b) 'On the estimation of the investment potential of informal investors: a capture–recapture approach', *Journal of Small Business and Entrepreneurship*, 5(4), pp. 26–40.

Riding, A., P. Dal Cin, L. Duxbury, G. Haines and R. Safrata (1993) *Informal Investors in Canada: The identification of salient characteristics*, Ottawa: Carleton University.

Scottish Enterprise (1993) *Scotland's Business Birth Rate: A national enquiry by Scottish Enterprise*, Glasgow: Scottish Enterprise/Scottish Business Insider.

Short, D. M. and A. L. Riding (1989) 'Informal investors in the Ottawa–Carleton region: experiences and expectations', *Entrepreneurship and Regional Development*, 1, pp. 99–112.

Small Business Research Trust (1991) 'Small business finance', *NatWest Quarterly Survey of Small Business in Britain*, 7(4), pp. 19–21.

Texas Capital Network (TCN) (1994) *Capital Network Survey*, Austin, TX: TCN.

Van Peer, P. A. J. (1988) *Informal Venture Capital in the Netherlands*, Tilburg.

Venture Economics Canada Ltd (1990) *Financing Early Stage Companies*, Toronto: Venture Economics Canada Ltd.

Vyakarnam, S. and R. Jacobs (1991) 'How bank managers construe high technology entrepreneurs', paper presented at the National Small Firms Policy and Research Conference, Lancashire Enterprises Ltd/Manchester Business School.

Welles, E. O. (1991) 'The French connection', *INC*, November, pp. 96–109.

Wetzel W. E. Jr (1981) 'Informal risk capital in New England', in K. H. Vesper (ed.), *Frontiers of Entrepreneurship Research 1981*, Wellesley, MA: Babson College, pp. 217–45.

Wetzel, W. E. (1984) 'Venture Capital Network Inc.: an experiment in capital formation', in J. A. Hornaday, F. Tarpley, J. A. Timmons and K. H. Vesper (eds.), *Frontiers of Entrepreneurship Research 1984*, Wellesley, MA: Babson College, pp. 111–25.

Wetzel, W. E. Jr (1986a) 'Entrepreneurs, angels and economic renaissance', in R. D. Hisrich (ed.), *Entrepreneurship, Intrapreneurship and Venture Capital*, Lexington, MA: Lexington Books, pp. 119–39.

Wetzel W. E. Jr (1986b) 'Informal risk capital: knowns and unknowns', in D. L. Sexton and R. W. Smilor (eds.), *The Art and Science of Entrepreneurship*, Cambridge, MA: Ballinger, pp. 85–108.

Wetzel W. E. Jr (1987) 'The informal risk capital market: aspects of scale and efficiency', in N. C. Churchill, J. A. Hornaday, B. A. Kirchhoff, O. J. Krasner and K. H. Vesper (eds.), *Frontiers of Entrepreneurship Research 1987*, Wellesley, MA: Babson College, pp. 412–28.

CHAPTER 2

Informal investment business introduction services: some operational considerations

Colin M. Mason and Richard T. Harrison

Introduction

It is widely accepted that the market for informal venture capital is incomplete and operates inefficiently, and that, in particular, information on finance availability and investment opportunities does not circulate freely. Accordingly, as the previous chapter has demonstrated, and as the series of case studies in the remainder of this volume indicates, there has been considerable interest in the establishment of various forms of business introduction service to link investors and ventures and so contribute to improving the flow of informal venture capital. It is in recognition of this market inefficiency, for example, that in the United Kingdom the British Venture Capital Association has recently begun to publish an annual directory of and guide to business introduction services (BVCA, 1993; 1994), which gives details of 32 such services currently operating, and the Department of Trade and Industry has published a guide to setting up and running such a service, based largely on the results of the interim review of the demonstration projects run by five Training and Enterprise Councils in England (DTI, 1993; see also Chapter 14).

The influential Advisory Committee on Science and Technology has argued that 'an active informal venture capital market is a pre-requisite for a vigorous enterprise economy' (ACOST, 1990: 41). Business introduction services are essential if the informal risk capital market is to operate effectively (Mason and Harrison, 1992; Harrison and Mason, 1993). However, as the rapid demise of many private and public sector match-making services in the UK (and in the more developed informal venture capital market in the United States also; see Chapters 4 and 6) implies, the establishment of such operations is more complex than might appear at first sight, and success is by no means guaranteed. First and foremost, business introduction services must be perceived by their potential clients as offering a convenient, confidential and trustworthy service. To be credible among both investors and entrepreneurs the service must create a client base that is sufficiently large and diversified to be capable of providing a significant number of introductions. Among the key issues that require careful consideration by any organisation that is planning to establish a business introduction service are the following:

(a) *Organisation*

- What are the most appropriate types of organisation to operate a business introduction service?
- On what geographical scale is it appropriate for a business introduction service to operate?

(b) *Financing*

- How should business introduction services be financed? Specifically, can they successfully operate on a for-profit basis?
- What kind of fee structure is most appropriate?

(c) *Marketing*

- What strategies should be used to build up a client base of investors and businesses?

(d) *Operation*

- What kind of matching process should be used?
- How can the conversion rate – the number of introductions that result in deals being made – be maximised?

(e) *Evaluation*

- On what basis should the performance of business introduction services be evaluated? What performance targets are appropriate?

Each of these questions is examined in the following sections of this chapter. The discussion is based on four sources of information: secondary literature on business introduction services; detailed discussions with key individuals involved in running business introduction services in the UK, USA and Canada; responses to our own detailed surveys of informal investors (Mason *et al.*, 1991a; Mason and Harrison, 1994), including those registered with LINC, a long-established business introduction service in the UK (Mason *et al.*, 1991b); and a survey of businesses also registered with LINC (Mason and Chaloner, 1992; see also Chapter 7). The discussion is therefore uniquely able both to distil the considerable experience and practice of many of the pioneering business introduction services in the UK and North America and also to highlight the needs, preferences and perceptions of investors and entrepreneurs in the UK for such services. As such, it provides a valuable context for the series of case studies and analyses of business introduction services in North America (Chapters 3–6), the United Kingdom (Chapters 7–14) and Scandinavia (Chapters 15 and 16) which make up the remainder of this volume.

However, it is important to emphasise that we do not seek to be prescriptive. Business introduction services are still at the experimental stage, even in the USA where VCN has been operating since 1984, and no single 'blueprint' has yet emerged. Moreover, organisational forms and practices are likely to vary according to circumstances – for example, the scale of the service, financing and staffing resources, size and characteristics of the client base and a host of other factors. Geographical context is also likely to be important. What works in the USA may not work in the UK, and neither may work in other parts of Europe. Equally, what works in the South East region of the UK may be inappropriate in other UK regions, and vice versa. Rather, our concern is to review some of the major decisions which the organisers of business introduction services must make and, based on the experience of other match-making services and on the views of potential investors and businesses seeking finance, to consider the appropriateness of alternative formats and procedures.

Organisational considerations

Who should operate a business introduction service?

The type of organisation which operates a business introduction service is a critical factor in its success. There are, of course, some examples of private sector, for-profit business introduction services (see Chapters 8 and 11 below). However, our review of business introduction services indicates that in general the most appropriate type of organisation to operate such a service is a respected, disinterested, not-for-profit body which can claim broad-based community support. Examples include local enterprise agencies, chambers of commerce, universities, business innovation centres and economic development agencies. Such organisations are likely to have a high level of credibility with both investors and businesses, who will be comfortable that such organisations are genuinely interested in fostering local economic development, have no vested interest in encouraging inappropriate matches and will maintain strict confidentiality. Such organisations have two further advantages. First, they generally have a high level of visibility in the local community and so will be highly accessible to both investors and entrepreneurs. Second, they hold key positions in local networks, which is advantageous for promotional purposes (Government of Ontario, 1986).

Conversely, investors and businesses may be less comfortable in dealing with business introduction services that are operated on a for-profit basis. Such organisations may lack the credibility that is associated with broad-based community support and may be perceived as operating in a less disinterested fashion than a not-for-profit service. The ability of commercial organisations to generate referrals, which we argue below is fundamental to the success of such a service, may also be constrained by two factors in particular. First, private sector organisations may lack a sufficiently broad range of contacts to promote the service and attract clients. Second, commercial enterprises may be less willing to make referrals to privately run referral services, especially where they are in the same industry (e.g. accountants), than to those which are operated by not-for-profit organisations. Shorter's research on the establishment of a business introduction service by a Training and Enterprise Council (TEC) in the East Lancashire area (see Chapter 13) confirms that financial institutions, local authorities and other bodies would *without exception* be willing to introduce investors and businesses to the service. This observation is complemented by that of Blatt and Riding (Chapter 4), who suggest that COIN's close association with Price Waterhouse, a major accountancy firm, has contributed to its low awareness among investors and the low level of participation among those who are aware of COIN. They argue that 'financial advisers associated with other consulting or accounting firms would be understandably loath to refer a client to a competitor'.

Our survey of LINC clients in the UK supports our contention that both investors and entrepreneurs favour a business introduction service that is operated by a not-for-profit organisation. The majority of both investors and businesses registered with LINC clearly feel that its status as a not-for-profit organisation is appropriate (Table 2.1). But whereas nearly half of the business owners believe that LINC should be subsidised by government, the largest single category of investors believe that LINC should be self-supporting and less than one-quarter supported the government subsidisation option. This divergence of views between entrepreneurs and investors can be explained by the fact that in order to be self-supporting a business introduction service would probably raise its fees for business clients. However, our survey of informal investors, the

Table 2.1 Preferred status of LINC by investors and entrepreneurs registered with LINC

	Investors (%)	Entrepreneurs (%)
A private, for-profit organisation	16	12
A not-for-profit organisation which is self-supporting through its fees	41	13
Either of the above	2	*
A not-for-profit organisation supported by sponsorship	14	9
A not-for-profit organisation subsidised by another organisation	0	3
A not-for-profit organisation subsidised by government	22	48
Any of the three not-for-profit options above	2	*
Other	–	9
Status not relevant/no opinion	2	5

* This category was not included in the survey of businesses registered with LINC.
Source: Mason *et al.* 1991b; Mason and Chaloner, 1992.

Table 2.2 Type of business referral organisation preferred by informal investors

	Number of investors	%
A private, for-profit organisation	16	18.8
A not-for-profit organisation which is self-supporting through its fees	11	12.9
A not-for-profit organisation supported by public and/or private grants	7	8.2
A local or central government agency	3	3.5
It's not important	42	49.4
Don't know	6	7.1
Total	85	

Source: Mason *et al.* (1991b).

majority of whom had not been members of a business introduction service, elicited contrasting views. For most, the issue was largely an irrelevant consideration, although a private, for-profit organisation was the most favoured form among those expressing a preference (Table 2.2).

What should be the geographical scale of operation of a business introduction service?

Informal risk capital investments are characterised by a high level of geographic localisation. Nearly three-quarters of such investments in the USA are made in firms within 50 miles of the investor's home or office (Gaston, 1989). A similar pattern holds in the UK, where two-thirds of investments are in companies located within a radius of 100 miles from the investor's home or office (Mason *et al.*, 1991a). Investments which have been made through LINC are characterised by a high level of geographic localisation, even though investors have access to information on investment opportunities in other parts of the country (Mason *et al.*, 1991b). This characteristic of informal investment activity is a product of three factors. First, most business angels become aware of investment opportunities through informal channels which tend to be highly localised (see Chapter 5). Second, because of the time taken up in the appraisal process, investors will seek to minimise travelling time by excluding all but the most promising investment opportunities that are located beyond some distance or time threshold. Third, and in similar vein, the active role which most investors play in the companies in which they invest is likely to require relatively frequent contact and will discourage investments in companies located some distance away on account of the travelling time involved. Thus, from a regional development perspective, informal investments are valuable because they help to retain and recirculate wealth *within* a region.

The strong preference of informal investors for investing in businesses in the same region, and often the same locality, clearly implies that business introduction services should operate on a subnational scale or, as in the case of LINC, as a national organisation with a decentralised operating structure: as the negative experience of COIN in Canada demonstrates (see Chapter 4), an avowedly national service is unlikely to work. Businesses, on the other hand, are less concerned that their investors should be local. Nearly two-thirds of businesses that have raised finance from informal investors regard the geographical proximity of a private investor as unimportant and none regarded it as essential. Thus whereas investors are likely to prefer a local/regional introduction service, businesses may favour a nationally organised service. However, as we argue below, recruiting investors to a business introduction service poses a greater challenge than attracting businesses. It therefore follows that, in situations where the preference of investors is contrary to that of businesses, it would be sensible to design a service which meets the needs of investors (Riding and Short, 1987). So in this particular case, the preference of investors for a regional service should override the preference of businesses for a national service.

It is difficult to be precise about the most appropriate geographical scale of operation for a business introduction service, beyond noting that if the area of operation is too small there may be insufficient investors and too limited a variety of investment opportunities for a viable service. Conversely, if the operating area is too large then investors may find that a substantial proportion of the investment opportunities are of no interest because of their location, leading to their disenchantment with the service. A complicating factor is that the role of distance as a constraining factor on informal investment activity will vary according to such factors as the quality of the road network, population density and the degree of regional identity. Thus, investors in rural areas may make investments over greater distances than investors in large urban agglomerations because of differences in the number of potential investments within a given radius. Conversely, it could be argued that investors in heartland regions will make investments over greater distances than their counterparts in peripheral regions because the superior road network reduces time distances. Areas with a strong sense of local or regional identity, such as Cornwall in the UK (see Chapter 14) or the Knoxville region in the USA (see Chapter 5), might also be characterised by a highly localised pattern of investments. In short, the most appropriate spatial coverage of a business referral service will depend upon the local geographical context. However, *in most circumstances* the appropriate size of operational area for a business introduction service in the UK will lie somewhere between the county scale and the regional scale. Some of the imprecision concerning the appropriate spatial unit for a business referral service can be removed by an exchange of information both between neighbouring organisations and also between local/regional business referral services and those which operate on a national basis (see Chapters 6 and 14 for a further discussion). The case of VCN may be instructive in view of its longevity. It operates in New England, which has a population of 15 million. Wetzel and Freear (Chapter 3) estimate that this region contains at least 10,000 *active* private investors and a population of self-made, high-net-worth individuals – which can be considered to represent the pool of *potential* business angels – of at least 80,000.

There are, however, two specific circumstances in which business introduction services should operate at more than the local and subregional scale necessary to meet investor needs and behaviour. First, many organisations that might wish to operate a business introduction service, and possess the appropriate attributes, have operating areas which are too small to be effective. In such cases the establishment of a business introduction service will require effective collaboration between neighbouring organisations: as the discussion of the TEChINVEST case in the UK demonstrates (Chapter 14), such collaboration works best where the organisations already have a tradition of working together and where the service established develops a local presence in each of the constituent parts of the operating area to ensure that the creation of a viable scale of operating area is not at the expense of local identity.

Second, a significant minority of investors have few, if any, geographical constraints on their investment activity and so are willing to invest regardless of the location of the business. Thus, many businesses do raise finance from non-local investors. Entrepreneurs would therefore benefit from gaining access to both local and non-local investors, so that they can present their ideas to as many business angels as possible. Similarly, a number of investors would be interested in examining non-local investment opportunities. For this reason there are advantages in establishing co-operative arrangements with similar services in other parts of the country and with national business introduction services. Such collaborative arrangements will enable entrepreneurs to reach more investors than can be found in their local area (without the costs and duplication involved in registering with several services), and enable investors to receive information on a larger number of investment opportunities than are available locally. As a number of contributors to this volume make clear (see Chapters 3, 6, 8 and 14), the establishment of national or quasi-national networks of business introduction services is now being actively pursued in both the UK and the USA. However, as the Canadian experience demonstrates (see Chapter 4), it is important to retain a local element in the delivery of the service.

Financing considerations

How should a business introduction service be financed?

The experience of financial match-making organisations in the USA and Canada suggests that such services cannot be operated as a profit-making activity. For example, Robert Gaston, director of Applied Economics Group Inc. which established the Seed Capital Network in 1988 from its base in Knoxville, TN, is quoted by Postma and Sullivan (1990: 39) as stating that 'I have yet to make a nickel out of this'. The rapid disappearance of most of the private sector match-making services that have been established in the UK would also seem to indicate the difficulty of operating such an activity on an on-going commercial basis. This is confirmed by Richard Hulse of Venture Associates, who commented in an interview that 'it was abundantly clear fairly quickly that I was certainly not going to make any money out of it'.

For-profit business introduction services have only been able to survive as part of a larger organisation which provides some form of cross-subsidisation. For example, Lucius Cary, founder of *Venture Capital Report*, one of the few organisations that has successfully operated a commercial business introduction service, admits that it is not genuinely profitable in the sense of paying proper salaries (Chapter 8). In similar vein, commercial match-making services that are operated by accountancy firms and other organisations are not profitable in their own right. Such organisations seek to make their profits, particularly on smaller deals, by establishing an on-going relationship with their clients in order to provide them with additional fee-based services, including basic professional services such as auditing, the preparation of the business plan, valuation of the business, structuring the deal and value-added services which enhance the quality of the business, and various financial products for which they will receive commissions (Chapter 11). However, the more that a business introduction service requires to sell additional services to its clients, the greater the risk that it will lose its credibility with investors and businesses for the reasons outlined earlier. Moreover, many organisations wishing to establish a business introduction service will lack services to cross-sell to clients.

The costs involved in running a successful business introduction service significantly exceed the revenue that can be derived from fee income. The operation of a business introduction service is a labour-intensive activity requiring skilled and committed staff to recruit investors and entrepreneurs on a continuous basis, largely through face-to-face channels, to manage the matching process, screen potential business clients and advise businesses on how to present their investment opportunity to investors. They also require a sizeable marketing budget on an on-going basis. The only source of income is likely to be the fees levied on investors and businesses. As we note in the next section, the upper limit that both investors and businesses are willing to pay is normally no more than £200, although *Venture Capital Report*, and some of the TEC-based demonstration projects linked with VCR in the UK, have demonstrated that investors will pay more if the service justifies the higher charges (see Chapters 8 and 14). As we also discuss below, there are likely to be difficulties in levying a 'success fee' on businesses which raise finance via an introduction made through the service. In the case of VCN, at its peak in 1989 it had an operating budget of $130,000, comprising mainly staff costs,[1] of which 60 per cent was covered by client fees. This was sufficient to cover the basic operating costs, but not marketing or research and development (Chapter 3). The President of COIN stated in an interview that its subscription fees are barely enough to cover operating costs, and are insufficient to cover the costs of reprinting publicity material or promotional expenses (see also Chapter 4). Business introduction services must therefore rely on a combination of a subsidy (generally an in-kind contribution) from their sponsoring organisation (e.g. economic development agency, chamber of commerce, university, enterprise agency), corporate sponsorship and government grants to meet the gap in their operating budgets that is not covered by revenue from subscriptions and fees.

There are strong arguments for local authorities and other public sector bodies responsible for local and regional economic development to provide financial support to business introduction services. First, it is an initiative which works with the market, trying to make the market work more efficiently. Thus, it is an 'ideologically acceptable' form of intervention in the present political climate. Second, business introduction services can be considered as an element of local economic infrastructure, which is traditionally regarded as a legitimate item for public expenditure to promote economic development. Third, genuine economic benefits arise by enabling businesses which would otherwise have abandoned the search for finance to raise finance from informal investors and from the know-how which business angel investors contribute to the businesses in which they invest. Fourth, the amount of public money required to support a business introduction service will produce 'a bigger bang for the buck' than if the same sum were used to invest directly in small businesses by means of a public sector venture capital fund. With the latter approach, the amount available for investment is finite and is reduced by significant appraisal and monitoring costs. Financing a business introduction service, by contrast, has no monitoring costs (since monitoring is carried out by the investors) and the amount available for investment is not limited in the same way. In similar vein, promoting informal venture capital is a more cost-effective approach to closing the equity gap than the use of tax incentives. This can be illustrated by a comparison of the cost of the Business Expansion Scheme in terms of tax revenue forgone, which we estimate at over £600 million in the period 1983/4 to 1989/90,[2] with the estimated average annual cost of running a business introduction service, which has been within the range £50,000–£60,000 for the first year of operation of the DTI-sponsored TEC demonstration projects in the UK (see Chapter 14).

The experience of VCN, COIN and LINC confirms that it is also possible for business introduction services to attract sponsors. In each case the sponsors have included banks, accounting firms and computer companies. However, as the experience of all three demonstrates, sponsorship has generally been insufficient to prevent closure (COIN), movement of the service (VCN) or restricted expansion capability (LINC). Wetzel and Freear argue (Chapter 3) that sponsorship should be sought on the basis of the marketing opportunities it provides rather than as a *pro bono* activity, and for-profit business introduction services place considerable value on the marketing and promotional benefits of the service (Chapter 11).

What kind of fee structure is appropriate?

The level and structure of the fee charged by business introduction services is intimately associated with its financial objectives. The size of the fee and method of charging investors and businesses will be influenced by whether the service is intended to be subsidised, cover its costs or make a profit. We consider three key issues. First, is a subscription fee necessary? Second, what form should the fee take and what is the appropriate level of fee? Third, should the charging structure be based on a registration fee, which is paid by all clients, or a 'success fee', which is only paid by business clients who are successful either in receiving introductions or in raising finance?

Clearly, only those organisations that are very well resourced through sponsorship or subsidised by another organisation will have the luxury of considering whether they *need* to charge for the service provided. However, even where there is no financial requirement to make a charge, it can be argued that a fee is desirable for at least two reasons. First, the value that users place on a service is related to its cost. Thus, a service which is provided at no cost is likely to be held in lower esteem than one which must be paid for. Second, a fee acts as a filter to eliminate non-serious clients. All but two of the North American computerised match-making services charge subscription fees (see Chapter 6). Two other services charge businesses but not investors, on the grounds that it is easier to recruit businesses seeking finance than investors, and that the development of an investor client base is a crucial factor in the success of a business introduction service. Postma and Sullivan (1990) suggest that it may make strategic sense for new business introduction services to waive registration fees for investors until a reasonable number have been recruited. VCN successfully adopted this strategy in its first year of operation in order to build up an investor clientele (Chapter 3).

In most business introduction services the charge takes the form of a registration fee. In the case of computerised match-making services, the fee entitles the investor and the business to have their details entered on the computer. For other types of business introduction service, the fee gives investors a subscription to an investment bulletin and may allow them to attend investors' clubs meetings, and entitles businesses to have their details listed in the investment bulletin and be considered for an investor meeting presentation. Most US computer matching services charge different rates for investors and businesses. The typical fee for investors is $200 per annum, although many services do not charge investors, compared with an average fee for businesses of $100 for six months' registration (see Table 1.7 in the preceding chapter). It is quite a common practice for such services to adopt differential pricing for individual and corporate investors and for local and overseas investors. For example, VCN charges private investors $250 for a year's subscription, $500 for venture capital funds, corporations and other institutional investors, and $1,000 for overseas investors (Chapter 3). Similarly, COIN's fees are $295 (Cdn) per annum for private investors and \$395 (Cdn) for institutional investors (Chapter 4). COIN is also unusual in adopting a differential fee for businesses: the fee for individuals – that is, pre-start-ups – is \$195 (Cdn) per annum compared with \$295 (Cdn) for established companies. Compared with North American practice, LINC's annual subscription rate of £50 for entrepreneurs (now raised to £150 by one member agency and to £200 by two others) and £120 (£100 if paid by standing order) for investors looks underpriced.

An alternative approach to charging which is adopted by some commercial business introduction services is to levy a fee on businesses that are successful in raising finance through the introductions provided, perhaps in combination with a one-off registration fee for businesses and investors. The fee is calculated on the amount of finance raised, usually on a sliding scale. Following a recent simplification, for example, VCR's success fees are charged on the basis of £1,000 plus 2.5 per cent of the finance raised (see Chapter 8), and this formula is now being used by those TEC-based introduction services in the UK which are linked with VCR. VCR also charges businesses a flat fee for appearing in the magazine, and in addition *Venture Capital Report* is only available to investors on subscription (see Chapter 8 for details). Blackstone Franks adopts a Lehman scale fee structure, levying a percentage fee based on the size of the capital sum raised, but with a much higher scale of charges, although it makes no charge on investors (see Chapter 11). The unsuccessful Venture Associates in the UK adopted a registration fee of £25 for investors and £100 for businesses, and charged a 3 per cent fee (minimum of £3,000) on completed deals. In practice, businesses are likely to build such a fee into the amount that they raise from investors.

There are some problems with the 'success fee' method of charging. First, this approach is time consuming to monitor, particularly since negotiations between investor and entrepreneur may extend over a long period of time (six months is not uncommon). The long period of time over which negotiations are conducted also creates potential cash-flow problems for the business introduction service, especially in its early stages of operation. Furthermore, as companies are unlikely to volunteer the information that they have successfully raised finance, the monitoring activity is likely to be both difficult and expensive in terms of time commitment. Second, matching may be particularly difficult to monitor in situations where, as in the case of VCR, investors are able to contact businesses directly. Thus, the match-making service may be unable to identify all of its introductions that have led to investments being made. Third, even where monitoring is successful, a further difficulty concerns a definition of the amount of finance provided. VCR adopts a broad definition: 'all capital provided by the investor in whatever form, plus other capital provided by banks or other lenders for which the investor provides a guarantee' (Cary, 1991: 67). Fourth, there may in any case be legal constraints on the use of this form of charging structure for business introduction services that are not authorised under securities legislation. For example, one of the criteria under which a business introduction service can gain exemption under the Financial Services Act is that it has 'no direct or indirect pecuniary interest in . . . any investment agreement' other than such as to recover the cost of providing the service (Figure 2.1). This does not rule out charging a success fee; what is important in determining whether the service benefits from the exemption is whether the fee is intended or likely to produce a profit over and above cost recovery (see Chapter 12). Finally, the use of a success fee, and the consequent implication that the service does have a vested interest in the outcome of introductions, may damage its image in the eyes of both investors and businesses as being independent and impartial, with implications for the longer-term credibility of the service.

A less common variant on the 'success fee' method of charging for the service is to levy a fee on businesses at the point at which an introduction is made. This approach was to be adopted by the proposed but abortive Grapevine service in the UK: they were to charge businesses a £500 fee (as being a one-off fee rather than a fee for *each* introduction) if an appropriate match was made with an investor. The service was to be free for investors. The Seed Capital Network in Knoxville, TN, operates in a similar way: there is no initial registration fee, but businesses pay $195 for the details of their investment opportunity to be sent to 'matched' investors (Postma and Sullivan, 1990). For this approach to work, however, it is important that both parties are confident that the introductions will be of a high quality with a significant likelihood of leading in due course to an investment.

Overall, the basis for setting fees is unscientific. However, in setting the level of fee the service should take into account the cost of alternative sources of information, and the savings in time and legwork which the client derives from the service. Certainly, most investors who register with a business introduction service appear to be aware of the benefits that are likely to result. For example, our survey of investors registered with LINC indicates that they expected to benefit from access to information on a better-quality and wider range of investment opportunities than they could obtain from other sources, and one respondent specifically commented that 'LINC was a more cost-effective approach than a personal search for investment opportunities' (Mason *et al.*, 1991b).

Any body corporate which has as its principal object or one of its principal objects the promotion or encouragement of industrial or commercial activity or enterprise in the United Kingdom or in any particular area of it or the dissemination of information concerning persons engaged in such activity or enterprise requiring capital to become so engaged being a body corporate which has no direct or indirect pecuniary interest in the arrangements or in any investment agreement which may be entered into by persons participating in them except any such interest as may arise from the receipt of such sums as may be reasonably regarded as necessary to meet the costs of making the arrangements in an exempted person as respects any arrangement it makes which fall within paragraph 13 of Schedule 1 of the Financial Services Act 1986.

Figure 2.1 Extract from the Financial Services Act 1986 (Miscellaneous Exemptions) (No. 2) Order 1988.

Nevertheless, our survey evidence suggests that a majority of informal investors are not willing to pay for information on investment opportunities even if it is pre-screened according to their investment criteria (Table 2.3). Only 36 per cent of informal investors are willing to pay for such information. However, it must be remembered that this survey comprised both the once-in-a-lifetime and the active/frequent ends of the informal investment spectrum. A business introduction service is only likely to be of interest to serious investors with a substantial amount available to invest. This is confirmed by our finding that the proportion of active investors in our survey (defined as those who have made three or more investments during the previous three years) willing to pay for information on investment opportunities is higher than for the less active investors (44 per cent compared with 33 per cent). Similarly, we found that those investors with £50,000 or more available for investment are more willing to pay for information on investment opportunities than those with lesser amounts (40 per cent compared with 26 per cent).

Our survey of LINC clients provides some indication of how much investors and businesses may be willing to pay to participate in a business introduction service. Almost two-thirds of the investors who responded to our survey considered the then membership fee of £75 per annum to represent good value for money. Moreover, of the 68 per cent of respondents who considered that LINC's existing services can be enhanced in some way, nearly three-quarters would be willing to pay a higher membership fee (Mason *et al.*, 1991b). Thus, the level of the fee clearly cannot be set independently of the services provided to investors. However, a figure of £150 appears to be an upper threshold for most LINC investors. LINC investors were equally divided on whether they preferred a single, all-inclusive fee or separate fees for each service provided (e.g. to be registered on a computer database, to receive an investment bulletin, to attend presentations by businesses seeking finance) (Mason *et al.*, 1991b). These figures may, of course, be significantly coloured by investors' experiences with LINC in particular. As evidence from VCR suggests (Chapter 8), investors will pay higher

Table 2.3 Willingness of investors to pay for information about investment opportunities from a business referral service

	Number of investors	%
Would only pay for unscreened information	5	5.6
Would only pay for pre-screened information	14	15.6
Would pay for either screened or unscreened information	13	14.4
Would not pay for any information	50	55.6
Don't know	8	8.9
Total	90	

Source: Survey of informal investors.

fees if they believe that they continue to get value for money in terms of the service offered. Although there is no systematic evidence on the degree to which investor utilisation of business introduction services is sensitive to the level of the fee charged, there is some evidence to suggest that those services with the highest fees (and correspondingly high levels of service) are also the most successful (see Chapter 14).

Nearly two-thirds of the entrepreneurs registered with LINC also considered that the registration fee (£50) represented good value for money. Moreover, three-quarters of those respondents who considered that LINC could offer additional business introduction services indicated that they would be prepared to pay a higher registration fee. However, there was little unanimity on how much more they would be prepared to pay: 44 per cent indicated that they would be willing to pay a registration fee of £100, but a further one-third stated that they would be prepared to pay a registration fee of up to £200 (Mason and Chaloner, 1992). Entrepreneurs are also attracted to the notion that business introduction services should be free to register, with the fee payable only if an acceptable offer of finance is received. Over three-quarters of entrepreneurs registered with LINC stated that they would probably or definitely consider joining such a service (Table 2.4).

Table 2.4 Willingness of businesses to join a referral service which was free to register and only charged a fee if they were successful in raising finance[a]

	Number of businesses	%
Definitely *would not* join	2	1.3
Would *possibly* join	17	21.8
No opinion	0	–
Would *probably* join	24	30.8
Would *definitely* join	35	44.9
Total	75	

[a] The question suggested a fee that was 2% of the amount raised.
Source: Survey of businesses registered with LINC (Mason and Chaloner, 1992).

Marketing considerations: how to build a client base

Developing and maintaining a client base is clearly of crucial significance in the success of a business referral service. The client base must possess the following three characteristics in order to produce an acceptable number and quality of introductions:

- *Large size.* Because of the hit-or-miss nature of matching investor preferences to business characteristics, it is necessary to maximise the numbers of investors and businesses which register with the service, not least because not all investors will be equally active and committed to making investments or have liquid funds (see Chapter 11). Wetzel (1984) has estimated that the minimum number of investors for an effective service is approximately 200. Table 2.5 indicates the number of clients of some referral services in North America and the UK (see also Chapter 6).
- *Diversity.* Business referral services must attract a wide range of businesses (stage of development, industry, amount of finance sought, 'high tech' vs 'low tech') and a range of investor types (e.g. amount available to invest, investment preferences, skills) in order to avoid the risk of an imbalance between the investment preferences of investors and the types of business seeking finance.
- *Quality control.* In order to minimise the risk of dissatisfaction by either investors or businesses, the service must attempt to screen out those businesses that are obviously 'lemons'. There is also a case for seeking to filter out investors seeking to buy themselves into a job (effectively through a management buy-in), business brokers primarily interested in buying and selling businesses, investors who are unable, or do not wish, to make a 'hands-on' contribution to the firms in which they invest, and investors who do not currently have liquid funds. However, it is in practice much more difficult to screen investors, and investor screening is rarely used by business introduction services.

Table 2.5 Client base of some business referral services

Name	Time period	Number of clients	
		Investors	Businesses
Tennessee Venture Capital Network[c]	After 6 months	20	50
Venture Capital Exchange[d]	After 16 months	52	190
Venture Capital Network[e]	July 1984 – October 1985	>300	>130
Venture Capital Network[f]	1984–1990	800[a]	1,200[a]
LINC[g]	At September 1993	200	<200
Venture Capital Report[h]	At September 1993	458[b]	n.a.

[a] These are cumulative figures.
[b] Private companies outnumber private individuals in a ratio of approximately 2:1; however, in the majority of such cases the managing director received the report. There are also a number of quoted companies, venture capital companies and other finance-based organisations in the client list.

Sources:
[c] Postma and Sullivan (1990).   [f] Chapter 3.
[d] Hisrich (1988).   [g] Chapter 7.
[e] Wetzel (1986).   [h] Chapter 8.

The establishment of a business introduction service involves a 'chicken and egg' problem. The service needs to recruit investors in order to attract businesses, but without businesses it cannot attract investors. One way around this problem is to buy in an initial client base of either investors or businesses. For example, Blackstone Franks used business brokers to develop an initial list of businesses seeking finance in order to attract investors (Chapter 11). However, the quality of bought-in client lists is likely to be poor (as Blackstone Franks found) and so this can only be a short-term measure to give the service the time to recruit its own clients.

It has already been noted above that entrepreneurs have more interest in a business introduction service than investors (Riding and Short, 1987).[3] Thus, fewer difficulties are likely to be encountered in recruiting businesses than investors. However, the turnover of business clients will be higher than for investors. Businesses are unlikely to remain clients for more than about six months. Some will have successfully raised finance either through the referral network or from other sources; those which have been unable to raise finance are likely to be unattractive to investors and, in all probability, will have abandoned their project. Indeed, the view of one director of a business referral service is that it is unlikely to be worthwhile retaining any business which has not received an offer of finance after being registered for more than six months or so. Thus, a business referral service is likely to experience close to a 100 per cent turnover of business clients every six months. In the case of LINC, 63 per cent of business clients had been registered for less than one year (Mason and Chaloner, 1992). Conversely, many investors are likely to retain their membership of a referral service for considerably longer. For example, 30 per cent of the investors registered with LINC in May 1991 had joined prior to 1989 (Mason *et al.*, 1991b). Thus, a reasonable estimate of the annual turnover of investors in a business referral service is between one-third and one-half.

It is probable that the majority of business clients attracted to an introduction service will be start-ups and early stage ventures. In the case of LINC, 61 per cent of registered businesses were pre-start-ups, start-ups or had been trading for less than two years (Mason and Chaloner, 1992).

Should a business introduction service be selective in the firms and investors that it recruits?

The key challenge in building a client base of investment opportunities is to recruit quality businesses rather than those whose request for finance has been turned down by institutional lenders and investors, and which turn to a business introduction service as a last resort. Richard Hulse, founder of the unsuccessful Venture Associates service, notes that, while there is no difficulty finding businesses, there is a problem in finding good-quality projects. As a result, he spent 'an awful lot of time looking through business plans for pretty hopeless projects'. Wetzel and Freear (Chapter 3) argue that business introduction services should devote their marketing efforts to recruiting *high-potential firms*, those that grow rapidly and are likely to exceed £10 million or more in sales, and *foundation firms*, those which grow more slowly but exceed £1 million in sales and may grow to £5 million to £10 million, and avoid the traditional, stable *lifestyle firms* because their limited growth prospects make them unattractive to investors.[4]

There is a debate concerning whether business introduction services should screen businesses seeking registration with a view to filtering out those that are unlikely to be successful in raising finance. Blatt and Riding (Chapter 4) argue that a match-making service should incorporate minimum 'listing requirements' in order to filter out 'lemons', otherwise investors will be discouraged and leave the service, leading to its degeneration. For-profit match-making services undertake rigorous filtering. Blackstone Franks estimate that they accept only 10 per cent of potential deal flow; while many companies are rejected because they do not look promising, others filter themselves out because they are not willing to meet Blackstone Franks' criteria (Chapter 11). VCR only accepts about one-third of the businesses that submit a business plan, but includes around two-thirds of the entrepreneurs that it meets: Cary (1991: 67) states that VCR will not include projects that it believes have fatal weaknesses. In the case of LINC, as the entry point is an enterprise agency, each business which is listed in the bulletin should have been referred by an enterprise counsellor, who plays both a positive role by assisting businesses in preparing their business plan summary, and acts as a filter for businesses judged to be unsuitable. However, LINC's experience suggests that the strength of this filter varies across the LINC member agencies and also between individual enterprise counsellors.

In contrast, computer matching services in North America do not undertake any screening or evaluation. For example, VCN literature includes the following statement:

> VCN neither evaluates nor endorses the merits of investment opportunities presented through its services. VCN conducts no investigations to verify either the accuracy or completeness of information provided by entrepreneurs and investors.

The reasons for this are partly philosophical, partly practical and partly regulatory (see Chapters 3 and 6). A philosophical position was adopted that investors themselves were presumed to be the best judges of investment opportunities and entrepreneurs were advised to do their own evaluations of potential investors. The practical consideration was the cost of employing qualified staff to screen investment proposals and investor qualifications. Finally, the decision not to undertake any screening enabled VCN to operate without registering as an investment adviser or broker/dealer with the US Securities and Exchange Commission.

There is also a case for investor screening, although this tends to receive less consideration. A significant minority of businesses registered with LINC complained that investors to whom they were introduced either were intermediaries or else were considered to be 'not serious' (Mason and Chaloner, 1992). Moreover, our survey of LINC investors identified some – admittedly a small minority – who joined because it provided a source of information on new business ideas rather than in order to identify investment opportunities (Mason *et al.*, 1991b). We also know of some investors who have been made redundant from management positions whose motive in joining LINC was to find a company in which they could invest their redundancy settlement to 'buy themselves a job' rather than to act as a bona fide 'hands-on' investor. Wetzel and Freear also suggest (Chapter 3) that business introduction services should be wary of accepting inexperienced and passive investors as they are unlikely to add value to investments and are prone to investor fatigue. This view is supported by findings from our survey of businesses registered with LINC. This study noted that the majority of businesses were specifically looking for an investor who would play an active role in their business: for example, on the board of directors, providing consultancy help or working part time or, less commonly, full time in the business. Businesses were typically seeking their investors to contribute financial and marketing expertise, although sales and general management skills were also sought (Mason and Chaloner, 1992; see also Chapter 7).

Recruitment strategies

Businesses can be recruited by advertising, although the danger is that this approach will attract a large response weighted towards low-quality businesses and so will require considerable filtering by the staff of the match-making service. A more promising approach is to seek referrals from professional intermediary organisations in the same region/locality as the match-making service, including solicitors, accountants and business consultants (particularly those delivering government schemes such as the Enterprise Initiative) and also from enterprise agencies, economic development units and universities (e.g. business schools, technology transfer and advisory units, industrial liaison officers, managers of incubator units and science parks). Clearing banks may refer businesses to the introduction service that they are unwilling to finance – for example, because they are too highly geared. Similarly, venture capital funds may be willing to refer businesses that do not fit their investment criteria or where there are opportunities for parallel investing by the venture capital fund and an experienced participative informal investor (as may occur with funds such as the Boston-based Zero Stage Capital; Kelley, 1992). The referral service may itself also be able to identify investors who will invest alongside a venture capital fund. Studies in the USA report that between one-third and one-half of investors are willing to invest in conjunction with a venture capital fund, with a smaller proportion (5 per cent to 25 per cent) willing to invest alongside a government economic development agency (Wetzel, 1981; Tymes and Krasner, 1983; Myers and Moline, 1988). Riding and Short (1987) also note that informal investors in

Canada often invest alongside venture capital funds and government economic development agencies. The attraction to the investor is the sense of security provided through participation with a venture capital fund; for the fund, the attraction of this arrangement is that the 'angel' can act as its 'eyes and ears', thereby reducing its monitoring costs. As Standeven (1993) has recently suggested, if measures were taken to help informal investors get to know the formal venture capital community (through the creation of special membership categories and networking events by national venture capital associations), more deals might be done, particularly those deals which, for want of a little capital and a lot of solid nurturing from a knowledgeable and committed investor, could be attractive to a venture capitalist.

Our study of LINC highlights the overwhelming importance of referral networks in generating awareness of the service (Chapter 7). However, it should be noted that LINC does no advertising, relying instead on editorial coverage. By contrast, VCR has generated a higher proportion of business clients from advertisements and listings in directories (36 per cent and 12 per cent respectively) than from referrals (36 per cent) (Chapter 8), although no evidence is available on the relative quality of businesses recruited through these different channels.

The recruitment of investors requires an equally proactive approach. A number of operators of business referral services have noted the difficulty in recruiting investors. The first challenge is to identify actual and potential informal investors, the majority of whom, it will be recalled, are successful business owners or entrepreneurs who have recently sold (or floated) their business (Mason *et al.*, 1991a, 1991b). Three approaches are possible. The first approach is by means of paid advertising. However, VCN's experience of advertising in a variety of media, including the *Wall Street Journal* and US Air's in-flight magazine, was not a cost-effective marketing technique (Chapter 3). A second approach is to undertake a mailshot using well-targeted mailing lists. Our experience of using mailing lists to identify informal investors for research purposes suggests that lists which target speculative investors (e.g. USM and OTC investors) are likely to produce the best response, although the 'hit rate' is only about 1 per cent (see Mason *et al.*, 1991a: table 1). Additionally, sports car owners and yacht and boat owners may be effective in identifying self-made, high-net-worth individuals who comprise the majority of business angels (Wetzel, 1986a, 1986b). A third approach is to seek referrals from local/regional accountancy firms, solicitors and other professional intermediaries (see Chapter 11). Finally, the importance of recruiting investors by means of personal recommendation should not be overlooked. Research has noted that investors tend to be found in clusters, thus finding one investor often leads to the identification of others (Wetzel, 1981; Mason *et al.*, 1991a). Postma and Sullivan (1990) suggest that at the outset business referral services should seek to recruit a handful of respected investors who will, in turn, convince their associates of the merits of participating in the service. Once the service is operating successfully, its existing investors are likely to be the most effective means of attracting new investors. The case of LINC highlights the importance of personal recommendations, referrals from institutions and also editorial coverage in the media as being the ways in which investors became aware of the service (Chapter 7). As recent UK experience suggests (see Chapter 14), most business introduction services use a diversity of approaches rather than relying on one or two only, and the mix varies considerably from one service to another.

Although efforts to recruit investors should have a strong local/regional focus in view of the geographical localisation of the informal investment process, there is nevertheless scope for attracting some long-distance investors to the service. These are of three kinds. First, tax havens such as the Channel Islands and the Isle of Man are likely to contain informal investors. Second, successful emigrants may be interested in investing in their 'homeland', particularly where cultural ties remain strong (e.g. those of Scottish and Irish descent in the USA, Canada and Australia). Third, investors who specialise in investing in technology-based businesses are likely to place less emphasis on location because of the scarcity of investments that are based on their specialist technology.

Having identified potential investor clients, the second challenge is to 'sell' them the concept of a financial 'marriage bureau' as a valuable service that minimises their cost of searching for investment opportunities and will generate good-quality deals that they could not find themselves. Selling the service to investors, in the words of a director of the Tennessee Venture Capital Network, requires 'a personal contact approach' (quoted in Postma and Sullivan, 1990: 37).

In summary, in order to develop a client base successfully, a business introduction service must achieve a high visibility in the local business and professional community, and develop networks with organisations that can be a source of high-quality referrals. This is best undertaken by face-to-face dialogue – for example, by speaking engagements at a variety of professional and civic organisations. In addition, it is important to maximise public relations opportunities. VCN's single most effective marketing technique was to use press releases to generate media interest, leading to articles in newspapers and the media (Chapter 3), an approach which also proved effective for some of the TEC demonstration projects (Chapter 14).

Operational considerations

What kind of matching mechanism?

As we have noted earlier, there are three main ways in which the matching process can be undertaken: by computer matching; through a publication giving details of businesses seeking finance; and by means of presentations by entrepreneurs to an audience of investors. These approaches are not mutually exclusive. For example, LINC undertakes all three matching mechanisms (Chapter 7).

In this section we consider some of the advantages and disadvantages of each approach.

Computer matching is a proven and widely used business referral mechanism in North America. One of the reasons for its popularity is that the materials (questionnaires, literature) and software can be bought off the shelf from VCN for a relatively modest charge ($4,000). VCN also provides a short training course. Nevertheless, use of the VCN system does not guarantee success. As we emphasised in the previous section, the crucial factor in determining the success of a business introduction service is the recruitment of clients: some attempts to replicate VCN in other regions of the USA have been unsuccessful because of the failure to recruit sufficient investors and businesses (see Chapter 6). However, there would appear to be little doubt that, when combined with the successful recruitment of investors and entrepreneurs, the use of computer matching does generate significant numbers of introductions for its investors and entrepreneurs. For example, 90 per cent of entrepreneurs registered with COIN have received several first-stage matches (*Financial Post*, 13 July 1990). In the case of VCN, about three-quarters of its entrepreneur clients received introductions to an average of four or five potential investors (Chapter 3) (see also Table 2.8 below). About half of the firms registered with LINC report an interest in presenting their investment opportunity to investors through computer matching (Table 2.6).

The main criticism of computer matching is that its major objective, namely to provide investors with a convenient screening system for receiving investment opportunities *that meet their screening criteria* (Wetzel, 1986a), involves an extremely delicate balancing act. Screening categories which are too broad will result in the investor receiving details of many investment opportunities that are

Table 2.6 Interest of entrepreneurs in alternative methods of presenting their investment proposition to investors

	Would be interested (%)	Indifferent (%)	Would not be interested (%)
60-word description in investment bulletin	48	23	30
Two-page description in investment bulletin	58	19	22
Complete business plan circulated to registered investors	48	10	42
On a video tape	33	29	38
Meeting in which several entrepreneurs make presentations	57	11	32
Personal meeting with individual entrepreneur	95	4	1
On-line access to database of opportunities	58	31	11
Computerised matching process	51	27	22

Source: Survey of businesses registered with LINC (Mason and Chaloner, 1992).

of little or no interest. Conversely, if the screening categories are too narrow, investors may not receive details of investment opportunities which would interest them. It would appear on the basis of a study of the early operation of VCN that the former is the case: Foss (1985) notes that two-thirds of both investors and entrepreneurs considered that they were receiving too many matches.

Computer matching also presupposes that investors are able to express positive investment preferences. But in reality, many investors only have clear opinions on what they will *not* invest in; with these exceptions they are generally fairly open-minded about what types of investment they are willing to consider, and investors often make investments in businesses that are very different to their initial criteria (see Chapter 11). Coon also cites examples of investors who have made a major investment which fits their criteria, but who have also made a second investment in a business which is far removed from their stated investment criteria but nevertheless 'catches their eye'.

Investment bulletins have been the most widely used matching mechanism in the UK. The key issue in their design is to achieve a balance between the number of investment opportunities and the amount of detail that is provided. For example, the LINC bulletin contains brief summaries on between 75 and 100 investment opportunities (the majority having appeared in previous issues), whereas *Venture Capital Report* has five-page articles on about ten businesses (none having been previously published). Although our surveys of both informal investors and LINC investors highlight considerable diversity of opinion on the appropriateness of different forms of providing information on investment opportunities, it is nevertheless clear that there is greater interest in a two-page summary than in a 50–60 word summary (Table 2.7). Businesses registered with

Table 2.7 Interest of investors in alternative methods of first learning of investment opportunities

	Would be interested (%)		Indifferent (%)		Would not be Interested (%)	
	(1)	(2)	(1)	(2)	(1)	(2)
Complete business plan	73	55	15	23	12	28
50-word description	35	60	36	31	28	10
Two-page description	61	84	27	14	12	2
Five-minute video tape	24	32	34	34	41	36
Personal meeting with individual entrepreneur	75	46	13	25	12	29
Meeting in which several entrepreneurs make presentations	45	44	29	34	26	22
On-line access to database of opportunities	40	39	29	22	30	39

Note:
Column (1)   Responses from sample of informal investors.
Column (2)   Responses from investors registered with LINC.
Sources: Surveys of informal investors and investors registered with LINC.

LINC also report greater interest in a two-page description than in a short summary (Table 2.6). However, there is also evidence that investors can be subject to 'information fatigue' (see Chapter 11), and in these circumstances personal proactive matching becomes important (see below).

Investors' meetings are widely used as an introduction mechanism in both the UK and the USA. However, fewer than half of the respondents to each of our investor surveys reported that they were interested in this method of learning of investment opportunities (Table 2.7). Among businesses registered with LINC, opinion was only slightly more favourable, with 57 per cent reporting that they were interested in this matching method (Table 2.6). One of the major problems of investors' meetings, particularly where this is not the sole matching mechanism used by the referral service, is therefore to attract a reasonable attendance by investors. Our survey of LINC investors found that half had never attended any investor meetings and only one-quarter had attended more than two meetings. However, attendance by investors who live in the South East is greater, with only 36 per cent never having attended any meetings and 52 per cent having attended three or more meetings. This reflects the greater frequency of meetings organised at the London Enterprise Agency.

Our surveys of investors found limited interest in alternative methods of receiving information on investment opportunities. Only about 40 per cent of investors in each survey reported that they would be interested in receiving such information via on-line access to a database, and between one-quarter and one-third stated an interest in receiving such information on video tape (Table 2.7). Entrepreneurs registered with LINC were equally unenthusiastic about the use of video, but over half registered their interest in having their details on an on-line database (Table 2.6). American experience, however, suggests that the use of video technology may be justified, and VCN, now renamed the Technology Capital Network since its move to MIT, is currently exploring the use of video technology, particularly for those businesses with a strong technology focus which can be readily demonstrated and illustrated. Furthermore, in the UK, the video taping of investor meeting presentations, and their circulation, has been discussed by some of the TEC demonstration projects (see Chapter 14). Further explorations of enhanced technological options for the matching process, particularly to overcome the constraints of distance without losing the personal element valued by investors may include the use of teleconferencing and related approaches to investor presentations (Bracker *et al.*, 1994). However, in the absence of a 'live' demonstration of video and teleconferencing approaches, there is no reliable means of assessing the extent to which either investors or entrepreneurs will respond positively to such developments.

A number of operators of business introduction services advocate the need to supplement these conventional matching mechanisms with proactive matching, in which they bring investment opportunities to the attention of those investors who are likely to be interested in that particular business venture. This requires that the operators of business introduction services get to know the investment preferences of their investors in some detail, and develop a trust so that they will follow up the opportunities that are put to them (see Chapter 11). However, there are limits to the adoption of this practice. First, it is generally not feasible for computer matching services to adopt this approach. Second, it is a labour-intensive, and therefore expensive, practice. Third, there is a limit to the number of investors that any individual can know. Thus, it is most appropriate in situations where the investor client base is small, or where the case load can be shared among a number of staff (for example, see Chapter 11). Business introduction services with a large number of investors that wish to undertake proactive matching must therefore give their staff responsibility for various segments of the client base. Finally, business introduction services which undertake proactive matching must also be careful not to make any implied endorsement or recommendation of investment opportunities to avoid falling outside the Financial Services Act Exemption Order (see Figure 2.1 and Chapter 12).

How can the conversion rate be maximised?

It is difficult for business introduction services to monitor the results of the introductions that have been provided. They may lack the resources to follow up the outcome of introductions, and former clients may be uncontactable (e.g. because of a change of address) or may be unwilling to divulge information on any investments that have resulted from introductions. As a result, their records of completed deals will, in all probability, be an underestimate. But even with this important caveat, the track record of various business introduction services indicates that the number of investments that have resulted is surprisingly small, given the large number of entrepreneurs who have been introduced to investors, and vice versa (Tables 2.5 and 2.8).

Business introduction services must be concerned with ensuring that a high proportion of the introductions that they make result in investments. Indeed, it is the number of deals that result from their activities that determines their impact on local/regional economic development. Thus, it is essential that business introduction services see their role as being wider than simply the management of a business introduction service. This will involve adopting a broader range of functions than simply managing the match-making process while ensuring that they conform to the relevant legal constraints on their activities.

Our survey of LINC clients (see Chapter 7) highlights two factors which contribute to the low conversion rate and, in turn, contribute to dissatisfaction among investors with the service. First, there is concern among investors about the quality of business opportunities and a demand that a business seeking to register with the service should be screened (Mason *et al.*, 1991b). Equally, as we noted earlier, some entrepreneurs complain that the investors to whom they are introduced either are 'not serious' or else are intermediaries. They propose that investors should also be screened for their motives (Mason and Chaloner,

Table 2.8 Performance of some business referral services

Name	Time period	Number of introductions[a]	Number of investments/amount invested[b]
Tennessee Venture Capital Network[e]	After 6 months	n.a.	1
Venture Capital Exchange[f]	After 16 months	>3,000 stage one	9
Venture Capital Network[g,h]	July 1984–October 1985	12,000 stage one 2,500 stage two 765 stage three	5
	1984–90	35,000 stage one 3,500 stage three	31/>$12m
COIN[i]	After 16 months	16,000 stage one 3,900 stage three	'few dozen'
Venture Capital Report[j]	December 1978–October 1990	n.a.	277[c]
	November 1990–November 1993	n.a.	19[d]
LINC[k]	1989–1991	n.a.	22/£1.19m
	1992		27/£1.27m

[a] Computer matching networks generate a three-stage matching process. Stage one matches are those produced by the computer: the investor receives details of the entrepreneur's investment opportunity profile. Stage two matches occur when the investor responds positively to the profile and requests the executive summary of the entrepreneur's business plan. Stage three matches occur when the investor responds positively to the business plan summary and requests to be introduced to the entrepreneur (Wetzel, 1986a; 1986b).

[b] As match-making services typically do not become involved in investment negotiations, they have no systematic method for tracking the outcome of introductions other than through occasional follow-up surveys. Consequently, these figures are likely to represent conservative estimates of the number of investments.

[c] This comprises 168 businesses that received an offer for all of the money they sought from a VCR subscriber and a further 109 businesses which received an offer for some of the money that they sought.

[d] These are companies which have raised all their funds from VCR subscribers. Overall, 30% of companies appearing in a full write-up receive all their funds (15% directly from a VCR subscriber and 15% from other sources), and a further 17% receive some funds.

Sources:

[e] Postma and Sullivan (1990).

[f] Hisrich (1988).

[g] Wetzel (1986).

[h] See Chapter 3.

[i] COIN press release, May 1990.

[j] Cary (1991; 1993); see also Chapter 8.

[k] See Chapter 7.

1992). While there are both financial and legal constraints on the amount of screening that can realistically be undertaken by business introduction services, businesses should be required to pass certain 'hurdles', notably the submission of a business plan, before being accepted by the service. It is harder to identify a simple but effective filter that can be applied to investors wishing to join a business introduction service. One approach may be to encourage firms to report any unsatisfactory investor to whom they have been introduced. The service would investigate such complaints. Any investor who was subject to a certain number of complaints that were upheld would have their registration terminated (Mason and Chaloner, 1992). However, the most effective means of increasing the number of deals is simply well-targeted marketing to enhance the quality of businesses and investors that register with the service.

The second factor that contributes to a low conversion rate is simply the lack of experience of investors and entrepreneurs in the investment process. This leads to a variety of failings. For example, investors indicate that the presentation of investment opportunities by entrepreneurs is often poor (Mason *et al.*, 1991b). This view is supported by the manager of the Investorlink scheme, who noted that one of the biggest difficulties was that many of the businesses which sought to use the service were unable to explain their business proposition to a potential investor. In other cases, introductions failed to lead to deals because the two parties could not agree on the equity stake, the risk/reward ratio or the investor's role in the company (Mason and Chaloner, 1992).

A number of steps can be taken to alleviate these difficulties. First, entrepreneurs can be given greater assistance in the preparation of their business plans and presentations. Second, businesses need to be given feedback. A frequent complaint among entrepreneurs registered with LINC is that they often do not receive any response from investors who are sent their business plan summary. The practice of VCN in informing businesses of the reasons for the lack of interest by investors (Wetzel, 1986a) is certainly worthy of replication. Third, it is appropriate for business referral organisations to undertake a generic education function. One respondent to our survey of LINC investors commented as follows: 'many informal investors are inexperienced and would probably be more prepared to invest and invest more wisely with the benefit of a support group'.

In this context, another practice by VCN which is now being replicated by some other business introduction services is to run professional workshops which provide information on the pricing and structuring of equity investments, in order to raise the competences of investors and entrepreneurs and increase their confidence in their ability to negotiate the price and other terms and conditions of a venture investment. Such workshops – which are sponsored – are also effective in raising VCN's visibility as a respected service for both investors and entrepreneurs, thereby helping to reach potential investors and entrepreneurs (Chapter 3). Finally, we have noted elsewhere (Harrison and Mason, 1992) that in comparison with the USA a much smaller proportion of informal investments in the UK are made by groups or syndicates of business angels. The consequence is that firms which are seeking to raise more than £50,000 to £100,000 – the maximum that most individual investors are prepared to invest in a single business – will encounter difficulties. Thus, business introduction services should also seek to encourage the formation of informal investor syndicates to invest larger amounts.

Evaluation considerations

It is appropriate that the activities of business referral organisations are evaluated, particularly where they are in receipt of public funds or sponsorship. However, the evaluation of business referral organisations poses two difficulties. First, on what basis should they be evaluated? And second, against what targets should their performance be evaluated?

There are a number of possible criteria on which such services can be assessed. The most appropriate basis for evaluating the performance of business introduction services is in terms of the number of introductions made and the average number of introductions received by each investor and business. The amount of finance that investors have available for investment would be a useful additional indicator of the effectiveness of the service. Some measure of client satisfaction should also be included as a performance indicator. Conversely, the performance of a business introduction service should *not* be assessed in terms of the number of deals that have resulted from the introductions provided by the service. The role of such services is to provide *information*: their objective is to provide *introductions*. Thus, it is inappropriate to judge the performance of an organisation on the basis of an outcome that is not its primary objective. Moreover, the outcome of negotiations between an investor and an entrepreneur is outside the control of a business introduction service to influence. Nevertheless, we believe that this information should be collected. To overcome some of the monitoring problems encountered by match-making services in collecting this kind of information, it should be part of the conditions of joining the service that businesses and investors agree to provide details of any investments that result from the introductions provided.

It is also important to recognise that some businesses which are unsuccessful in raising finance through a business introduction service nevertheless derive some benefits from the experience. This reflects the fact that business introduction services generate 'ripple effects' in addition to the immediate aim of effecting successful introductions between investors and entrepreneurs. Three such effects, or benefits, can be identified. First, business introduction services can provide a coaching role for business clients, advising them on business plan preparation and presentation, the preparation of information for potential investors, presentation skills and negotiating skills. Investor feedback may form an additional input into this coaching role. Second, business introduction services can provide a pathfinding role for business clients which are not appropriate for informal venture capital, but may have other support needs. Third, business introduction services may provide a wider evaluation function by raising businesses' and entrepreneurs' awareness of the role and function of equity finance, and by providing guidance on the deal-making and pricing process (see Chapter 3). Evidence in the UK from LINC suggests that almost half of the businesses registered with LINC but unsuccessful in raising finance nevertheless reported that they had derived some benefits from their registration (Mason and Chaloner, 1992; see also Chapter 7).

Establishing meaningful performance targets for a business introduction service is even more problematic. The information that we have provided on the performance of business introduction services in North America and the UK, notably in Tables 2.5 and 2.8, but also in various places throughout subsequent chapters, provide guidelines to the scale of performance that it may be reasonable to expect. However, it is important to compare like with like when setting targets: thus, the performance of a computer matching service is likely to provide a misleading guide to setting the target for an introduction service that uses a different matching mechanism. Similarly, it is unrealistic to use the performance of national service as a basis for setting the target for a local/regional business introduction service.

Conclusion

Various studies have highlighted the important contribution played by informal venture capital in filling the equity gap. Increasingly, new and growing businesses are finding that informal venture capital may be the only source of potential finance available after they have exhausted their own personal financial resources and those of family ('love money'), as a result of the more cautious attitude that is being adopted by the banks and the increasing pressures on the venture capital industry (Murray, 1991a, 1991b). In view of this, it becomes all the more important that the inefficiencies which characterise the informal venture capital market are reduced. One promising approach is the establishment of local or regional business introduction services, which provide a channel of communication between investors seeking investments and entrepreneurs looking for sources of risk capital, thereby reducing the search costs for each party. There is considerable interest at the present time among both the public and private sectors in the UK (and also elsewhere in Europe) in developing such services, and the government has indicated its support for this development by providing some financial support to enable five TECs to establish business introduction services.

The many unsuccessful attempts to establish match-making services in the UK over the past decade, and the limited success of others which have become established, indicates that the successful development of such services is a major challenge. It is therefore essential that any organisation seeking to form a business introduction service must have a thorough understanding of the nature of the informal venture capital market and learn from the experiences of both unsuccessful and successful business introduction services elsewhere. This chapter has sought to assist in this learning process by reviewing various aspects of the operations of some business introduction services in North America and in the UK, in order to highlight a number of issues that are of central importance in the design and operation of a business introduction service.

In conclusion, a business introduction service, while making an important contribution, does not provide a complete solution to the problems faced by entrepreneurial ventures seeking equity capital. First, it is not a 'quick fix': a business introduction service will not generate instant results. It takes time to develop the visibility, credibility, referral networks and critical mass that are essential for a viable service. In setting up a business introduction service, the initiators and sponsors must therefore be prepared to make a long-term commitment. The VCN experience in the USA (Chapter 3) suggests that at least five years are necessary to build an organisation with a reputation for effectively serving the needs of entrepreneurs and private investors. Second, the economic impact of a business introduction service is much broader than simply facilitating introductions. Businesses also benefit from the coaching and pathfinding roles that a business introduction service undertakes, and both businesses and investors (and hence the operation of the informal capital market) benefit from education and training provided by the service. Thus, many of the outcomes are intangible and can be overlooked in assessments of its contribution to local/regional economic development.

Third, a business introduction service should not be established as an isolated attempt to address the financing needs of small firms. As the ACOST (1990: 30) report noted, 'in a well developed capital market there will be a spectrum of institutional mechanisms to finance business experimentation and growth'. The informal venture capital market is appropriate for only one part of the spectrum of SME financing needs. It is most effective in meeting the initial financing needs of new and recently established companies seeking amounts of up to about £100,000 (although some larger investments do occur). A business introduction service is therefore less appropriate in meeting the financing needs of larger established SMEs. Moreover, most business angels do not have deep pockets and so may not be willing or able to provide follow-on finance to businesses that need a second round of external financing. Most business angels are seeking a minority stake and limited involvement, so a business introduction service is also unable to assist companies in receivership or seeking an outright sale; nor is it appropriate for investors who are seeking a management buyin situation.

Finally, it is clear that although the concept is sound and the need is increasing, the design and operation of business introduction services are still at the experimental stage. Thus, there is considerable scope for refining existing practices and for further experimentation with formats and sharing experiences with other business introduction services. The series of North American, British and Scandinavian case studies which constitute the remainder of this volume represent an initial attempt to elaborate on the issues discussed in this chapter and thereby contribute to developing this shared experience.

Implications for practice

- The key issues to be considered in the establishment of a business introduction service are as follows:
  - What kind of organisation should manage the service? Should it be the private, public or voluntary sector? Should it be a commercial, for-profit organisation or on a not-for-profit organisation?
  - What should be the geographical scale of operation of a business introduction service? Should it operate on a local, regional or national basis?
  - How should a business introduction service be financed? Is it possible to operate such a service on a commercial basis? Should introduction services be subsidised by the public sector? If so, what is the justification for this?
  - What kind of fee structure should be adopted? Should a 'success fee' be used?
  - What are the most effective ways of building a client base? What are the most productive marketing techniques? How can a business introduction service develop a high-quality client base?
  - How effective are the various matching mechanisms?
  - How can the conversion of introductions to deals be maximised?
- The evaluation of business introduction services should not be on the basis of deals done, but in terms of introductions. It should also capture the varied indirect benefits of a business introduction service.

Notes

1. Prior to its move to the MIT Enterprise Forum, VCN staff comprised two full-time staff, namely a project director and an operations manager, two half-time staff, namely an assistant operations manager and a secretary/office manager, and four work/study students who served in a variety of capacities. Wetzel himself, who is President of VCN and its principal external spokesperson, held a full-time position at the Whittemore School of Business and Economics and the University of New Hampshire and so served without pay (see Chapter 3).
2. We have derived this estimate from the following information: (1) £579 million was invested through the BES between 1983/4 and 1986/7 when the top marginal

rate of tax was 60 per cent, and a further £832 million was invested between 1987/ 8 and 1989/90 when the top marginal rate was 40 per cent; (2) approximately three-quarters of BES investors are upper-rate taxpayers (Mason *et al.*, 1988).
3. This also implies that business introduction services will have to offer greater inducements to investors than to firms – for example, in terms of the fee structure (Riding and Short, 1987). See the earlier discussion on fees.
4. The terminology follows Timmons (1990): his dollar sales values have been converted into approximate sterling equivalents.

References

Advisory Council on Science and Technology (ACOST) (1990) *The Enterprise Challenge: Overcoming barriers to growth in small firms*, London: HMSO.
Bracker, J. S., G. H. van Clouse and R. A. Thatcher (1994) 'Teleconferencing business forums: an approach to linking entrepreneurs and potential investors', *Entrepreneurship and Regional Development*, **6**, pp. 259–74.
British Venture Capital Association (BVCA) (1993) *A Guide to Business Introduction Services*, London: BVCA.
British Venture Capital Association (BVCA) (1994) *Sources of Business Angel Capital 1994/95*, London: BVCA.
Cary, L. (1991) *The Venture Capital Report Guide to Venture Capital in Europe*, 5th edn, London: Pitman.
Cary, L. (1993) *The Venture Capital Report Guide to Venture Capital in Europe*, 6th edn, London: Pitman.
Department of Trade and Industry (DTI) (1993) *Increasing the Supply of Informal Venture Capital: A guide to setting up a business introduction service*, London: DTI.
Foss, D. C. (1985) 'Venture Capital Network: the first six months of an experiment', in J. A. Hornaday, E. B. Shils, J. A. Timons and K. H. Vesper (eds.), *Frontiers of Entrepreneurship Research 1985*, Wellesley, MA: Babson College, pp. 314–24.
Gaston, R. J. (1989) *Finding Private Venture Capital for your Firm: A complete guide*, New York: Wiley.
Government of Ontario (1986) *The Ontario Investment Network*, Small Business Advocacy Report No. 9, Toronto: Small Business Branch, Ministry of Industry, Trade and Technology.
Harrison, R. T. and C. M. Mason (1992) 'International perspectives on the supply of informal venture capital', *Journal of Business Venturing*, **7**, pp. 221–31.
Harrison, R. T. and C. M. Mason (1993) 'Finance for the growing business: the role of informal investment', *National Westminster Bank Quarterly Review*, May, pp. 17–29.
Hisrich, R. D. (1988) 'New business formation through the Enterprise Development Center: a model for new venture creation', *IEEE Transactions on Engineering Management*, **35**, pp. 221–31.
Kelley, P. (1992) 'USA today: an update', in Proceedings of the 6th European Seed Capital Fund Network Seminar, Palais des Congres, Liège, December 1992, pp. 3–6.
Mason, C. and J. Chaloner (1992) *The Operation and Effectiveness of LINC (Local Investment Networking Company). Part 2: Survey of businesses*, Southampton: Urban Policy Research Unit, University of Southampton.

Mason, C. M. and R. T. Harrison (1992) 'The supply of equity finance in the UK: a strategy for closing the equity gap', *Entrepreneurship and Regional Development*, **4**, pp. 357–80.

Mason, C. M. and R. T. Harrison (1994) 'Informal venture capital in the UK', in A. Hughes and D. J. Storey (eds.), *Finance and the Small Firm*, London: Routledge, pp. 64–111.

Mason, C. M., R. T. Harrison and J. Chaloner (1991a) 'Informal risk capital in the UK: a study of investor characteristics, investment preferences and investment decision-making', Venture Finance Research Project, Working Paper No 2, Southampton: Urban Policy Research Unit, University of Southampton.

Mason, C. M., R. T. Harrison and J. Chaloner (1991b) *The Operation and Effectiveness of LINC. Part 1: Survey of investors*, Southampton: Urban Policy Research Unit, University of Southampton.

Mason, C. M., J. Harrison and R. T. Harrison (1988) *Closing the Equity Gap? An Assessment of the Business Expansion Scheme*, London: Small Business Research Trust.

Murray, G. (1991a) 'The changing nature of competition in the UK venture capital industry', *National Westminster Bank Quarterly Review*, November, pp. 65–80.

Murray, G. (1991b) *Change and Maturity in the UK Venture Capital Industry 1991–95*, Coventry: Warwick Business School.

Myers, D. D. and M. D. Moline (1988) 'Network and participation interest of Missouri informal investors', paper presented at the 8th Babson Entrepreneurship Research Conference, Calgary.

Postma, P. D. and M. K. Sullivan (1990) *Informal Risk Capital in the Knoxville Region*, Knoxville, TN: Centre of Excellence for New Venture Analysis, College of Business Administration, University of Tennessee.

Riding, A. and D. Short (1987) 'Some investor and entrepreneur perspectives on the informal market for risk capital', *Journal of Small Business and Entrepreneurs*, 5(2), pp. 19–30.

Standeven, P. (1993) 'Financing the early stage technology firm in the 1990s: an international perspective', Six Countries Programme Discussion Paper, Montreal, Canada.

Timmons, J. A. (1990) *Planning and Financing the New Venture*, Dover, MA: Brock House Publishing Co.

Tymes, E. R. and O. J. Krasner (1983) 'Informal risk capital in California', in J. A. Hornaday, J. A. Timmons and K. H. Vesper (eds.), *Frontiers of Entrepreneurship Research 1983*, Wellesley, MA: Babson College, pp. 347–68.

Wetzel, W. E. Jr (1981) 'Informal risk capital in New England', in K. H. Vesper (ed.), *Frontiers of Entrepreneurship Research 1981*, Wellesley, MA: Babson College, pp. 217–45.

Wetzel, W. E. Jr (1984) 'Venture Capital Network Inc.: an experiment in capital formation', in J. A. Hornaday, F. Tarpley, J. A. Timmons and K. H. Vesper (eds.), *Frontiers of Entrepreneurship Research 1984*, Wellesley, MA: Babson College, pp. 111–25.

Wetzel, W. E. Jr (1986a) 'Entrepreneurs, angels and economic renaissance', in R. D. Hisrich (ed.), *Entrepreneurship, Intrapreneurship and Venture Capital*, Lexington, MA: Lexington Books, pp. 119–39.

Wetzel, W. E. Jr (1986b) 'Informal risk capital: knowns and unknowns', in D. L. Sexton and R. W. Smilor (eds.), *The Art and Science of Entrepreneurship*, Cambridge, MA: Ballinger, pp. 85–108.

PART II

North American experiences

Promoting informal venture capital in the United States: reflections on the history of the Venture Capital Network

William E. Wetzel Jr and John Freear

Introduction

In 1979, the output of the Fortune 500 companies accounted for 58 per cent of gross national product, up from 37 per cent in 1954. The 500 employed 16 million people. Between 1979 and 1994, employment in Fortune 500 companies fell by 4·5 million. Over the same period, entrepreneurial ventures created 24 million jobs, many of which were in high-technology manufacturing and services. The impact of these ventures has been considerable. The *Economic Report of the President* (1989) estimated that innovation and its diffusion has accounted for about half the historical increase in the standard of living in the United States. Further, Romeo and Rappoport (1984) have estimated that the median private rate of return to technological innovation has been of the order of 25 per cent, compared to the median social rate of return of 56 per cent (see also Robert R. Nathan Associates Inc., 1978; Tewksbury *et al.*, 1980; Mansfield, 1983). Furthermore, these studies suggest that the innovations carried out by smaller firms involved even larger gaps between private and social rates of return, as smaller firms were less able than larger firms to appropriate the economic gain from their innovations.

Until the late 1970s, little was known about how these entrepreneurial ventures raised equity funds. What has emerged from the research conducted over the last 15 years particularly is an increased knowledge and understanding of a huge, informal and not very efficient capital market, with entrepreneurial ventures and individual investors as its principal participants. In the United States, there is a population of about two million individual investors, each of whom has a net worth of more than $1 million, excluding principal residence. Their equity investments, in which they have no management interest, lie in the range $100 billion to $300 billion. Individual investors invest more than $30 billion each year in over 100,000 ventures. This chapter assesses the nature, composition and efficiency of the market, its importance and its participants. In addition, it evaluates the role played by a venture capital network in improving local market efficiency, together with some of the lessons learned from its start-up and subsequent operation.

Entrepreneurial ventures and small businesses

Entrepreneurial ventures are distinguished from small businesses in that they define themselves by their growth potential rather than by their size. They have a vision and a business plan to realise that vision – to become a significant business with 50 or more on the payroll within five to ten years. Unless a venture can offer the prospect of at least $10 million in revenues, growth of at least 20 per cent annually, and pre-tax margins of at least 15 per cent within five years, it is unlikely to be of interest to any external supplier of equity capital, whether a venture capital fund or an individual investor.

Entrepreneurial ventures offering a good prospect of meeting those minimum expectations represent fewer than 10 per cent of the one million business start-ups each year. The remaining businesses are so-called 'lifestyle' companies, which are intended to provide a reasonable living for their owners, without the risks or prospects of rapid growth. They are unlikely to seek external equity financing.

At the other end of the spectrum from the 'lifestyle' businesses are the high-potential ventures representing less than 1 per cent of start-ups. They anticipate annual growth rates in excess of 50 per cent, with five-year revenue projections above $25/50 million, and may require several financing rounds, each in the six- or seven-figure range. They expect to be traded publicly within five years, and are the strongest candidates for professional venture capital financing, although individual investors may be involved at the very early stages.

In between the 'lifestyle' and the high-potential businesses are the approximately 50,000 'middle market' ventures, often having anticipated growth rates in excess of 20 per cent, and five-year revenue projections of $10 million to $25/50 million. They are the backbone of the entrepreneurial economy, and often rely heavily on 'bootstrap financing' – the term given to financing provided by such sources as the founders' personal savings, credit cards, second mortgages, customer advances and extended credit terms from vendors. These ventures are likely to be interested in, and of interest to, individuals with risk capital to invest, who are not otherwise connected to the venture or its founders. Who are these individual investors, and what do they seek from a venture investment opportunity?

Individual investor profiles

Individual investors, known as 'business angels', are high-net-worth individuals (worth at least $1 million, excluding their principal residence), often self-made, who are interested in investing equity capital in entrepreneurial ventures (Freear and Wetzel, 1992). Typically, individual investors are male, with a median age of 48 years. They hold at least a baccalaureate degree, with over half holding an advanced degree. Most have moderate to substantial business experience, and more than half have entrepreneurial experience. They have a median annual return expectation of 32.5 per cent over the median expected life of the investment (about five years), which is lower than the median annual rate of 40 per cent expected for venture capital fund investments over approximately the same period. Individual investors are willing to invest between 5 per cent and 50 per cent of their investment portfolio in venture investments. Non-financial factors, such as environmental concerns or reducing unemployment in a particular area, may play a part in the willingness to accept a lower rate of return. The evidence on geographical proximity to the investment suggests that individual investors seem to have a preference for investments located within about 100 miles of their home (Freear and Wetzel, 1989; Haar *et al.*, 1988). Their interest in providing 'know-how' as well as capital to ventures may explain, at least in part, this geographical preference.

Evidence from several studies in the United States over the years suggests that individual investors invested in financing rounds that were early stage and less than $250,000 in total. Often several investors each invested around $50,000, usually following a lead investor, who tends to be more knowledgeable about the particular industry, technology, product or market. Typically, the lead investor will change from deal to deal. The importance of knowledge and experience on the part of individual investors cannot be overemphasised. Individual investors bring more than money. Their expertise and their willingness to become involved, in varying degrees, in the operation of the venture can make the difference between success and failure. There must be a good and clearly defined relationship between the entrepreneur and the investors if the line between helpful advice and assistance and downright meddling is not to be crossed. Commonly, an individual investor will take a seat on the board of directors, and may offer, in addition, informal consulting help, and, in some cases, will even work full time or part time for the venture. Three-quarters of the entrepreneurs in one survey reported that they found the working relationships with their investors moderately or very productive.

Compared to venture capital funds, individual investors supply much more equity capital in total by making many more investments in much smaller amounts. Yet there is another potential source of private equity funding – the high-net-worth individuals who do not invest in entrepreneurial ventures. Research has indicated that there are three groups of high-net-worth individuals: individuals experienced in investing in entrepreneurial ventures; interested potential investors with no venture investment history who express a desire to enter the market; and uninterested potential investors who would not in any circumstances consider investing in entrepreneurial ventures (Freear *et al.*,

1994). Actual investors represent no more than 20 per cent of high-net-worth individuals. Among those who have not yet made any venture investments, interested potential investors outnumber uninterested potential investors by about 3:1. The actual and interested groups have broadly similar preferences for existing ventures that are close to home, and similar exit horizons. Clues to ways in which these interested investors may be activated are to be found in their stated intention of investing in small amounts compared to actual investors, in their expressed need for assistance in pricing, structuring and monitoring the performance of an investment, and in their willingness to participate with other investors in a venture investment opportunity.

The great majority of ventures fall below the screening criteria of size, risk, financing stage and liquidity set by venture capital funds. Some of these ventures tend to look towards individual investors for their external equity financing needs – but they need to be able to find them. How efficiently does the informal venture capital market work? Can venture capital networks help to improve the information flows about available capital and investment opportunities?

The market for venture capital

Entrepreneurial ventures in the 'middle market' and 'high potential' categories offer the prospect of significant growth to attract the investors who will be needed to finance that growth. The growth prospects must be sufficient to offset the high risks and lack of liquidity associated with these ventures, particularly in their early stages.

Potential investors need to be made aware of the entrepreneurial ventures, and the ventures need access to the potential investors. In other words, there needs to be a capital market of at least reasonable efficiency if these ventures are to be in a position to attract the equity financing necessary to promote or sustain growth.

The principal equity capital sources are two: one visible, the other close to invisible. The visible suppliers are financial institutions, notably the professional venture capital funds. The more than 500 professional venture capital funds manage a total portfolio of about $35 billion, and are listed in published directories such as *Pratt's Guide to Venture Capital Sources* (Morris *et al.*, 1992).

Much less visible are the individual investors or 'business angels'. These high-net-worth individuals do not list themselves in public directories; nor do they court other forms of publicity. Lack of visibility does not imply, however, lack of importance in the supply of equity capital. The best estimates suggest that there are some two million individual investors, each with a net worth exceeding $1 million, excluding their principal residences (Ou, 1987; Avery and Elliehausen, 1986). The evidence suggests that, in any one year, about 250,000 of these individuals invest a total of $10 billion to $20 billion in over 30,000 ventures. To put this in perspective, it was noted earlier that, annually, about

100,000 business start-ups offer good prospects of meeting the minimum expectations of outside equity investors.

In contrast, the much more visible venture capital funds, in the early 1990s, invested only about $2 billion annually in entrepreneurial ventures, approximately the sum that changes hands in an average morning on the New York Stock Exchange. Their impact is even more restricted by the fact that they invested the $2 billion in only 2,000 companies (usually the perceived high-potential companies), and two-thirds of the investments were supplementary investments in companies already in their portfolios. Thus, although there may be some overlap between venture capital funds and individual investors, the degree of complementarity in their functions is probably much more significant (Freear and Wetzel, 1990). Individual investors tend to supply early stage capital in amounts that are well below the normal venture capital fund minimum. If the venture grows, then it may attract the attention of the venture capital fund at a time when it is beyond the means of its earlier individual investors.

A frequently identified market inefficiency is the 'equity financing gap' between the needs of those seeking capital and the requirements of those supplying capital (Obermayer, 1983; Wilson, 1984). Specifically, the equity financing requirements of many entrepreneurial ventures are said to be too small, too illiquid and/or too risky to meet the investing criteria of professional venture capital funds and other financial institutions, but too large for the resources available to the venture's owners and their families. The Small Business Investment Act of 1958 sought to fill this gap by creating the Small Business Investment Company (SBIC) programme. Other initiatives since then include the Small Business Investment Incentive Act 1980, the Small Business Innovation Development Act 1992, and the SEC's Regulation D. In the United States in particular, there is evidence that this gap is where many business angels tend to invest.

A second market inefficiency arises when market mechanisms either fail to bring together potentially willing investors and eager entrepreneurs, or operate too slowly. Market efficiency depends upon the free and timely flow of information about sources of finance and about investment opportunities. The search for individual investor financing or venture capital fund investing normally takes at least six months from start to finish. Venture capital funds are easier to find than individual investors, but it takes longer to meet with a managing partner of a venture capital fund (a median of 1.75 months) than to meet the individual investor (a median of one month). Between the first meeting and the receipt of funds, the differences are greater. The median elapsed time was 2.5 months for individual investors and 4.5 months for venture capital funds. In the first case, the entrepreneur will be dealing with a small, close group of individual investors who would rely on the expertise of the lead investor, thus enabling decisions to made relatively rapidly. In the case of venture capital funds, the entrepreneur will be dealing with an organisation holding other people's money, so the managing partner will have a fiduciary duty to follow established consultative procedures. At the very least, it seems to take four months to raise financing from individual investors *once they have been found*, and six months from venture capital funds (Freear *et al.*, 1990; Freear and Wetzel, 1989, 1992). Such inefficient information flows impede the ability of market forces to allocate scarce capital to the most productive of the competing uses.

Given the serious inefficiencies in the venture capital market, what role can venture capital networks play?

Venture Capital Network Inc.

Finding individual investors is a major problem for entrepreneurs. There are no public lists, and there is no formal market mechanism. Thus, building a viable, financially self-supporting, private investor network itself requires a long-term entrepreneurial commitment by the sponsoring individuals or organisation. The network will require at least five years to build its organization and its network. During this period, significant financial support will be needed to supplement client fees.

There is likely to be a high degree of asymmetry in the client base of the network. The number of entrepreneurial ventures seeking the help of the network in meeting their equity capital needs will tend substantially to exceed the number of potential private individuals interested in new ventures in which to invest. These private individuals are hard to find, and reluctant to participate unless and until the network can demonstrate an adequate flow of potential investment opportunities and a high degree of confidentiality and professionalism. As a result, the network is in the classic 'chicken and egg' situation. To attract the investors, it must have the ventures. To attract and maintain the ventures as clients, it must have the investors. To be successful, it must be able to offer the prospects of a reasonable deal flow.

Venture Capital Network Inc. (VCN) was organized in 1984 as a not-for-profit corporation affiliated to the Center for Venture Research at the University of New Hampshire. VCN defined itself as being in the information business, for reasons that were partly philosophical, partly practical and partly regulatory. By being solely in the information business, VCN's mission excluded any effort to evaluate either the merits or the risks of investment opportunities submitted by entrepreneurs, or the qualifications of potential investors. Investors themselves were presumed to be the best judges of investment opportunities, and entrepreneurs were advised to do their own evaluations of the qualifications of potential investors. VCN based its operations on the philosophy that a market comprising many well-informed participants will facilitate optimal investment decisions.

Practically, the cost of maintaining a staff to screen investment proposals and investor qualifications would have been enough to deny access to most of VCN's prospective clients. From the regulatory standpoint, VCN operated without registering with the US Securities and Exchange Commission (SEC) as an investment adviser or broker/dealer. As VCN provided no investment advice and received no compensation based on the outcome of entrepreneur/investor introductions, the SEC provided VCN with two 'no action' letters, thus permitting VCN to operate without registering under the Investment Advisors Act of 1940 or the Securities and Exchange Acts of 1933 and 1934. Under the SEC's Regulation D, VCN required all its listed investors to self-certify that they qualified as 'accredited investors' under Rule 504, or, under Rule 506, that they had sufficient knowledge and experience in business and financial matters that they were capable of evaluating the merits and the risks of investment opportunities.

VCN's operations and clients

Entrepreneur clients completed a registration form, and VCN required them to submit an executive summary of their business plan. VCN provided a sample outline of a business plan and other guidance to assist entrepreneurs. The registration form contained a series of questions on: industry category; financing stage (seed, start-up, etc.); the amount of capital needed; actual and projected sales and profits; the extent to which managerial or technical assistance would be needed; the extent to which the entrepreneur would involve the investor in the venture; the state in which the venture was located; and whether the entrepreneur wished to have the details sent only to interested individual investors or to financial institutions (e.g. venture capital funds), or both. The ventures seeking funding were clustered in manufacturing, especially high-technology manufacturing, services, and the medical and health care fields.

VCN asked investor clients to complete a registration form that reflected similar data to those requested from the entrepreneurs. It asked investors to identify whether they were individual investors, institutional investors or venture capitalists. The form sought information about the geographic regions in which they would consider investing; the stage or stages of financing in which they were most interested; their preferred industry categories; and the maximum amounts they would consider investing in any one venture. The form asked also whether or not investors were willing to participate with other investors in financing ventures. In addition to asking about investors' financing criteria, the form sought basic biographical information, to help VCN accumulate broad investor profiles. As with entrepreneurs, investor interest was strongest in manufacturing, especially high-technology manufacturing, service industries, and the medical and health care industry. They expressed interest also in real estate (this was the 1980s!), financial and high-technology related services, computer software and publishing and communications.

VCN maintained a confidential database, using the registration forms of investors and entrepreneurs, and the investment opportunity profiles and investment interest profiles submitted by investors. VCN submitted to investors those investment opportunities that met their screening criteria. Both parties remained anonymous throughout this process. At the conclusion of the process, entrepreneurs were introduced to those investors who had expressed an interest in their venture. VCN's role terminated with the introduction of investor and entrepreneur.

Of VCN's 409 investor clients in the 1985–92 period, 72 per cent were individual investors and 19 per cent were venture capitalists. Overall, the characteristics of VCN's individual investors were similar to those found by other studies (Freear and Wetzel, 1989; Krasner and Tymes, 1983; Aram, 1987, 1989; Harr *et al.*, 1988; Postma and Sullivan, 1990; Gaston and Bell, 1988). Sixty-one per cent lived in New England, and 70 per cent held a master's degree or doctorate. Typically, the investors had professional backgrounds in executive positions, entrepreneurial ventures, venture capital, engineering, technology, marketing, finance or operations. They sought venture investments in New England and the Middle Atlantic states, with only 12 per cent expressing a willingness to invest outside the United States and Canada. Individual investors had lower growth expectations ($1 million to $5 million over five years) than did the venture capitalists in the VCN database ($5 million to $40 million over five years). Individual investors expressed little interest in single investments of over $1 million, and venture capitalists showed no interest in investments of under $50,000. As individual investor interest declined at about $500,000, so venture capitalist interest began to pick up. This complementary relationship was identified by another study (Freear and Wetzel, 1990). Both groups offered more than financing; they offered assistance in financial management and marketing, and to a lesser extent in production, personnel, and research and development.

VCN's registration form asked investors how many entrepreneurial ventures (excluding their own) they had invested in over the past five years. Most had made at least one investment, and many had made several. Only 18 per cent had never made an entrepreneurial investment, and this percentage of 'new' investors declined in the latter part of the period, 1989–92, as the recession set in. Growth expectations generally followed a similar declining pattern. Investor interest in the various financing stages indicated a willingness to consider all stages and remained stable over the 1985–92 period. The amounts that investors were willing to invest remained somewhat stable, although the higher amounts ($500,000 and over) declined relative to the smaller amounts, especially in the $100,000 to $250,000 range. As other studies have found, most of the investors were willing to participate with other investors in funding ventures in greater amounts than they could invest individually. Investors offered non-financial assistance in the form of membership of the board of directors or informal consulting help. Less often, they worked part time, or even full time, for the venture. In only a few cases was the participation limited to the receipt of periodic reports and attendance at stockholder meetings.

Promoting, financing and staffing VCN

VCN considered its geographical market to be the six New England states, with a population of about 15 million. The total number of active individual investors in the region was estimated to be at least 10,000. The total number of self-made, high-net-worth individuals (potential individual investors) in the region was estimated to be about 80,000.

During the first 14 months of operations, VCN permitted private investors to enrol for one year at no charge. Over 300 investors enrolled during that period. Many were curious observers rather than serious investors. The number of investors dropped to about 100 when VCN introduced enrolment fees. Despite the high attrition rate, open and free enrolment was an effective way of building an initial investor clientele.

VCN experimented with paid advertising in the media, including the *Wall Street Journal* and US Air's in-flight magazine. The *Wall Street Journal* generated fewer enquiries but more clients. The US Air magazine generated many more enquiries but fewer clients. Neither was cost-effective. VCN aggressively sought opportunities to speak about its mission and its services before professional and civic organisations of all kinds, including annual meetings of state bar associations and CPA societies, and regional meetings of commercial loan officers. These financial intermediaries were frequent sources of client referrals, as were accountants, attorneys, bankers and venture capitalists. The implied or explicit endorsement of VCN by a referral from these groups added a valuable element of credibility to VCN in the minds of investors and entrepreneurs.

Several organisations provided significant funding to help launch VCN. The Business and Industry Association of New Hampshire provided seed capital for VCN in the form of a $5,000 non-interest-bearing loan, to be amortised over two years by allocating a portion of client fees to that purpose. Thereafter, the US Economic Development Administration provided funds averaging $30,000 annually, to augment the funding supplied by sponsors. Initial sponsors, the Shawmut Bank of Boston, Peat Marwick Mitchell, Price Waterhouse, and Deloitte, Haskins and Sells, each provided one-time grants of $5,000. VCN acquired two new sponsors three years later: the law firm of Nutter, McClennen and Fish provided $2,500 per year over three years and assistance with VCN's workshops; and Digital Equipment Corporation granted $5,000 annually for three years. The Ellis L. Phillips Foundation provided a developmental grant of $10,000. In addition to its sponsorship, Digital Equipment Corporation contracted with VCN to present workshops on university campuses, which were designed to inform software programmers of VCN's networking assistance and Digital's interest in developing working relationships with programmers. The workshops met with limited success and were discontinued after two campus presentations.

The University of New Hampshire gave VCN considerable assistance by providing office space and all utilities except telephone charges. In the three years prior to VCN's move to MIT, the university also gave $15,000 for operating support. Client fees supplied about 60 per cent of VCN's operating budget. At the time of its transfer to MIT, VCN was charging entrepreneurs $125 for a six-month registration. It charged individual investors $250, institutional investors $500 and overseas investors $1,000, for a twelve-month registration. At its peak, VCN's operating budget was about $130,000.

VCN's operating budget supported a staff of two full-time employees, two half-time employees and four work/study students, each working ten hours per week. VCN's president and principal external spokesperson served without pay while maintaining full-time faculty responsibilities at the Whittemore School of Business and Economics at the University of New Hampshire. The full-time positions consisted of a project director and an operations manager. The half-time positions comprised an assistant operations manager and a secretary/office manager. The work/study students provided a variety of support services, were an integral part of the team, and obtained valuable work experience.

Measuring VCN's performance

Between 1984 and 1990, VCN served about 1,200 entrepreneur clients and 800 investor clients. Approximately 35,000 computer matches resulted in about 3,500 investor requests for introductions to entrepreneurs. Some 25 per cent of VCN's entrepreneur clients received no introductions, principally because the submitted plans were poorly developed or inadequately thought through. VCN's 'no action' letters from the SEC precluded it from pre-screening entrepreneur registrations.

Leaving aside the entrepreneurs who received no investor introductions, the typical entrepreneur met between four and five potential investors. Once the introductions were made, VCN was precluded from playing any further role, and thus lost systematic contact with its clients at that point. Systematic contact ended also when the entrepreneurs' registrations expired. Thus, it has proved impossible to measure accurately the number of actual investments that occurred as a result of VCN introductions.

Nevertheless, VCN arranged more than 1,000 introductions for over 200 entrepreneurs from 30 states and over 300 investors from 33 states. VCN learned, through follow-up telephone interviews and other informal sources of information, that 31 ventures had raised some $12 million from about 50 investors, as a result of registration with the network. About 80 per cent of those ventures were technology-based ventures, which is perhaps a reflection of the nature both of the New England economy and of its self-made, high-net-worth individual investors. VCN also encouraged and assisted in the formation of other similar networks across the country and in Canada. Currently, six networks are in operation.

Recent developments

In late 1988 and early 1989, VCN attempted to raise about $300,000 to underwrite the costs associated with achieving its goal of becoming the major financing resource in New England for entrepreneurs and individual investors. The University of New Hampshire provided $10,000 to support the fund-raising effort, which targeted three potential sources: the US Department of Commerce Office of Technology Administration, multinational firms with strategic business interests in both emerging high-growth ventures and high-net-worth individuals, and large private foundations.

VCN's quest for this funding was unsuccessful. Discussions then began with the MIT Enterprise Forum, with which it had enjoyed a six-year history of collaboration on programmes promoting the entrepreneurial cause. The Enterprise Forum had no capital formation process of its own. This, and VCN's reputation among entrepreneurs and individual investors, coupled with the fact that over 80 per cent of the ventures that raised funds through VCN were technology based, led MIT to decide to establish VCN as a not-for-profit affiliate of the Enterprise Forum of Cambridge. The move to MIT was completed in December 1990. VCN was renamed Technology Capital Network Inc. (TCN) in 1992.

Conclusion

What conclusions may be drawn from the informal venture capital market in the United States and from the VCN experience?

Those hoping to establish a venture capital network would usually know that there are entrepreneurial ventures seeking equity financing. More importantly, they must believe that there are indeed individual investors out there interested in making such investments, even though they may shun publicity and are difficult to find. Economic, financial and social conditions differ from country to country, yet it seems likely that most countries would have potential if not actual individual investors within their populations. Helping to make the market in which investors participate is a major aim of a network. Another worthy aim is to find ways of mobilizing potential investors to become active investors. All of this requires greater knowledge of the attitudes, behaviour and characteristics of active and potential investors.

Networks, and entrepreneurs, should remember that investors frequently bring business knowledge and experience to the table as well as money.

Networks are not a panacea. Most owners of ventures do not seek external equity capital (those owning 'lifestyle' ventures may be willing to trade growth prospects for retention of full control over their venture).

Financing gaps, including efficiency gaps, will persist as long as the overall market for equity and debt capital remains segmented, with poor information flows within and among the various segments.

Just as it is difficult and time consuming for the individual entrepreneur to find an individual investor, so it is difficult and time consuming for a network to find individual investors. In other words, there is a marketing and information problem. However, once the network has found the investor, and has proved its ability to provide a confidential, efficient and effective service, it has made the investor potentially available, long term, to many entrepreneurs.

Starting a network requires a mixture of staying power and zeal. Knowing that the idea of a network is good means little if you cannot persuade the many other players of its value and potential. Its problems are like those of any business start-up. A new network will require seed and start-up capital to set up its operations, to become known and to build its client base to a self-supporting level.

VCN's involvement in individual financing situations ceased at the introduction stage. The deal participants need professional help in pricing, structuring and monitoring the deal. Again, VCN, being in the information business, was able to offer help. This it did principally through workshops, although it contemplated also producing an instructional video-tape series.

Given that many of the deals are struck between ventures and investors located within a few hours' travel of each other, there is a strong argument in favour of defining a network's probable 'catchment area'. Linkages among networks would allow for those investors willing to invest further afield.

Implications for practice

- Not all small businesses necessarily require, or are attractive for, external equity investment, and business introduction services should be selective in the client businesses they include in the service.
- Informal investors, or business angels, are more likely to finance early stage financing rounds, in smaller amounts, than are venture capital funds.
- The information gap, which prevents entrepreneurs and potential investors from getting together, is a major constraint on the growth of entrepreneurial ventures, which business introduction services can work to close.
- Entrepreneurs should allow around four months to raise finance from individual investors once they have been found.
- To attract potential investors to register with a network, it is necessary to demonstrate an adequate flow of potential investment opportunities and ensure confidentiality and professionalism.
- Attraction of sponsorship funding, contributions in kind and endorsements from professional and financial intermediaries is vital to ensure adequate resourcing of an introduction service, and support the attraction and retention of clients.

References

Aram, J. D. (1987) *Informal Risk Capital in the Eastern Great Lakes Region*, Washington, DC: Office of Advocacy, US Small Business Administration.

Aram, J. D. (1989) 'Attitudes and behaviors of informal investors toward early stage investments, technology based ventures and co-investors', *Journal of Business Venturing*, **4**, pp. 333–47.

Avery, R. B. and G. E. Elliehausen (1986) 'Financial characteristics of high income families', *Federal Reserve Bulletin*, **72**, pp. 163–77.

Economic Report of the President (1989), Washington, DC: US Government Printing Office.

Freear J. and W. E. Wetzel Jr (1989) 'Equity capital for entrepreneurs', in R. H. Brockhaus, N. C. Churchill, J. A. Katz, B. A. Kirchhoff, K. H. Vesper and W. E. Wetzel Jr (eds.), *Frontiers of Entrepreneurship Research 1989*, Wellesley MA: Babson College, pp. 230–44.

Freear J., and W. E. Wetzel Jr (1990) 'Who bankrolls high-tech entrepreneurs?', *Journal of Business Venturing*, **5**, pp. 77–89.

Freear J., J. E. Sohl and W. E. Wetzel Jr (1990) 'Raising venture capital: entrepreneurs' view of the process', in N. Churchill, W. D. Bygrave, J. A. Hornaday, D. F. Muzyka, K. H. Vesper and W. E. Wetzel Jr (eds.), *Frontiers of Entrepreneurship Research 1990*, Wellesley MA: Babson College, pp. 223–37.

Freear, J., J. E. Sohl and W. E. Wetzel Jr (1994) 'Angels and non-angels: are there differences?', *Journal of Business Venturing*, **9**, pp. 109–23.

Freear, J. and W. E. Wetzel Jr (1992) 'The informal venture capital market in the 1990s', in D. L. Sexton and J. D. Kasarda (eds.), *The State of Art of Entrepreneurship*, Boston: PWS-Kent, pp. 462–86.

Gaston, R. J. and S. E. Bell (1988) *The Informal Supply of Capital*, Washington, DC: Office of Economic Research, US Small Business Administration.

Haar N. E., J. Starr and I. C. MacMillan (1988) 'Informal risk capital: investment patterns on the East Coast of the USA', *Journal of Business Venturing*, **3**, 11–29.

Krasner, O. J. and E. R. Tymes (1983) 'Informal risk capital in California', in J. Hornaday, J. A. Timmons and K. H. Vesper (eds.), *Frontiers of Entrepreneurship Research 1983*, Wellesley, MA: Babson College.

Mansfield, E. (1983) 'Entrepreneurship and the management of innovation', in J. Bachman (ed.), *Entrepreneurship and the Outlook for America*, New York: The Free Press.

Morris, J., S. Isenstein and A. Knowles (1992) *Pratt's Guide to Venture Capital Sources*, New York: SDC Publishing Inc.

Obermayer, J. H. (1983) *The Capital Crunch: Small high-technology companies and national objectives during a period of severe debt and equity shortages*, Cambridge MA: Research and Planning Inc.

Ou, C. (1987) 'Holdings of privately-held business assets by American families: findings from the 1983 Consumer Finance Survey', unpublished manuscript, Washington, DC: Office of Economic Research, US Small Business Administration.

Postma, P. D. and M. K. Sullivan (1990) 'Informal risk capital in the Knoxville region', unpublished report, Knoxville: TN: University of Tennessee.

Robert R. Nathan Associates Inc. (1978) *Net Rates of Return on Innovation*, Washington, DC: National Science Foundation.

Romeo, A. A. and L. Rappaport (1984) *Social Versus Private Returns to Innovation by Small Firms Compared to Large Firms*, Washington, DC: Office of Advocacy, US Small Business Administration.

Tewksbury, J. G., M. S. Crandall and W. E. Crane (1980) 'Measuring the societal benefits of innovation', *Science*, **209**, 658–62.

Wilson, I. G. (1984) *Financing High Growth Companies in New Hampshire*, Concord, NH: Department of Resources and Economic Development, State of New Hampshire.

CHAPTER 4

'. . . Where angels fear to tread': some lessons from the Canada Opportunities Investment Network experience

Rena Blatt and Allan Riding

Introduction

In recent years, it has become abundantly clear that the early stages of corporate growth are obstructed by firms' inability to access equity capital. The perception of an 'equity gap' has led to a number of initiatives. One such initiative has been the development of match-making systems. The first such system was the Venture Capital Network (VCN). It was pioneered by William Wetzel in the north-eastern United States. Described more fully elsewhere (Wetzel, 1983, 1984; see also Chapter 3), VCN uses computer software to link investors with entrepreneurs. The purpose of match-making systems is to complete a marketplace which is intrinsically fragmented.

In 1986, the Ontario Chamber of Commerce (OCC) advanced the idea of an Ontario (now Canadian) version of VCN. The 'Computerised Ontario Investment Network', or COIN, was established soon afterwards. COIN was initially sponsored by the government and a number of firms in the private sector in addition to the OCC. Subsequently, COIN was expanded to a national basis as the 'Canada Opportunities Investment Network' (still COIN) with substantial additional support from the federal government.

At the time it was established, a paradox was noted. On the one hand, there was an unsatisfied demand by growing firms for equity capital; on the other hand, a large pool of private savings was understood to exist. Accordingly, COIN was initiated as a mechanism to connect investors and entrepreneurs in an inchoate marketplace. Three understandings formed the foundation of the initial governmental support for COIN. First, support for COIN was forthcoming because COIN embodied an opportunity to 'greatly facilitate the flow of capital from RRSP and Pension Funds'. Second, COIN looked to be a community-based initiative. Support was also predicated on the active involvement of the OCC and the expectation that COIN would be self-sufficient and would operate independently of government. The intent was to establish a community-based instrument to deliver relatively small amounts of start-up and expansion capital. The extent to which COIN has succeeded in accomplishing its goals is not clear.

This chapter has three purposes. First, it reviews the theoretical rationale for the establishment of intermediaries such as COIN. Second, the history of COIN is documented. Third, the chapter presents the findings of an external analysis of the efficacy of COIN. This analysis is based on the results of a survey of informal investors.[1] These findings are then related to the theoretical requirements for successful intermediation.

To accomplish these tasks, the chapter is organised as follows. The next section examines previous work, including the theoretical reasoning behind the establishment of intermediaries. This is followed by a chronology of the development of COIN. The methodology of the empirical aspect of this study is then presented, and is followed by the findings. The chapter closes with a summary and conclusion.

Previous research

The theory of intermediation in primitive markets

In a classic article, Akerlof (1970) presents an analysis of markets which are characterised by imperfect information. Akerlof illustrates his reasoning by considering the market for cars. He distinguishes between new cars and used cars and between good cars and bad cars (lemons). The sellers of used cars are able to assess the likelihood that their car is a lemon with greater accuracy than can a potential purchaser. This information asymmetry has several implications.

First, it explains why there is such a large disparity between the average prices of new cars and of old cars. Second, it leads to a market in which good used cars sell at the same price as bad used cars. This is because a buyer cannot a priori tell the difference between the two: only the seller knows. In such a market, Gresham's law applies to the point that bad cars drive out the good (they sell at the same price). Under these conditions, potential buyers exit the market. Without intermediation, the market degenerates.

Akerlof went on to liken the 'market for lemons' to a capital market in an underdeveloped country. This analogy has been pursued by others and the analysis extended to underdeveloped markets, even those in developed countries. For example, Campbell and Kracaw (1977) introduce a financial intermediary able to distinguish good firms from bad in a credit market. Without such an intermediary, these researchers show that the market deteriorates in the manner predicted by Akerlof. In the presence of such an intermediary, however, firms' true values are reflected in the market.

Chan (1983) explicitly considers financial intermediation in a venture capital marketplace in which information is imperfect. Chan's model postulates the existence of entrepreneurs who put effort into a firm and who use a portion of the returns from the firm to satisfy current consumption. Potential investors cannot observe either the level of effort or the entrepreneurs' draw without an investigation. The investigation is assumed to have a cost. Chan shows that, without a particular form of intermediation, such a market will fail. Entrepreneurs will present only inferior projects. Investors would then have to conduct additional (costly) searches before finding a non-inferior opportunity. The total cost of serial searches reduce investors' anticipated rates of return. Investors then exit the market in favour of alternative investments.

In Chan's model, the market is salvaged if it includes either a perfectly informed investor or an investor for whom search costs are zero. Under this condition, entrepreneurs are induced to bring better investments to market and investors remain active.

This theory helps us to understand better the role of intermediaries such as COIN. Theory identifies how match-making services aid the market for informal equity capital and also how such mechanisms fall short. In the context of Chan's model, COIN reduces the costs associated with making first contact between investors and entrepreneurs. Accordingly, it *might* diminish a portion of the search costs faced by investors. However, the most significant portion of search costs is not abated. The investigation of the quality of the project remains the investors' responsibility. Hence, such services are unlikely to provide the type of intermediation which Chan and his precursors advocate. At best, COIN may be a step towards enhancing the market *if* it reduces the investors' costs of making initial contact. A consideration of the research on informal investors, however, suggests that even this impact is negligible.

Informal investors in Canada

Seminal research on the informal market for risk capital was carried out by William Wetzel (1983). Wetzel provided evidence, based on US data, which suggested that the size of the pool of informal risk capital may exceed that of the institutional venture capital industry. Wetzel and his colleagues conducted additional studies of the characteristics of US informal investors. Gaston and Bell (1986) and Tymes and Krasner (1983) have also documented some characteristics of US investors.

In Canada, the only study of informal investors yet reported in the academic literature is that conducted by Short (1987) and Riding and Short (1987a; 1987b). According to Riding and Short, preliminary estimates of the size of the pool of risk capital in the Ottawa–Carleton region are consistent with Wetzel's contention that the market for informal risk capital is of a significant size.

There are several areas of agreement in this literature. Previous studies have shown that the informal market is very much a *local* marketplace and a *personal* marketplace. Interactions among investors form an important part of informal risk-capital-investing decisions. Investors are part of a loosely connected network of market participants. Informal investor profiles show that investors are well-educated individuals of means who have had prior experience, at the management level, in the start-up of new business ventures. They typically prefer to invest geographically 'close to home'. Investors prefer to invest in common stock and to participate with other informal investors in financing deals. Research concurs that investors hold realistic expectations regarding the outcome of their risk capital investments. While investors recognise risks inherent in investing in young or start-up companies, they do not appear obsessed with those risks.

Ottawa–Carleton investors differ in a few respects. They display higher levels of activity, lower levels of involvement in the management of the firm, and higher rates of rejection of possible deals than their counterparts in the United States. Investors in the Ottawa–Carleton region also have higher amounts of capital committed to individual investments than did US investors, although they typically assume minority positions in investee firms.

Informal investors tend to invest in those areas experiencing so-called capital market gaps. Riding and Short (1987a) found that investors did not perceive capital market gaps. Investors indicated that they were exposed to a more than sufficient deal flow. If this is true, then match-making services have negligible impact on reducing the investors' costs of search. Investors expressed a low level of interest in match-making systems. If models such as that advanced by Chan make sense, then further intermediation is required.

Conversely, entrepreneurs perceived the marketplace for informal risk capital to be inefficient and found that gaps were significant impediments to growth. While the perception of 'gaps' is understandable, actual shortages in the supply of risk capital may not exist. It was on this basis that COIN was established: to improve upon the disorganised and fragmented marketplace for informal capital. Prior to a consideration of COIN's evolution and performance, it is useful to consider the legal infrastructure for the Canadian market for informal capital. It will be seen that the legal setting potentially places serious limitations on the viability of match-making services.

The legal setting for the Canadian market for informal capital

Securities regulation in Canada falls under provincial rather than national jurisdiction. There is, therefore, a plurality of practices. However, most provinces, to a greater or lesser extent, follow the lead of the Ontario Securities Commission (OSC), the body which monitors Canada's largest stock exchange, the Toronto Stock Exchange. According to the Securities Act of the Province of Ontario, any firm, large or small, which tries to raise capital by distribution of securities must file a prospectus with the OSC. This is a costly procedure ($300,000 to $500,000) and can be avoided only under some very specific exemptions.

One exemption is known as the 'Private Company Exemption'. Such companies are defined by a term in their corporate charter which prohibits any invitation to the public to subscribe for its shares. Excluding employees, the number of shareholders permitted in a private company is limited to 50. The essential legal issue in determining if a firm can avoid the prospectus requirement is the determination of whether or not a prospective investor is a 'member of the public'. Thus the sale of securities to people already closely associated with the firm would be permissible. Prospective investors discovered through a match-making service would, in general, not qualify.

A second exemption is the 'Private Placement' exemption. If an investor in Ontario invests more than $150,000, he or she is deemed to be a sophisticated investor and the protection supposedly proffered by a prospectus is not required.[2] The OSC must be appraised of such trades and the corporation may be required to supply a (somewhat costly) offering memorandum. The investor receives the rights of action for damages or recision in the event of misrepresentation in the memorandum. This is the most frequently used exemption. COIN may be useful if the Private Placement exemption can be used. However, COIN's usefulness is limited with respect to smaller deals.

A third exemption is the 'Seed Capital' exemption. Under the terms of this release, an invitation can be made to no more than 50 potential investors and no more than 25 of these may actually invest. Investors must be 'reasonably informed' and firms may only use this exemption once. It does not appear that a listing on COIN meets the terms of this exemption.

There are other exemptions. For example, the 'Isolated Trade' constitutes a means by which a firm could change owners. However, frequent or repeated trades of a like nature are not permitted. The OSC can designate an exempt status to certain potential investors. Some financial institutions may also purchase shares without the prospectus requirement. Finally, employees may also purchase shares, so long as such purchases are not coerced.

From this description, it is clear that the legal environment in Canada differs from that in the USA. In the USA, a prospectus is not required if investors qualify as sophisticated under the terms of Regulation D. This regulation identifies such investors according to their personal backgrounds, education and experience. Because of these differences in the legal environment, it might be reasonable to suppose that match-making services in Canada are in a more tenuous position than are their counterparts elsewhere: that the development of Canadian networks may be impeded.

The evolution of COIN

In 1986, the OCC advanced the idea of an Ontario (now Canadian) version of the VCN. Known as the Computerised Ontario Investment Network (COIN), it later expanded its operation to a national basis as the 'Canada Opportunities Investment Network' (still COIN).

Background and premises

The setting for COIN is grounded, on the one hand, in the well-documented problems that small firms face when seeking growth (equity) capital. On the other hand, there is a large pool of capital held by individuals. Three understandings initially formed the foundation for COIN's support. First, support for COIN was forthcoming because COIN embodied an opportunity to promote the flow of capital from RRSP[3] and Pension Funds. Second, COIN looked to be a community-based initiative. The premise that government funding would only be required for start-up was also a factor in governments' support for COIN.

As a result, the 1986 Ontario Government Speech from the Throne announced COIN. The Ontario government committed initial funding. On 13 August 1986, the Ontario Securities Commission ruled that COIN was exempt from prospectus requirements. The OSC did stipulate that COIN play no screening role and provide no investment advice. COIN also had to include a disclaimer that network participants must themselves be in compliance with the Securities Act.

The launch of the Computerised Ontario Investment Network occurred in November of 1986. A significant media advertising programme and a 'road show', which involved the programme management, accompanied the launch. The goal of the promotional campaign was to enlist 1,000 users. This was premised on the belief that 'The *identified* number of potential users of the system during the first year is estimated to be 17,000' (8,000 entrepreneurs and 9,000 self-directed RRSPs; emphasis that of the original)[4] and that 'the credibility of the OCC . . . will further enhance the image of COIN'. The advertising was a 'broad brush' approach. The thinking behind this strategy was exemplified by assertions such as 'it's believed that one insertion weekly in the Toronto papers will be needed to generate sufficient inquiries to meet our goal of 1,000 users'.[5]

COIN's financial statement data for the four months of operation ending April 1987 reported fee incomes of $9,450 and $13,450 from entrepreneurs and investors respectively. The fee rates were $150 per entrepreneur and $250 per investor, less discounts ($50 to OCC members) and subsidies to local Boards of Trade ($25 to local branch). These data imply an initial registration of approximately 60 to 75 investors and about 75 to 125 entrepreneurs.[6] These registrations fell far short of the 1,000 participant goal.

In later years, it does not appear that the number of COIN participants increased according to projections. COIN's financial statement data for 1989 and 1990 report total fee revenues of $51,775 and $48,583 respectively.[7] The $48,583 fee revenues for 1990 embrace $30,578 from entrepreneurs (implies 200 to 400 entrepreneurs) and $18,005 from investors (implies 80 to 100 investors).[8] These data provide some potential insights into COIN's efficacy.

In 1990, COIN's advertising stated that 'about $250,000,000 . . . from investors in Canada and up to $25,000,000 from offshore investors' was available in COIN.[9] COIN's own documentation[10] breaks down the availability of funds from investors according to Table 4.1. These data imply that the average COIN

Table 4.1 Availability of investment capital through COIN

Amounts available	Availability from investors (%)
Under $10,000	0
$10,000 to $25,000	6
$25,000 to $50,000	6
$50,000 to $100,000	17
$100,000 to $250,000	28
$250,000 to $500,000	14
$500,000 to $1,000,000	16
More than $1,000,000	13

investor has about $450,000 available for investment. (The median COIN investor has less than $250,000, according to this table.) If COIN indeed had $275,000,000 available, the COIN database must have represented at least 600 investors. This would imply an annual fee income from investors alone of at least $125,000. The data are reconciled if one supposes that the 13 per cent of investors who have 'more than $1,000,000' to invest include one or more institutional venture capitalists who, in principle, may have access to very large pools of funds. However, COIN would not be needed for entrepreneurs to locate such investors; nor does previous research indicate that these investors are much interested in the low end of the equity market.

COIN has been unable to achieve self-sufficiency. COIN's financial statement data do not reflect the claims of success in its promotional literature. At this point, examination of the findings of a preliminary investigation of COIN's impact on the informal market for risk capital is in order.

The impact of COIN on the market for informal risk capital: a preliminary analysis

This section reports some interim findings from a survey of participants in the Ontario market for informal risk capital. This analysis uses the responses of 187 individuals, 126 of whom are informal investors. Contact with these investors occurred by a variety of means. Personal references in the Toronto area were invaluable. In other areas (Collingwood, North Bay, Niagara, Kingston), the good offices of local Boards of Trade or Economic Development Corporations identified investors. Personal interviews were employed in more than 50 per cent of these cases. COIN also sent questionnaires to the investors on their database. Fifteen responses resulted from the COIN mailout. One of these respondents did not complete the questionnaire and is not among the 126 investors in the sample.[11]

Awareness of and satisfaction with the COIN programme
Awareness of COIN is estimated using the responses of the 112 investors *not*

contacted through COIN. The distribution of these responses is as follows. Investors were asked if they were aware of COIN. If they were aware of COIN, they were asked if they had used COIN. The breakdown of the replies to these questions is shown in Table 4.2.

These results imply that COIN's advertising is ineffective. More than half the active investors surveyed in this research were unaware of the existence of COIN. Moreover, less than one in five of the investors who did report awareness of COIN had participated in the programme. One of the reasons advanced for this lack of participation is COIN's close identification with Price Waterhouse, a major accounting firm. Financial advisers associated with other consulting or accounting firms would be understandably loath to refer a client to a competitor.

Of course, an alternative reason for the low rate of COIN usage is the prospect that investors do not need COIN. As structured, COIN may not be suited to their requirements. According to one respondent, the investor's pursuit of the entrepreneur (with COIN, the onus is on the investor to initiate contact) weakens the investor's subsequent bargaining position.

A consistent finding of all previous research has been the propensity for informal investors to invest within 50 miles of home or office. Another pervasive finding is that business associates and friends are the primary sources of information about potential opportunities. These colleagues do not simply provide an alternative match-making facility. They also act as mentors of the investing process. This personal aspect of the market is important. Instituting an impersonal (computer-based), centralised (Toronto-based), match-making service is dissonant with the innate nature of the market.

Investors who had used COIN were asked if they would use COIN again. Table 4.3 breaks down the responses to this question according to the source of the response. These results show that satisfaction was mixed. One respondent to the COIN mailing did not complete the questionnaire, but wrote as follows:

> After filling out already two questionnaires from COIN and paying the $250 for their services (0 contacts, 0 recommendations during one full year), it was the last thing I wanted to receive an other [sic] form to complete from COIN. If you wish please look at the previous forms.

On the other hand, half the respondents were sufficiently pleased to be willing to use COIN again.

Table 4.2 Awareness and use of COIN in Ontario

Response	Number of investors
Not familiar with COIN	58
Aware of COIN, have not used COIN	44
Have used COIN	9
No response	1

Table 4.3 Willingness to use COIN again

	Respondents to COIN mailing	Respondents to main survey	Total
Would use COIN again	7	2	9
Would *not* use COIN again	3	7	10
Registered with COIN, but have made no investments	4	0	4

Further insight arises from analysis of respondents' ratings of COIN *vis-à-vis* other potential sources of investment leads. The questionnaire asked investors to respond (on a five-point scale where 1 = not often, 5 = very often) about how frequently that had employed each of 11 possible sources of investment leads. Figure 4.1 presents the means of the responses to this question. It shows these responses for the 18 investors who had used COIN and 95 investors who had not used COIN. (Not all respondents answered this question.) From these data, active personal search, lawyers or accountants, business associates, and friends were all used more frequently than COIN. This is true of both sets of investor respondents and is fully consistent with previous research findings.

The questionnaire also asked investors which of these sources had been the most useful means of generating leads. Respondents cited business associates most frequently (59 investors). They cited active personal search second most frequently (29 investors). As *the* most useful source of leads, none cited COIN. In view of Akerlof's and Chan's arguments about the need for a filter in the

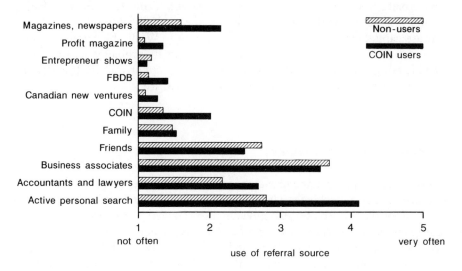

Figure 4.1 Informal investment deal referral sources.

marketplace, these findings ought not to be surprising. Business associates informally provide the review of projects which is so essential to preserving the integrity of the marketplace. There are no real listing requirements for COIN; thus, COIN fails to provide protection against 'lemons'.

COIN's impact in the informal market

The questionnaire asked respondents to describe the process by which they decided about investments. Investors accepted an average of 5 per cent of the opportunities presented to them. The most common reason for rejecting a proposal was a perceived lack of faith in the managerial abilities of the principals of the firm.

Two-thirds of the investors reported a scarcity of 'investment opportunities in which they would seriously be interested'. Only 12 per cent perceived an abundance of such opportunities. While there is no shortage of entrepreneurs seeking capital, most investors are less than impressed with the quality of deals.

This situation is one that COIN has not redressed. Sixty per cent of the investor respondents perceived that, compared with five years ago, it is now *more* difficult to find high-quality investment opportunities, COIN notwithstanding. Among the 40 per cent of respondents who reported that it was now easier to find such opportunities, only one cited the availability of exchanges and databases (e.g. COIN) as a factor in the perceived improvement. From the investors' viewpoint, then, the problem with the informal market for risk capital is not an inability to make contact. Rather the problem they report is a scarcity of high-quality opportunities.

A further indication that COIN was not meeting the needs of the informal marketplace has been the formation of alternatives. Table 4.4 provides a listing of such alternatives with a short description of each.[12] In addition, a number of venture capital clubs are also in active operation.[13] While the extent to which such clubs invest on behalf of their members is legally problematic, such clubs provide points of contact and on-going educational opportunities. It is striking that, in every case, these alternatives are local in nature.

Summary and conclusions

Conceptually, a programme to match investors and entrepreneurs makes sense in a market that is inchoate. The informal market for risk capital, however, is not a national marketplace. All previous research shows that investors venture more than 50 miles from home or office only by exception. Informal investors invest close to home. It is a *local*, and also a *personal* market. Investors rely on personal contact and recommendations. The integrity and knowledge of other participants incline them to invest, usually as members of syndicates.

Table 4.4 Alternatives to COIN

Investment Matching Service of Alberta	Operated by the provincial department of Economic Development and Trade, the service provides business–investor introductions (2 offices)
FACE Business Opportunity Database	Business opportunities are listed with the Foundation for the Advancement of Canadian Entrepreneurship and published in FACE's *Venture Source* magazine.
FACE Enterprise Funding Board	After professional review of business plans, opportunities with sufficient merit are presented to FACE's Funding Board. Those accepted by the board are provided with intermediation assistance.
The Market Place Bulletin	Published by the Ontario Ministry of Industry, Trade and Technology, the bulletin lists certain types of business opportunity in Ontario. The bulletin is distributed to about 9,000 Ontario business executives.
British Columbia Investment Matching Program	Operated by the BC Ministry of Economic Development, Small Business and Trade, the programme provides a listing of business opportunities in each region of the province. It provides match-making services and also aids with joint ventures, etc.
Ontario SBDC Program	This attempts to match a profile of an entrepreneur's company with listed SBDCs (small business development corporations)/PVCCs (provincially sponsored venture capital companies).
The Investment Exchange, Calgary	A private sector initiative, the exchange claims to have more than 550 potential investors on its computerised database. Onus is left to the entrepreneur to contact potential investors.
Entinex Inc	Provides (at a cost) a computerised listing of Canadian business opportunities.
Locating Investors for Niagara Companies (LINK)	Publishes a bulletin and helps Niagara-based manufacturing firms locate investors
Investment Opportunities Project, St John's Board of Trade	The IOP not only provides a match-making facility; it assists with the negotiation process and provides advocacy.

Establishing a *national* and *impersonal* referral service is fundamentally at odds with the nature of the market.

In general, investors do not report COIN to be an essential, or even important, element of their investment sourcing. Investors use alternative leads to potential investments more frequently than they use COIN – even investors registered with COIN. The importance of local leads and referrals may be one explanation of why COIN has failed to achieve financial self-sufficiency and has been unable to approach its targeted number of participants. The deterioration of COIN as a marketplace is fully consistent with Akerlof's and Chan's predictions.

On the other hand, COIN has undoubtedly resulted in some degree of investment activity. However, to make better use of a computerised match-making service, there are several steps that might be considered.

First, the emphasis needs to be at the local level. In particular, the presence of individuals respected by the community and known to be persons of integrity is crucial. Such people, by their own involvement in a deal, lend credibility to the opportunity. Other investors are then willing to follow. Such individuals need not be 'lead investors'. Members of economic development agencies can also play an advocate role. In several communities such a role is evolving.

Second, a match-making service ought to incorporate well-known minimum 'listing requirements'. Studies in classical financial economics (e.g. Akerlof, 1973; Chan, 1983) have identified the need for an intermediary which filters out the 'lemons' from the spectrum of investment opportunities. In the absence of such filtering, investors exit the market and the market degenerates. In a very real sense, this is part of what a 'lead investor', mentioned above, also accomplishes.

Third, consideration could be given to amendments to the legislative environment. In the USA, entrepreneurs do not need to comply with costly prospectus requirements if investors qualify as 'sophisticated' investors under the terms of 'Regulation D'. This regulation identifies sophisticated investors in terms of their personal qualities, education and experience. No such provision exists in the provincial securities acts. While there are conditions under which entrepreneurs can avoid prospectus preparation, these conditions are much more restrictive than are those in the USA.

Systems similar to COIN, such as the VCN, have operated with greater success in the USA. Such systems, however, have remained more local in scope, have operated in a less restrictive legal setting, have usually been associated with small business research centres or incubators (or universities), and have incorporated greater advisory capability than is permitted under Canadian laws. A match-making service, one with well-known minimum 'listing requirements' can, under such circumstances, then become a useful adjunct to easy syndication and investment.

Implications for practice

- Informal investment is, in part, a personal process, and purely impersonal (computer-based) and centralised (national) match-making services may fail to meet the needs of the market.
- Without some measure of quality control on the nature of the business registering with the service, investor dissatisfaction is likely.
- There is no shortage of entrepreneurs seeking capital, but most investors are less than impressed with the quality of the deals.

- The informal market for risk capital is not a national marketplace, but a local and personal market.
- A successful match-making service should be based on two principles:
  - The emphasis should be on the local level.
  - The services should include 'minimum listing requirements' or quality filters.

Notes

1. According to Wetzel, active involvement of informal investors is crucial to the success of match-making services.
2. The dollar limit varies across different provincial jurisdictions. In the province of Alberta, for example, the limit is set at $25,000.
3. In the early 1970s, the Canadian government recognised the need for individuals to provide for their own post-retirement financial security. Therefore, the concept of a Registered Retirement Savings Plan (RRSP) was introduced. Up to an annual limit (a limit which varies with economic policy), individuals may defer taxation on that portion of income contributed to an RRSP. These contributions, together with the interest earned on them, are taxable on withdrawal from the RRSP, presumably on retirement, and at lower tax rates in effect of retirement income.
4. *COIN Marketing Plan*, 27 August 1986, p. 5.
5. *COIN Marketing Plan*, 27 August 1986, p. 15.
6. It is interesting that, at this early point in its development, COIN applied for and received a charter by letters patent (applied February 1987, granted 25 March 1987) not as the Computerised Ontario Investment Network, but as the Canada Opportunities Investment Network. The proposal to form a Canada-wide investment network was not advanced until October 1987. That proposal sought $500,000, citing that the programme 'has proven to be an unqualified success in bringing together entrepreneurs and investors for face to face negotiations' (The Ontario Investment Network, *An Innovative Approach to Small Business Risk Capital Formation*, p. 3, attached to correspondence related to proposal for 'COIN Canada').
7. A letter of 22 September 1988 from COIN to the then minister, Monte Kwinter, asserted that 'the Ontario [COIN] program has undercovered [*sic?*] a hitherto undisclosed pool of available capital within your province of between $65 to $80 million'. The COIN file did not contain financial statement data for 1988, so it is not clear how many investors participated in COIN in that year. Other data in the COIN file suggest an average of $450,000 of funds available per investor. Together, these data imply a 1988 investor population in the order of 200.
8. Canada Opportunities Investment Network, *COIN Budget 1991*.
9. Canada Opportunities Investment Network, 'Overview' in *How? What? Where? When? and How Much?*, p. 2.

10. Canada Opportunities Investment Network, August 1990 Business Plan, Appendix C. This same appendix specifies the ratios of investors to entrepreneurs across a variety of industrial categories. In no industry is the ratio less than 1:1. The highest ratio is 8:1. One interpretation of these ratio data is that, on average, there are 3.9 times as many investors as entrepreneurs, when in fact the ratio of entrepreneurs to investors was between 2:1 and 5:1.
11. In mailed survey research, a response rate of 15 to 26 per cent is the norm. A return of 15 questionnaires from the COIN database therefore implies a population of COIN investors of 60 to 100 individuals.
12. A more detailed listing can be found in Williamson (1992).
13. The Venture Capital/Entrepreneur Club of Montreal, the Toronto Venture Group, and the York University Venture Capital Showcases and Forums are among these groups.

References

Akerlof, G. (1970) 'The market for 'lemons': quantitative uncertainty and the market mechanism', *Quarterly Journal of Economics*, **84**, pp. 488–500.

Campbell, T. and M. Kracaw (1977) 'Information production, market signalling, and the theory of financial intermediation', *Journal of Finance*, **37**, pp. 215–32.

Chan, Y.-S. (1983) 'On the positive role of financial intermediation in allocation of venture capital in a market with imperfect information', *Journal of Finance*, **38**, pp. 1543–68.

Gaston, R. S. and S. Bell (1986) 'Informal risk capital in the Sunbelt region', Knoxville, TN: Applied Economics Group.

Riding, A. L. and D. M. Short (1987a) 'Some investors' and entrepreneurs' perceptions of the informal market for risk capital', *Journal of Small Business and Entrepreneurship*, 5 (2), pp. 19–30.

Riding, A. L. and D. M. Short (1987b) 'On the estimation of the investment potential of informal investors: a capture–recapture approach', *Journal of Small Business and Entrepreneurship*, 5 (4), pp. 26–40.

Short, D. M. (1987) 'A preliminary investigation of the informal risk capital market in Ottawa–Carleton', unpublished Masters of Management Studies thesis, Carleton University, Ottawa, Canada.

Tymes, E. R. and O. J. Krasner (1984) 'Informal risk capital in California', in J. A. Hornaday, J. A. Timmons and K. H. Vesper (eds.), *Frontiers of Entrepreneurial Research*, Wellesley, MA: Babson College.

Wetzel, W. E. Jr (1983) 'Angels and informal risk capital', *Sloan Management Review*, summer, pp. 23–4.

Wetzel, W. E. Jr (1984) 'Venture Capital Network Inc.: an experiment in capital formation', Entrepreneurship Research Conference, Georgia Institute of Technology, Atlanta, GA, April.

Williamson, I. (1992) *Your Guide to Raising Venture Capital for Your Own Business in Canada*, Toronto: Productive Publications.

CHAPTER 5

Local networks and informal venture capital in Tennessee

Mary Kay Sullivan

Introduction

Early studies of informal venture capital in the United States tended to focus on New England and the East coast (Wetzel, 1981; Haar *et al.*, 1988) and California (Tymes and Krasner, 1983). It could be argued, however, that these areas may not be representative of the United States as a whole, due to their higher-than-average median household income, heavy concentration of industry, and primarily urban setting. Before generalising the results of these studies to other populations – and before assuming that a large potential pool of informal venture capital exists in various geographic areas – it is important, as Wetzel has suggested (1986a), to study the informal venture capital activity of other regions.

This chapter is an attempt to do just that, to look at a very different geographic and demographic area – a four-county area of the state of Tennessee – and examine the extent of informal investments being made there. In addition, we will attempt to learn something about the investors themselves, how and why they made these investments, and what sources of information they drew upon. It should be noted that there are no active formal match-making programmes in this area, so that any networks would be, perforce, informal and not highly organised.

The region and the sample

The eastern part of the state of Tennessee is an area which in many ways approximates the 'heartland' of middle America. The median annual family income here is close to the US national median income ($35,350 in 1990, according to the US Bureau of the Census), there are no large urban areas (the largest city is Knoxville with a population of 165,121 in 1990) and there is little major industry.

In terms of social networks, the area has been described as traditionally 'closely-knit' (Rothrock, 1972). There is not a high rate of immigration into the area, or much out-migration (Tennessee Statistical, 1993); many families are fourth- and fifth-generation residents (Rothrock, 1972). Further, a relatively small number of professional associations allow considerable interaction among community leaders. For example, most corporate executives belong to one of two area chambers of commerce and interact fairly frequently.

While very 'average' in some ways, the area is distinct in others. There is a high concentration of institutions of higher education in the area; the state university with 26,000 students is located here, as are four smaller private colleges and several two-year community colleges. The area is also home to a number of research and technology-based enterprises, among them Oak Ridge National Laboratories, Martin Marietta, Tennessee Valley Authority, and the Tennessee Technology Foundation. The research activities in this area have spawned a number of new ventures attempting to commercialise some of the results. In fact, this area has been described as one with a significant cluster of new venture activities (Federal Reserve Bank of Atlanta, 1983).

To determine the role of informal venture capital in the economic development of the region, a questionnaire was mailed to 900 individuals in the four counties including and surrounding the Knoxville/Oak Ridge area of Tennessee. The sample was not randomly selected, but made up of community leaders, business executives and occupational categories associated with informal investing in other studies. Some of the sample were known to have provided venture capital on occasions; others were selected simply because of their occupation category or active involvement in the community and therefore, presumably, greater access to networks or information sources. Data drawn from these questionnaires form the basis of this chapter.

A total of 493 questionnaires were returned, yielding a response rate of 55 per cent. Of these, there were 473 usable responses (52.5 per cent). Of the usable responses, 214 respondents reported having made an informal venture capital investment at some time in the past five years, 190 had never invested informally, and 69 had invested at some time in the past, but not within the past five years (Table 5.1). This five-year time period was chosen to permit comparison with past studies and to facilitate more accurate investor recall.

Table 5.1 Number of households which have made informal investments

	Number	%
Informal investor	214	45
(have made an informal investment in past five years)		
Previous investor	69	15
(have made an informal investment, but not in five years)		
Non-investor	190	40
(have never made an informal investment)		
Total	473	100

A profile of the typical informal investors in this sample points to an investor in the 45–54 year-old bracket (Table 5.2), working in the field of technology/engineering, health care or law (Table 5.3). Interestingly, the vast majority (72 per cent) of informal investors indicated that they themselves were entrepreneurs, having started a business at some time (Table 5.4).

Table 5.2 Age group by respondent categories

	Informal investor (%)	Previous investor (%)	Non-investor (%)
Under 35 years	4	2	12
35–44	28	16	24
45–54	33	29	31
55–64	23	31	22
65 and older	12	22	11
Total	100	100	100

Table 5.3 Occupational field of respondents

	Number	%
Accounting	8	3.8
Banking/finance	13	6.2
Communications/entertainment	5	2.4
Education	6	2.9
Food service	3	1.4
Insurance	7	3.3
Law	26	12.4
Manufacturing	17	8.1
Health care	27	12.9
Real estate/construction	16	7.6
Retailing/wholesaling	15	7.1
Services	18	8.6
Technical/engineering	38	18.1
Other	11	5.2
Total	210	100

Table 5.4 Entrepreneurial backgrounds of respondent categories

	Informal investor (%)	Previous investor (%)	Non-investor (%)
Have started a business	72	50	50.5
Have not	28	50	49.5
Total	100	100	100

Reasons for investing

Why did these individuals decide to commit funds in what is widely considered to be a highly uncertain and risky investment situation? Certainly, the hope of financial gain is one obvious motivation. And yet previous studies have suggested that there might be factors other than purely financial incentives influencing informal venture capital decisions (Wetzel, 1983). Factors such as personal satisfaction and the desire to help others or the community have been proposed in the past, but these typically reflected investors' attitudes rather than actual behaviours. Discussions with a focus group of known informal investors as a part of the questionnaire development supported these early studies. The investors described instances of specific investment behaviour and enumerated 11 possible motives for investing. Respondents to the questionnaire were then asked to rate the importance of each of these motives in their own most recent informal investment. On a scale of 1 (little or no importance) to 5 (very important), the following, in order of overall importance, were reasons for actually having made an investment:

- The potential for capital appreciation.
- The potential for an increased income stream.
- Tax benefits.
- To help a friend or family member.
- To have some influence or 'say' in an investment.
- The enjoyment of playing an entrepreneurial role.
- The enjoyment of having/observing an interesting investment.
- To support new business in the community.
- To support a needed or socially desirable product.
- To gain positive recognition in the community.

The primary reasons, as we might have expected, were clearly financial, but non-financial reasons were important to some investors. A factor analysis pointed to three separate factors inherent in these motives: an economic motive, an altruistic motive, and an enjoyment or 'fun' factor. (See Sullivan (1990) for details of this analysis.) When asked to select the one most important reason for investing, 72 per cent (143 of the 198 respondents who answered this question) indicated that they were motivated to invest primarily by a financial reason: that is, for capital appreciation, income or tax benefits. The other investors were influenced primarily by altruistic motives (17 per cent) or by the perceived enjoyment that they might derive from their investment (11 per cent).

   While the overwhelming majority of these investors were seeking primarily financial rewards, it is interesting to note that one in four of those responding indicated a primary interest in something other than strictly economic return. The desired rate of return, not surprisingly, was less for individuals interested in non-financial benefits than for the strictly financially motivated investors: the former sought an average return of 18 per cent, the latter 24 per cent.

The informal investments made

The sample reported a total of 525 informal venture capital investments in the past five years. Respondents gave more detailed descriptions of 487 investments. Of these, 194 investments were in service industries, 105 in manufacturing, 76 in wholesaling or retailing, 55 in communications or entertainment, 32 in natural resources, and 25 were listed as 'other', which were variously described as banking or other financial services, research, or construction (Table 5.5). About 20 per cent of the 525 investments were considered to be 'high-technology' products or services.

A little over one-third of the respondents reported having made only one informal investment, another one-third had made two investments, and the remainder had made three or more (Table 5.6). The majority of these investments were in area businesses, described as businesses within 100 miles of the respondent's home or office. Most of the investments were relatively small, with 50 per cent (262) involving amounts of $25,000 or less. Another 30 per cent were greater than $25,000 but less than $100,000. Only 9 per cent of the investments were over $250,000 (Table 5.7).

Appendix 5.1 contains some detailed analysis of the characteristics of the most recent reported investment, which confirms the diversity of investors' investment behaviour, but suggests that this sample of informal investors are slightly more likely to invest in start-up ventures using straight equity producing low or

Table 5.5 Informal investments of past five years by industry category

	Number	%
Services	194	40
Manufacturing	105	22
Retailing/wholesaling	76	16
Communication/entertainment	55	11
Natural resources	32	7
Other	25	5
Total	487	100

Table 5.6 Number of informal investments made per household in past five years

Number of households	Number	%
Making only 1 investment	77	36
Making 2 investments	74	35
Making 3 investments	26	12
Making 4 investments	8	4
Making 5 or more	29	13
Total	214	100

Table 5.7 Size of the investments in US dollars

	Number	%
Less than $10,000	132	25
$10,000 to $24,999	130	25
$25,000 to $99,999	154	30
$100,000 to $249,999	57	11
Over $250,000	50	9
Total	523	100

moderately innovative and complex products/services with which the investor is likely to have some familiarity. Investors are likely to become actively and significantly involved in the business. Of more specific interest, almost three-quarters (72 per cent) of investors have co-invested with others personally known to them, re-emphasising the importance of informal networks in the opportunity identification and evaluation process.

The investment process

Word of the investment opportunity came primarily through sources close to the investor: 47 per cent of investments were mentioned first by a close friend or family member and 24 per cent by co-workers. Professional sources (primarily brokers, attorneys and bankers) accounted for 18 per cent of investments. Only 6 per cent of investments were the result of contact from a non-family representative of the firm seeking finance (Table 5.8).

In an attempt to learn more about the process of gathering information and making the investment decision, respondents were asked to categorise themselves as one of four investor types. These types, representing varying degrees of self-reliance in the investment process, were described in the questionnaire as follows:

1. Lead Investor   I search for opportunities, make an independent decision to invest and often suggest investments to others.
2. Independent Investors I welcome investment leads from others but rely on my own investigation in deciding to invest. Other investors don't influence me.
3. Referred Investor   I ask some questions and read materials but am primarily influenced by a recommendation from a knowledgeable person.
4. Group Investor   I invest along with a group of associates. I'm likely to invest if there's group consensus, but I don't rely on a single individual.

Table 5.8 Primary referral sources for investments of past five years

	Number	%
Personal relationship (friend, family)	245	47
Business associate (co-worker)	121	24
Professional relationship (attorney, banker, etc.)	91	18
Representative of the firm	32	6
Active personal search	24	5
Total	513	100

Most investors considered themselves to be either independent (39 per cent) or referred (35 per cent), with only 12 per cent taking the role of lead investor and 14 per cent relying primarily on a group. Here we find investors to be fairly evenly divided between the more self-reliant lead and independent investor types and the referred and group investors who tend to rely on outside information sources and the opinions of others in making their investment decisions. However, 72 per cent of respondents indicated that they have at some time invested as part of a group that included associates or friends.

Reasons for not investing

The study also sought to learn why individuals reject some informal risk capital proposals. A total of 327 rejected investments were reported. Of these, a primary concern centred around a lack of information: 45 per cent of the rejections were attributed primarily to lack of sufficient or adequately trustworthy information. Another 38 per cent were rejected on the merits of the investment situation itself, with the investor having decided that the investment was too risky, lacked profit potential, was not a promising product, or lacked a strong management team. Only 16 per cent were rejected primarily due to the lack of available funds.

What have we learned?

What broader implications can we draw from this study? The results suggest several conclusions. First, in line with earlier studies, there is indeed a significant pool of informal venture capital at work, even in non-urban areas. The average informal investment in this region was approximately $80,000. With a total of 525 investments reported in the past five years, this indicates a conservative estimate of about $42 million recently invested in this one area. To project this figure nationally would suggest a possible $23 billion pool of informal risk capital in this five-year period, a figure not far from Wetzel's estimate of as much as $5 billion a year in the United States (1986b). This conservative figure would support speculation that informal risk capital does indeed constitute a large potential reservoir of capital for economic development.

Even in a relatively small community such as the area under study, however, informal venture capital is not readily visible. Several respondents to the questionnaire commented that they had never heard of venture capital investments in this area, but would like to be informed either of sources of funds or of investment opportunities.

Another finding was that Tennessee investors seem to rely on a rather unstructured system to learn of promising opportunities and to help evaluate the investment's potential. Lacking a formal mechanism for matching potential investors with companies seeking funds, investors tend to invest with others whom they know, often relying on the expertise or judgement of a lead investor. The sample was evenly split between those who seek out investments and evaluate the company themselves, and those who rely on the opinions of a knowledgeable source. Yet fully 72 per cent have invested with others. In a sense we have here an informal network which seems to have been successful in finding capital for firms seeking funds.

This leads to a second conclusion: a trustworthy information and evaluation source is vital to the venture capital process. In this sample, the lead investors seem to fill this role; we can certainly speculate that considerable capital might go untapped without someone or some institution providing this knowledge base. The informal network work here has clearly facilitated the exchange of information and increased the amount of venture capital invested.

A third finding emphasises that there are information gaps between those who might want to invest and those seeking venture capital. This study found such a lack in two situations: first, those who rejected an investment opportunity because they did not have sufficient information or expertise to evaluate the offering; and second, those who were not informal investors because they had never heard of investment opportunities in the first place. Each of these findings points to the potential for additional venture capital from those currently outside the informal networks, and suggests the scope for more formal initiatives to improve the flow of information in the informal venture capital market.

A final conclusion might be of help to the entrepreneur seeking venture capital. As other studies have suggested, individuals who have themselves started a business tend to be a likely potential source of capital for others. Indeed, 72 per cent of the informal investors in this study are entrepreneurs themselves. Also, it is important to note that different investors invest for different reasons, some strictly for the economic return, but others for more affective reasons. These differences appear to translate into different expected rates of return for the investor, and a possible potential lower cost of capital for the entrepreneur seeking funds. This has the potential for fruitful research with significant application.

Conclusion

In sum, the findings here confirm the findings of others: lack of information is a significant impediment in the informal venture capital process. Indeed, it is not so much the lack of funds which leads a potential investor to reject an investment, but rather the lack of adequate information. In this study, we find a loose and informal network of investors operating within a relatively small, interactive community. Even so, certain inefficiencies exist, with some potential capital overlooked. It is interesting to consider whether a more formal match-making system might enhance the efficiency of the process, thereby increasing the amount of venture capital available and strengthening regional economic development.

Implications for practice

- Informal investments are made primarily for financial return, but altruistic motives and enjoyment or 'fun' are also important – investment opportunities listed by a business introduction service should reflect the opportunity for financial gain.
- Personal, informal, networks and trust relationships are most important in informal investment activity – introduction services should therefore retain as far as possible the personal element in the process.
- Lack of trustworthy information is a major reason for rejection of an investment opportunity by an investor – business introduction services can help to improve the quality, appropriateness and reliability of this information.

Appendix 5.1 Characteristics of most recent investment

(a) Number of investors on board of directors of most recent investment

	Number	%
Serving on board of directors	78	38

(b) Types of investment vehicle for most recent investment

	Number	%
Equity	135	64
Straight debt	27	13
Debt convertible to equity	23	11
Other debt/equity combinations	25	12
Total	210	100

(c) Most recent investment by stage of company growth

	Number	%
Start-up (before first sale)	133	63
Early stage (after first sale but during first 2 years)	44	21
Growth (after 2 years but less than 8 years old)	20	9
Established (over 8 years old)	15	7
Total	212	100

(d) Degree of involvement in most recent investment

	Number	%
Respondents reporting no involvement	41	19
Little involvement beyond reading reports	30	14
Moderate amount	86	41
Very involved	42	20
Extremely involved (equivalent of full-time work)	12	6
Total	211	100

(e) Characteristics of most recent investment

	Number of investments	% of investments
Innovativeness of product or service		
Not at all innovative	26	12
Very little innovation	46	22
Moderately innovative	61	29
Very innovative	45	21
Extremely innovative	33	16
Total	211	100

	Number of investments	% of investments
Complexity of product or service		
Not at all complex	52	25
Very little complexity	33	16
Moderately complex	63	30
Very complex	36	18
Extremely complex	24	11
Total	208	100
Investors' familiarity with product or service		
Not at all familiar	25	12
Very little familiarity	49	23
Moderately familiar	56	27
Very familiar	60	28
Extremely familiar	21	10
Total	211	100
Co-invested with others personally known to respondents	153	72

References

Federal Reserve Bank of Atlanta (1983) 'Venture capital and economic growth in the Southeast', *Economic Review*, **66** (July), pp. 12–21.

Haar, N. E., J. Starr and I. C. MacMillan (1988) 'Informal risk capital investors: investment patterns on the East coast of the USA', *Journal of Business Venturing*, **3**, pp. 11–29.

Rothrock, M. U. (1972) *The French Broad-Holston Country*, Knoxville, TN: East Tennessee Historical Society.

Sullivan, M. K. (1990) 'Segmenting the informal investment market: a benefit-based typology of informal investors', unpublished Ph.D. dissertation, University of Tennessee, Knoxville.

Tennessee Statistical Abstract 1992/93 (1993) Knoxville, TN: University of Tennessee, Knoxville, Center for Business and Economic Research.

Tymes, E. R. and O. J. Krasner (1983) 'Informal risk capital in California', in J. A. Hornaday, J. A. Timmons and K. H. Vesper (eds.), *Frontiers of Entrepreneurship Research 1983*, Wellesley, MA: Babson College, pp. 347–68.

US Bureau of the Census (1992) Statistical Abstract of the United States (112th edn), Washington, DC.

Wetzel, W. E. Jr (1981) 'Informal risk capital in New England', in K. H. Vesper (ed.), *Frontiers of Entrepreneurship Research 1981*, Wellesley, MA: Babson College, pp. 217–45.

Wetzel, W. E. Jr (1983) 'Angels and informal risk capital', *Sloan Management Review*, **24** (Summer), pp. 23–34.

Wetzel, W. E. Jr (1986a) 'Informal risk capital: knowns and unknowns', in D. Sexton and R. Smilor (eds.), *The Art and Science of Entrepreneurship*, Cambridge, MA: Ballinger, pp. 85–105.

Wetzel, W. E. Jr (1986b) 'Entrepreneurs, angels and economic renaissance', in R. Hisrich (ed.), *Entrepreneurship, Intrapreneurship and Venture Capital*, Lexington, MA: Lexington Books, pp. 119–39.

CHAPTER 6

Private venture capital networks in the United States

Donald J. Brown and Charles R. B. Stowe

Introduction

A major question which every new and/or growing business must answer is: how will growth be financed? Most entrepreneurs are not wealthy when they go into business; nor do they have wealthy friends and relatives who can underwrite their capital needs. Therefore, those entrepreneurs who desire to expand and grow their ventures will at some point face the need to look 'outside' the group of close associates and family for equity financing. They may not face a more critical problem at any other point in the development of their venture, and unless they are lucky enough to meet an 'angel', they may never acquire the equity financing they desire.

Now as always, private investors (more recently referred to as angels) are the primary source of equity financing for small, developing companies. In most cases new start-up firms or existing young growing companies are not large enough to attract interest from the formal venture capital market and must depend on the less visible, informal market. Because of the limited amount of information available about this market's participants, the market may appear to be totally invisible to most entrepreneurs who are seeking financing. In general, the market operates today as it always has, by word of mouth, and the chance that a venture will receive financing may depend upon whom the entrepreneur knows. As a result of the limited flow of information in this market it is viewed as highly inefficient and underutilised. Many believe the potential for the market as a source of venture financing could be enhanced substantially if a sufficient level of information flow could be created. A review of the information available about the market reveals the amount being invested through private investors at present in a relatively inefficient market. The question is: what would be the potential of this market if it were efficient, and how can this be accomplished?

The informal market

Until the 1980s no formal attempt had been made to identify the size and structure of the informal venture capital market. However, in 1983, under a grant from the Small Business Administration, William Wetzel and his colleagues at the University of New Hampshire turned up 133 investors who fit the self-imposed description of a business angel. The objective of Wetzel's research was to find out 'where angels come from, how many there are, how to find them or what angels look for in a venture proposal' (Wetzel, 1983). One of the questions Wetzel asked the angels was whether they were satisfied with the effectiveness of existing channels of communication between bona fide entrepreneurs and investors like themselves. Using a Likert scale to measure the respondents feelings, he found that 'totally dissatisfied' respondents outnumbered 'definitely satisfied' respondents by more than 4:1 (Wetzel, 1983), confirming other studies reflecting general dissatisfaction of participants in the informal venture capital market with the flow of information (Brophy, 1982). This research was the initial step toward the creation of the Venture Capital Network at the University of New Hampshire (see Chapter 3). The Venture Capital Network and subsequent networks will be discussed later.

Venture capital has been described by Florida and Kenny (1988a) as serving the function of accelerating the process of technological change, and it has been argued that venture capitalists perform a gate-keeping function. They conclude that 'venture capital-financed innovation overcomes a variety of barriers which stymie technological progress including the risk aversion of established financial markets, the organisational inertia of large corporations, and the multifaceted technological, organisational and financial requirements of new business development' (Florida and Kenney, 1988a). Interestingly, while the researchers charted the roles of venture capital in terms of three phases – catalyst-organisational to assistance to liquidation – they did not describe 'angels' or identify the role of those willing to invest relatively small amounts of capital in seed or start-up entities. To the extent that angels make possible entities large enough to attract the investment interest of the professional venture capital industry, the existence of such angels may yet form another 'gatekeeper'. Citing research by Timmons and Gumpert, who surveyed 51 of the largest and most active professional venture capital firms, Wetzel noted that the study revealed that the size of a typical individual investment by a venture capital firm was $813,000. However, research by Gaston indicates that the average investment in the informal equity capital market is only $66,700 (Gaston, 1989). Unless ventures successfully make it through the first 'gate', they will not attain the size to attract financing from the second 'gatekeeper'.

In order to assess the importance of the informal venture capital market, it is important to note the research on the venture capital industry as a whole. In the United States, there are seven venture capital complexes: California (San Francisco/Silicon Valley), Massachusetts (Boston), New York, Illinois (Chicago),

Texas, Connecticut and Minnesota. Researchers have suggested that, although venture capital is not absolutely necessary to facilitate high-technology entrepreneurship, 'well developed venture capital networks provide tremendous incentives for entrepreneurship by lowering the difficulties of entering the industry' (Florida and Kenny, 1988b). If the existence of the professional venture capital industry is, as Florida and Kenny suggest, a self-feeding magnet that tends to attract more capital and more professional venture capitalists because professionals seek syndications, or the sharing of risk, or the sharing of information (Bygrave, 1987), and if the existence of such centres of venture capital help to promote new business formation, then the question of the economic impact of improving the efficiency of the informal market is all the more intriguing.

The overall importance of this market is further supported by a 1987 study by Wetzel, which suggests that private investors manage a portfolio of venture investments that in 1987 was about $50 billion and approximately twice the total capital managed by professional investors (Wetzel, 1987). He also contends that, due to the relative size of the investments in the two portfolios, the private investors finance over five times as many entrepreneurs as do professional venture investors: over 20,000 versus two or three thousand. Wetzel reaches this conclusion by first using data on wealth, income and asset distribution of all US households, and concluding that the top 1 per cent of these households have invested over $151 billion in non-public businesses in which they have no management interests. He believes 'it is not unreasonable to believe that venture-type financing in the portfolios of the top one percent may be at least $50 billion' (Wetzel, 1987). Then citing research conducted by Applied Economics Group Inc. (AEG), Wetzel notes that the typical firm in AEG's sample raised $220,500 of equity and near-equity financing, typically from three informal investors (Wetzel, 1987). Based on this data, Wetzel concludes 'informal investors commit some 10–24 per cent of their net worth to venture investments'. And 'if there are 345,000 informal venture investors in the US with an average net worth of $750,000, and with 10–24 per cent of their net worth available for venture investments, the aggregate informal venture capital pool is between $25 billion and $62 billion' (Wetzel, 1987).

More recent research by Gaston and Bell indicates that private investors may contribute substantially more than Wetzel estimated. This research was done as part of a Small Business Administration (SBA) study, which documents the size and importance of the informal venture capital market (Gaston and Bell, 1988). The SBA study aggregated three regional studies of informal investors into the first accurate national estimate of the informal supply of external equity capital in the United States.

Gaston used national survey data from the Informal Investor Microdata File in his analysis (Gaston, 1989). From this data he estimated that 720,000 investors make 489,000 equity capital investments per year, valued at an estimated $32.7 billion. When an additional investment of $22.9 billion of debt capital is included in the total, it is estimated that the informal market supplies annual informal capital of $55.6 billion (Gaston and Bell, 1988). The $32.7 billion of equity investment is estimated by Gaston to be about eight times the annual investment from the formal venture capital market. He believes that informal investment is the single largest source of small firm equity capital available, and is approximately equal to the amount raised from all other sources combined (Gaston, 1989). Nine out of ten investments by informal investments are devoted to small, mostly start-up firms with fewer than 20 employees according to the SBA study (Gaston and Bell, 1988). Gaston concludes that the total aggregate portfolio of the informal group may exceed $167 billion, with a 5.1-year mean holding period (Gaston, 1989). Also cited in the SBA report is a study by the Congressional Office of Technology Assessment, which estimates the total number of firms financed annually by private investors at 87,300, which is 42 times larger than the number financed by professional venture capital investors (Office of Technology Assessment, 1984: table 14). They estimate that $55 billion per year is invested by this group compared with only $3 billion invested by professional investors.

In spite of the size of the informal venture capital market, Wetzel's review of studies shows that the most common and reliable sources of investment information among the 'informal' or non-professional venture investors were friends and business associates (Wetzel, 1987). Most significantly, Wetzel cites many studies that document the inefficiency of the informal capital market, leading to what is described as 'a discouragement effect operating among unsuccessful seekers of venture capital, would-be seekers of venture capital, and would-be entrepreneurs' (Boylan, 1981; Wetzel, 1986). A study published in 1988 provides additional research evidence describing the 'informal capital risk investors-angels' and confirms that their most common entry into an investment is through associates or friends. The researchers confined their study to the US East coast and explored not only the issue of 'market efficiency', but also the issue of investment criteria and the decision-making process utilised. The results were achieved by surveying a sample population consisting of members of New York venture capital clubs, graduates of specific professional schools (NYU and Wharton MBA and medical graduates), personal referrals and NY Metropolitan dentists. From a sample of 2,989 potential respondents, 320 responded affirmatively to their study. The researchers developed a demographic profile reflecting the biases of their sample, but more intriguing was their analysis of the decision-making strategies used by the respondents in evaluating an investment (Haar et al., 1988).

Venture capital networks

During the past decade a major effort has been made by a small group of people to improve the efficiency of the informal market in North America, by creating networks through which vital information can flow. The first informal venture capital network was formed by William Wetzel at the University of New Hampshire's Whittemore School of Business and Economics in 1984, creating expectations that these networks held high promise as a vehicle through which entrepreneurial ventures in need of risk capital might acquire financing (see Chapter 3). The concept of organising the informal market in this fashion was hailed as 'the greatest thing since sliced bread'. During the period July 1984 to June 1986, venture capital networks arranged in excess of 1,000 introductions for over 200 entrepreneurs from 30 states with more than 300 investors from over 33 states (Wetzel, 1987).

The establishment of the Venture Capital Network in New Hampshire was not unnoticed by both trade and academic publications. One writer noted that 'taking the randomness out of matching angels with entrepreneurs would mean a wide range of opportunities for investors, while providing a badly needed pipeline to growth capital for small companies' (Blake, 1986). *Business Week* (1986), *D&B Reports* (Blake, 1986), *In Business* (Goldstein, 1987) and the *Boston Herald* (Katzeff, 1986) have all carried articles about the development of the Venture Capital Network and its spread through the country.

Based on the original model developed and implemented at Whittemore School by Wetzel, and with his assistance, 21 additional venture capital networks have been established in 19 other states and Canada (see Chapter 4) since 1984. These networks are designed to overcome the inefficiency of the informal market by creating a mechanism through which information can be disseminated. They are essentially a conduit through which information can flow, and contacts can be established between potential investors and entrepreneurs.

A review of the literature on informal venture networks reveals several key studies on the difficulties of identifying and measuring the informal venture capital investor (Tymes and Krasner, 1983; Haar *et al.*, 1988; Wetzel, 1983, 1987). The research cites the problems of market efficiency due to a lack of formal informational networking among needy companies and ready investors. The historical development of the Venture Capital Network and how it operates is fully described in many different studies (Brown, 1987; Shellenbarger, 1989, Wetzel, 1983; see also Chapter 3). However, there has been little assessment of the impact of all the venture capital networks, nor an assessment of the costs and benefits of such programmes, nor an analysis of what factors will account for higher participation or matches. One such recent study is reviewed in the following section (Brown and Stowe, 1991).

The Brown and Stowe study

The stated purpose of the Brown–Stowe study was 'to assess the Venture Capital Network concept using the very simple criteria of number of participants, the number of matches, the number of fundings and a subjective assessment of indirect benefits of the programme' (Brown and Stowe, 1991).

At the time of the original Brown–Stowe research in 1990, 17 venture capital networks had been organised based on the original model developed by Wetzel at the University of New Hampshire. At present only eight of these 17 can be confirmed as still operational. Of the remaining nine, six have been confirmed as no longer operating and three more do not answer their phone. The three who do not answer the phone may or may not still be operating. They may have new phone numbers or have changed locations since the original study in 1990. However, if this is the case the old numbers do not give a message of a number change as would be anticipated when numbers are changed. Therefore it is assumed that they are no longer operational. Three of the eight venture capital networks still operating have changed their names and two of these three have also moved to new locations (see Table 6.1).

Since the original study was done in 1990, four new venture capital networks have become operational. However, of these new venture capital networks only one appears to be doing well, one has become non-operational already, one does

Table 6.1 List of all venture capital networks and their present status

Name and location	Present status
Venture Capital Network, Durham, NH (now Technology Capital Network at MIT, Cambridge, MA)	Active
Venture Capital Network of New York Inc., Lake Placid, NY	Inactive
The Computerised Ontario Investor Network, Toronto, Canada (now Canada Opportunities Investor Network)	Active
Upper Peninsula Venture Capital Network, Marquette, MI	Inactive[a]
Wyoming Investor Network, Casper, WY	Inactive
Private Investor Network, Aiken, SC	Active
Heartland Venture Capital Network Inc., Evanston, IL	Inactive
Iowa Venture Capital Network, Council Bluffs, IA	Inactive[a]
Mississippi Venture Capital Clearinghouse, Jackson, MS	Inactive
Capital Formation Network, Houston, TX (now Texas Capital Network, Austin, TX)	Active
Northwest Capital Network, Portland, OR	Active
Mid-Atlantic Venture Capital Network, College Park, MD	Active
Nebraska, Venture Capital Network, Omaha, NB	Inactive
Tennessee Venture Capital Network, Murfreesboro, TN	Inactive[a]
Venture Capital Network of Minnesota, St Paul, MN	Active
Washington Investor Network, Olympia, WA	Inactive
Southwest Venture Capital Network Inc., Goodyear, AZ	Inactive[a]
Pacific Venture Capital Network, Irvine, CA	Active
Georgia Capital Network, Atlanta, GA	Inactive
Investment Capital Network, Frankfort, KY	Active
Venture Capital Exchange, Tulsa, OK	Active

[a] These are not positively confirmed as inactive but contact has not been made because no one answered the phone when several calls were placed to the numbers listed as their number.

not answer the phone and the other is operating on a very limited budget with only one part-time employee, and with the restriction of only listing entrepreneurs who are located in the same state as the venture capital network. At present, two additional venture capital networks are in the process of becoming operational. One of these will be located in northern California and the other in Washington State. Details about when these will be functional are not available at this time.

Why have venture capital networks in some areas of the United States prospered while many others failed? An analysis of the Brown–Stowe study can help answer this question. Several of the tables from the earlier research are used in this analysis. An examination of Table 6.2 shows that these are all relatively young organisations. If the assumption is that they will to some degree be similar to new business ventures, then it is understandable that a number will fail during the early part of their lives. The 'normal' failure rate for new business ventures may be as high as 70 per cent during the first five years of the business life. The failure rate for venture capital networks is less than 70 per cent, but apparently greater than 50 per cent during a comparable period. The smaller failure rate probably results from the fact that venture capital networks are not stand-alone organisations, but are somewhat subsidised by government during the start-up phase of their operation.

An analysis of Table 6.3 and Table 6.4 is also beneficial in understanding the failure rate for venture capital networks. These tables reveal that these venture capital networks were operating with very limited budgets and very small staffs. Without an operating budget large enough to hire full-time staff and with limited resources available for marketing their services it is difficult for them to offer the level of service needed to attract a sufficient number of investors and entrepreneurs necessary to make the venture capital network a viable venture. As with any other business venture, the success or failure of the venture capital networks is ultimately determined by how effective they are in meeting the needs of their clientele.

Table 6.2 Year of organisation of the venture capital networks

	Number organised in		
1986	1987	1988	1989
2	3	4	1

Table 6.3 Annual operating budget of the venture capital networks

$10,000 or less	$10,000–25,000	Greater than $25,000
5	3	2

Table 6.4 Number of employees of the venture capital networks

Full-time employees	Number of VCNs with Part-time employees	Volunteers
3	10	2

Tables 6.5 and 6.6 illustrate the results of venture capital networks being underfunded. If venture capital networks had the resources to market their organisations effectively, the number of investors and entrepreneurs should be higher for a larger number of venture capital networks. It takes time to build a viable investor network which is capable of reaching the stage where it can be self-supporting. Without the resources to survive in the short run, a network will never achieve the critical mass of investors and viable entrepreneurs needed to become self-supporting in the long run. It takes time and money to build a venture capital network's reputation and to build a track record of successfully meeting the needs of its clientele. It is apparent from the data presented here that a large majority of these venture capital networks lack the resources necessary to achieve the number of investors and entrepreneurs required for them to become viable organisations.

Brown and Stowe concluded that without a well-organised, aggressive marketing programme the high promise of venture capital networks would never be realised. They found a strong correlation between the level of funding and the initial success of venture capital networks. Because of limited operating funds, the networks could not develop an outreach to the potential entrepreneurs or the groups which are most likely to produce angels. They believed that if sufficient funding were available, the networks could become successful. More recent research involving venture capital networks partially bears out these conclusions, but also indicates that other issues may be equally important to the success or failure of a venture capital network. In fact one of the most successful venture

Table 6.5 Number of active investors on all networks

0–10	10–20	Number of VCNs with 20–30	Greater than 30
2	2	3	3

Table 6.6 Number of firms seeking capital

0–24 firms	Number of VCNs with 25–50 firms	Greater than 50 firms
3	3	5

capital networks stated that it does not do any marketing because it is attracting all the investors and entrepreneurs it desires without doing marketing. It maintains its investor and entrepreneur base at approximately 100 each without any marketing other than word of mouth. This strategy will not work for every venture capital network, but it does make the point that, if several other important factors are present, marketing may not be essential to the success of the venture capital network.

A careful analysis of Table 6.1 reveals that several factors must be present before a private investor network will become successful. Money is definitely one of the key ingredients, but unless the amount of money available for operations is unlimited for a very long period, it alone may not be sufficient to make a venture capital network viable. This point is borne out by an examination of the budgets of venture capital networks in the Brown–Stowe study. The venture capital network with the largest operating budget at the time of their research is now inactive. This venture capital network had good funding for the first two years, but was not able to establish a critical mass of investors and entrepreneurs during this period. If it had been located nearer one of the major venture capital complexes, its chances of success would have been enhanced.

Table 6.1 shows that most of the successful venture capital networks are located in an area with large population centres nearby, and in close proximity with one of the seven venture capital complexes: Massachusetts, Texas, California, New York, Minnesota, Illinois or Connecticut. These factors are important because they are part of an overall environment which makes the success of venture capital networks possible.

The venture capital network must be functioning efficiently for a long enough period to attract viable ventures and knowledgeable investors. There must be a period of building confidence in the network, which works to overcome the natural suspicion entrepreneurs and investors have about revealing confidential information.

The areas where private investors have been most successful are areas which bring several important factors together. There are larger numbers of high-tech firms in these areas than exist in areas where venture capital networks have realised less success. These high-tech firms are beneficial because they bring together the two important groups in a successful venture capital network: knowledgeable investors and viable entrepreneurs. The high-tech firms are more likely to spin off entrepreneurs with viable projects in need of financing. These individuals may have been working in high-tech industries and are more comfortable with revealing the needed information to help acquire financing. Also, there will be a larger number of knowledgeable investors who have made investments in similar firms in the past, or who have managed firms with operations which allow them to better understand and analyse potential ventures. Having larger numbers of both these groups available and in an environment more conducive to venture capital investing plays a major role in the success of the venture capital network. Money for marketing is important, but it is not the only critical ingredient.

The data in Table 6.7 are useful in understanding the differences between those venture capital networks which are successful and those which are not. The most successful ones have more full- and part-time employees, charge higher fees, have more corporate investors on their networks, have a larger number of investors and have a larger number of entrepreneurs on their networks than the less successful ones. They are also all located in environments with all the other important factors named above present.

When the characteristics of the successful venture capital networks are compared to those of the unsuccessful venture capital networks, it is apparent that more than operating budgets are important to their success. Those who failed to make it are generally in small population centres and are not close to a major venture capital complex or high-tech centre. Without the environment of venture capital investing, it is difficult for a venture capital network to succeed. Not only does the venture capital environment bring together the entrepreneurs and investors, but also it will make it easier for the venture capital network to supplement its operating budget with corporate sponsorship and additional government support.

Market efficiency

At present, the informal venture capital market is considered relatively inefficient. There is some increased efficiency from the limited success of venture capital networks, but it is unlikely that this market will ever be efficient in the same way we think of market efficiency in stock and bond markets. A concern for strict confidentiality is a major factor which will work to keep this market inefficient. Wetzel and Freear (Chapter 3) rightly point out that confidentiality is essential for a variety of reasons: high-net-worth private investors are not willing to be listed publicly; and there will never be a directory of private investors similar to *Pratt's Guide to Venture Capital Sources*. Investors have money to invest, but they do not have a strong reason to invest unless they feel a special link to the type of investment being offered. They can live very well without making any investments. Therefore, they can be very independent in their approach to the entire process. As Wetzel and Freear point out (in Chapter 3), 'private investors are both diverse and dispersed, and tough to reach through traditional marketing techniques. The energy and creativity required to mobilise the capital and the know-how of these investors should not be underestimated.'

Information flows are key to market efficiency, and by its nature the informal market is concerned about confidentiality. However, when venture capital networks are successful there is an opportunity to have a high level of confidentiality and also good information flows. The structure of the venture capital network allows confidentiality to the investor until they choose to reveal

Table 6.7 Performance averages for venture capital networks, 1989 and 1993

	Number of employees		Fees charged			Number of investors	Number of entrepreneurs
	Full	Part	Individual investor	Entrepreneur	Corporation		
VCNs in Brown–Stowe study, 1990[a]	0.3	1.2	$125	$100	–	42	73
The four most successful VCNs, 1993[b]	3	3	$238	$213	$625	128	238
Other VCNs, 1993[b]	0	1	$200	$100	–	45	36

Sources:
[a] The 1990 averages were computed from data in the Brown–Stowe study.
[b] The 1993 averages were computed from data gathered by phone during August and September 1993.

themselves to the entrepreneur. Therefore, these networks can improve overall efficiency without any loss of confidentiality to the potential investor.

Several events now occurring in venture capital networks may help increase efficiency in the informal market. A greater degree of networking among the various individual venture capital networks located in different areas of the country is developing. Some of the venture capital network directors indicate that they now contact other directors when they receive requests which they think could be better served by a network closer to the enquiring party. As the amount of informal networking increases, it will help the efficiency of the informal market in some areas, but this alone will do little to increase the overall efficiency of the market. Unless there are a great many more viable venture capital networks in the United States than exist at the present, the market will remain only marginally efficient.

If all the venture capital networks which have been formed to date were operational, it would help this market's efficiency, but the failure of such a large number of those previously formed illustrates that it is unlikely that a great many more will ever be available. The need for venture capital investment is so small in many areas of the country that it may be impossible even to have a viable venture capital network in all the areas which desire one. This is not to imply that these areas would not benefit from a viable network, but only to indicate that areas with a small pool of investors and entrepreneurs with viable ventures may be unable to create enough activity to make an independent venture capital network feasible. The lack of success of networks in the areas with smaller population bases and/or those outside the influence of a venture capital/high-tech complex appears to support this view.

The Texas connection

David Gerhardt, at the Texas Capital Network in Austin, Texas, is developing a programme which may help increase the overall efficiency of the informal venture capital market. At the present time, some venture capital network directors have indicated that, if they get an application from an entrepreneur that they think can be served better by another network, they will advise the entrepreneur to list on the other network. The programme now being developed by Mr Gerhardt would formalise this exchange of information. What his programme is designed to do is link up several of the existing venture capital networks. When an entrepreneur lists a proposal on one network, which is a member of the linked networks, the project can be viewed by all investors on all the individual networks in the linked group.

A national venture capital network such as this could help a great deal in market efficiency. It might make a difference in whether some marginal venture capital networks can survive for the long term. There is a possibility that, if marginal venture capital networks could link up with larger networks located in areas with a broader base of investor and entrepreneur participation, they could continue to operate as a part of this larger system. In other words, they may become more attractive to investors and entrepreneurs in their own areas because of the national link. It is too soon to speculate a great deal about the likely success or failure of a national system, but it does hold some promise for the informal market and it will be watched with interest.

Summary

Almost every new and growing venture is faced with the need to raise 'outside' equity capital at some point in their start-up or early growth phase. At this stage they are not able to issue shares of stock; nor are they attractive to venture capital firms. This creates a dilemma which, if not solved, can condemn the new venture to an early death. Family, friends and acquaintances are the most likely source of capital for many who find themselves in this situation. However, not everyone who has a promising venture has family, friends and acquaintances with the kind of wealth needed to fund a risky venture. Those who are lucky enough to meet an 'angel' may have an answer to their problem. But not everyone will be so lucky.

In the past decade, efforts have been made to develop computerised networks through which the entrepreneurs with promising ventures could be matched with investors who have an interest in new ventures. William Wetzel organised the first Venture Capital Network at the University of New Hampshire, in 1984. Since his original network was formed, 19 others have been organised in the United States and one in Canada.

The concept of organising the informal venture capital market in this way created high expectations for improved efficiency in this market, and for significant increases in the amount of funds which would flow through these networks to promising ventures. The success of several venture capital networks in the United States and Canada has demonstrated that the concept is a good one. However, the experience of several other venture capital networks which have failed also proves that the concept cannot be universally applied to all regions of the country. What is obvious from examining the evidence is that several important factors must be present if a venture capital network is to succeed. The environment within which the venture capital network is located must include a large population base, and a venture capital/high-tech complex in rather close proximity to the network. Also the network must be able to acquire sufficient funding to be able to operate long enough to develop a strong base of investors and entrepreneurs. Both of these groups are needed if the network is to succeed. Some of those networks which failed did so because they could not attract enough investors, but some also failed because they lacked a good pool of viable entrepreneurs.

The success of those which have prospered proves the worth of the concept, and recent developments at the Texas Capital Network may lead to greater success on a wider front. The idea of a national network linking several networks across the country has promise for this market and, as with the original idea, only time will tell as to how much it adds to the overall efficiency of the informal venture capital market.

Implications for practice

- Not all business introduction services/networks will survive or succeed – only half of those set up in the USA are still active.
- Without an operating budget large enough to hire full-time staff and support on-going marketing efforts, the level of service offered will not be sufficient to attract investors and entrepreneurs.
- It takes time and money (and committed personnel) to build a network's reputation and establish a track record of success.
- Successful networks share a number of characteristics: they are well resourced, they are based in or close to major population centres, they are close to centres of formal venture capital activity, and they have been in existence long enough to build up confidence in the network.

References

Blake, D. (1986) 'Making a deal with the angels', *D & B Reports*, May/June.

Boylan, M. G. (1981) 'What we know and don't know about venture capital', *Proceedings of the American Economic Association Annual Meeting*, 28 December.

Brophy, D. T. (1982) 'Venture capital research', in C. A. Kent, D. L. Sexton and K. L. Vesper (eds.) *Encyclopaedia of Entrepreneurship*, Englewood Cliffs, NJ: Prentice Hall, pp. 165–92.

Brown, D. J. (1987) 'Filling the gaps: sources of small business risk capital', *Business and Economic Review*, Pittsburgh State University, July.

Brown, D. J. and C. R. B. Stowe (1991) 'A note on venture capital networks: promise and performance', *Journal of Small Business Finance*, **1**, pp. 75–87.

Business Week (1986) 'Special report: raising money in 1987', 3 November.

Bygrave, W. D. (1987) 'Syndicated investments by venture capital firms: a networking perspective', *Journal of Business Venturing*, **2**, pp. 138–54.

Florida, R. and M. Kenney (1988a) 'Venture capital and high technology entrepreneurship', *Journal of Business Venturing*, **3**, pp. 301–19.

Florida, R. and M. Kenney (1988b) 'Venture capital-financed innovation and technological change in the USA', *Research Policy*, **17**, pp. 119–37.

Gaston, R. J. (1989) 'The scale of informal capital markets', *Small Business Economics*, **1**, pp. 223–30.

Gaston, R. J. and S. Bell (1988) 'The informal supply of capital', Final Report to the SBA, 29 January.

Goldstein, N. (1987) 'Where to go when raising dough', *In Business*, January/February.

Haar, N. E., J. Starr and I. C. MacMillan (1988) 'Informal risk capital investors: investment patterns on the East coast of the USA', *Journal of Business Venturing*, **3**, pp. 11–29.

Katzeff, P. (1986) 'Computer matchmaking unites firms with funds', *Boston Herald*, 22 December.

Office of Technology Assessment (1984) *Technology, Innovation and Regional Economic Development*, Washington, DC: US Congress Office of Technology Assessment, OTA-STI-238.

Shellenbarger, S. (1989) 'Wanted: small businesses to start rural revival', *Wall Street Journal*, September.

Tymes, E. R. and O. J. Krasmer (1983) 'Informal risk capital in California', in J. A. Hornaday, J. A. Timmons and K. H. Vesper (eds.), *Frontiers of Entrepreneurship Research*, Wellesley, MA: Babson College, pp. 347–68.

Wetzel, W. E. Jr (1983) 'Angels and informal risk capital', *Sloan Management Review*, **24**, (Summer) pp. 23–34.

Wetzel, W. E. Jr (1986) 'Informal risk capital: knowns and unknowns', in D. L. Sexton and R. Smilor (eds.), *The Art and Science of Entrepreneurship*, Cambridge, MA: Ballinger, pp. 85–105.

Wetzel, W. E. Jr (1987) 'The informal venture capital market: aspects of scale and market efficiency', *Journal of Business Venturing*, **32**, pp. 299–313.

PART III

United Kingdom experiences

CHAPTER 7

LINC: a decentralised approach to the promotion of informal venture capital

Colin M. Mason and Richard T. Harrison

Introduction

LINC – the Local Investment Networking Company – was formed in 1987 to integrate the existing local financial marriage bureaux of a number of local enterprise agencies into a *nationwide* business introduction service. LINC offers three types of matching service to help small businesses raise capital from private investors.

- A monthly *Investment Bulletin*, which provides a brief description (approximately 100 words) of businesses seeking finance and is distributed to investors who are registered with LINC. Investors can contact LINC to request a more detailed two-page summary of any investment opportunities featured in the bulletin. Some member agencies automatically send the two-page summary of businesses in their area to their local investors.
- An *investment database*: each month all new bulletin entries are matched by computer against investors' investment criteria. Investors are sent the detailed summary of all businesses that meet their investment preferences.
- *Investors' meetings*, which allow entrepreneurs to present their investment opportunity to a gathering of potential investors. The normal format is that between four and six entrepreneurs make half-hour presentations of their projects at each meeting. There are opportunities for questions and the meetings conclude with refreshments, which provides an opportunity for further informal discussions.

LINC is run by its member agencies – mostly enterprise agencies – under a federal-type structure. Its member agencies each pay a membership fee, initially £1,000 per annum but raised at the beginning of 1993 to £5,000 per annum, as a contribution to LINC's central budget. This entitles them to a seat on the LINC board. There is also a second-tier class of membership available, with no seat on the board, for a fee of £1,500 per annum. LINC's central budget covers the cost of its small head office staff based at the London Enterprise Agency, plus printing and circulation of all literature, including the *Investment Bulletin*, management of the investor database, national promotion of the service and the attraction of sponsorship. The key functions of the LINC member agencies are the promotion of the service in their local area to recruit businesses and investors, counselling to businesses which seek to register with LINC, both to filter out those that are inappropriate and to assist those businesses which are accepted to prepare a business plan, and the running of investor meetings in their area (although not every member agency runs these meetings). In addition, member agencies generally get to know their investors and businesses quite well and so are often able to undertake a more personalised, proactive matching process based on a sound knowledge of the investment preferences of their investors. One LINC agency even organises visits by investors to firms.

As at mid-1993, LINC had nine member agencies, comprising the London Enterprise Agency, Barrfield Enterprise Training Ltd (covering North London), Staffordshire Development Association (on behalf of a consortium of ten enterprise agencies in the West Midlands), Somerset Enterprise Services, Great Western Enterprise (based at Swindon), North Derbyshire Enterprise Agency, the Mid-Scottish Consortium and Sheffield Enterprise Agency (a second-tier member) plus TEChINVEST, one of the DTI informal investment demonstration projects (see Chapter 14), covering Cheshire and the Wirral. A number of agencies have dropped out in recent years, particularly following the increase in membership fees at the beginning of 1993. However, these agencies tended to be less active in promoting LINC. For example, in 1992 LINC facilitated 27 matches involving a total investment of £1.19 million; however, only six agencies were involved, with four agencies accounting for 25 of the matches (Somerset: 10; Staffordshire: 7; Mid-Scotland: 5; London: 3). Indeed, many of the other agencies which subsequently dropped out were not even producing cases for the *Investment Bulletin*. Thus, although LINC's geographical coverage is now very patchy it does comprise the most active member agencies.

LINC is open to businesses seeking funds of £250,000 or less, and which are willing to offer an equity share in the business to investors. They must provide a business plan showing the amount of funds required together with details of the business, its people and the nature of the product or service that is provided. Local enterprise agencies can provide guidance to entrepreneurs in the preparation of their business plan. Businesses which are considered suitable to join LINC are charged a one-off registration fee which entitles them to appear in the *Investment Bulletin* for six months. For a number of years this fee had been set at £50. However, in 1993 the London Enterprise Agency and Somerset Enterprise Services both raised this fee to £200 and Great Western Enterprise raised their fee to £150; other member agencies have retained the original fee. Investors should have between £10,000 and £250,000 available for investment to be eligible to register with LINC. They are charged an annual fee, raised from

£75 to £120 in 1993 (£100 if paid by direct debit). As in the case of other business introduction services, LINC's registration and membership fees do not cover operating costs, so LINC has always relied upon sponsorship to survive. In recent years its sponsors have been Lloyds Bank, British Petroleum plc and accountants Levy Gee. Each has contributed £10,000 annually to the central budget. However, both British Petroleum (on account of the company's well-publicised financial difficulties) and Levy Gee ended their notional sponsorship in 1993, forcing LINC to search for new sponsors.

In an attempt to reduce its reliance on sponsorship, LINC is proposing to charge those businesses which raise finance a success fee of 3 per cent of the amount raised. Had such a charge been levied in 1992, it would have raised £35,000. However, a number of LINC's member agencies are reluctant to enforce the success fee and it is recognised that it may be difficult to collect in some cases.

This chapter provides an evaluation of LINC. It is based on independent research undertaken on behalf of LINC.[1] Its objectives are: first, to examine the characteristics of investors and businesses registered with LINC, and the views of both investors and entrepreneurs on the services provided by LINC; second, to assess what impact LINC has had on the informal venture capital market in the UK; and third, to consider what changes in its operation are appropriate in order to serve better the interests of investors and businesses seeking finance, and, in turn, to enhance its impact. Although the analysis is based on a case study, the issues raised will nevertheless have general relevance for all business introduction services, since they share a number of common challenges and operating problems.

Data sources

This study is based on two separate postal questionnaire surveys of investors and businesses registered with LINC. Information on investors is derived from a postal survey of both current and 'lapsed' members of LINC. Questionnaires were sent out to all 211 current members of LINC plus 97 former members. A total of 53 usable questionnaires were received (after one reminder letter), giving a rather disappointing response rate of 17 per cent. Of the 53 questionnaires returned, 33 were from people who, according to LINC records, were current members and the remaining 20 were from lapsed members. However, respondents' perceptions of their membership status are at variance with LINC's records, since 42 respondents claimed to be current members of LINC and only 11 described themselves as lapsed members.[2]

Information on businesses registered with LINC was derived from a postal survey of businesses that had registered with LINC during 1990 and 1991. The survey therefore includes businesses that were registered with LINC at the time of the survey (of which there were between 80 and 100), and which were therefore still seeking finance, as well as those which were no longer registered either because they had succeeded in raising finance or for other reasons. A total of 78 usable responses were received from the 250 questionnaires that were sent out (after one reminder letter), a response rate of about one-third.

Characteristics of investors and businesses registered with LINC

Investors

LINC investors are predominantly male (only one female respondent), are mostly in the 35–54 age group (66 per cent), and have a business background, generally in service industries. Many have entrepreneurial experience: three-quarters had founded one or more businesses (over half of these respondents had founded more than one business). Two-thirds have annual incomes of over £50,000 and their average net worth (excluding principal residence) is over £200,000. In view of the entrepreneurial background of most entrepreneurs, we can assume that a substantial proportion of LINC investors are financially self-made.[3] There is a common perception that business introduction services attract redundant executives who have received 'golden handshakes' and who are seeking to make informal investments as a means of 'buying themselves a job': however, with only 6 per cent of respondents describing themselves as 'unemployed and looking for an investment opportunity', this perception would appear to be incorrect.

Comparison with other surveys of informal investors in the UK (Mason and Harrison, 1994), most of whom have not joined business introduction services, indicates that LINC investors are distinctive in a number of respects. First, they are younger. Second, they have higher annual incomes but lower net worth. Third, investors registered with LINC make larger investments (taking into account all of their investments, not just those made through LINC). Just under two-thirds of respondents had made informal investments during the preceding three years, of which only a minority were through LINC. These 33 active angels had invested an average of £100,000 in a total of 76 investments. The median size of investment per deal was £30,000. Comparative figures from other studies of informal investors in the UK are £22,000 and £10,000 respectively (Mason and Harrison, 1994).

LINC's investor membership comprises both recent and long-established members. Around one-third of the respondents to the survey have been members for more than two years, while a further 35 per cent had joined less than a year prior to the survey. Well over 80 per cent had joined LINC in a personal capacity, with the remainder joining on behalf of their company (e.g. accountancy firms, consultancies, investment companies). The main motive for joining LINC was, not surprisingly, for access to small business investment opportunities. However, many respondents elaborated on this point by indicating that they believed that LINC would provide information on either a better quality or a wider range of investment opportunities than they could obtain from other sources. In some cases the reason given for joining LINC was to identify investment opportunities in which they could have some management involvement. Other reasons given for joining LINC included access to 'intelligence' on the small business sector and opportunities to network with other informal investors.

Respondents who were no longer members of LINC had withdrawn for various reasons. However, the crucial point is that only one-quarter of these investors had discontinued their membership because of dissatisfaction with the service provided. In a further one-third of cases, investors terminated their membership because of a mismatch between their requirements and the services provided by LINC. One-quarter of investors discontinued their membership because of a change in their circumstances which meant that they were no longer in a position to make informal investments. The remaining investors (12 per cent) discontinued their membership because of factors beyond the control of LINC: examples given included high interest rates and the failure to agree investment terms with an entrepreneur.

Businesses

LINC is primarily serving new and recently started firms (Figure 7.1), with over 60 per cent of respondents classifying themselves as pre-start-ups (4 per cent), start-ups (30 per cent) or infant businesses (27 per cent), while at the other extreme just 16 per cent of respondents were established businesses. Not surprisingly, most firms are also small: 46 per cent had just one or two employees (including salaried directors), whereas only 11 per cent had more than nine employees. The small size of LINC businesses is also seen in terms of their turnover. Nearly one-third of firms had not completed their first financial year. Of the remainder, 41 per cent had annual sales of less than £100,000. At the other extreme, just one firm had annual sales of over £1m.

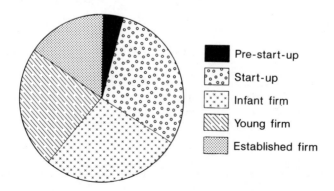

Figure 7.1 Stage of business development of companies registered with LINC.

LINC has attracted firms from a wide range of industrial sectors. Over 40 per cent of firms undertake manufacturing activities, a much higher proportion than in the small business population as a whole. Within the service sector, retail and wholesale distribution is the largest category, comprising 15 per cent of businesses, while finance, insurance and business service firms account for 11 per cent of the total.

The amount of finance sought by LINC-registered firms ranged from less than £25,000 to over £250,000. Just under half of all firms were seeking amounts in the £100,000 to £250,000 range, while a further 31 per cent were seeking less than £50,000 (Figure 7.2). There is little relationship between the amount sought and the stage of business development (Table 7.1).

Reflecting the youthfulness of most LINC clients, the main purposes for which finance was sought were associated with product development and initial marketing, funding start-up operations and working capital to allow expansion. Only a small proportion of firms required finance to overcome cash-flow difficulties or for rescue purposes (Table 7.2).

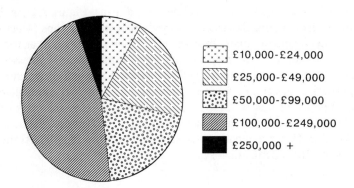

£10,000-£24,000

£25,000-£49,000

£50,000-£99,000

£100,000-£249,000

£250,000 +

Figure 7.2 Amount of finance sought by companies registered with LINC.

Table 7.1 Amount sought by firms registered with LINC, by stage of business development

Amount sought (£000)	Pre-start-up	Start-up	Infant firm	Young firm	Established firm	Total	%
10–24	0	1	4	1	1	7	91
25–49	2	6	3	3	3	17	22.1
50–99	1	2	6	3	2	14	18.2
100–249	1	13	6	10	5	35	45.5
250–499	0	1	2	0	1	4	5.2[a]

[a] No response from one firm.

Table 7.2 Purposes for which finance was sought

Purpose for which finance was sought	Number of firms	%
Develop an idea/build a prototype	7	9.0
Produce development/initial marketing	27	34.6
Fund full-scale operations at start-up	27	34.6
Working capital for expansion of young firm	33	42.3
Major expansion of mature firm	4	5.1
Cash-flow difficulties	12	15.4
Acquisition of another company	1	1.3
Rescue/company turnaround	1	1.3
Management buyout	0	–
Other purposes	8	10.3

Note: Multiple responses possible.

Most firms have registered with LINC as part of a wider search for finance. Two-thirds of firms registered with LINC at the same time as they sought to raise finance from other sources. Thus, only a minority of firms have regarded LINC as a 'last resort', registering after having failed to raise finance from other sources. However, most firms have undertaken a restricted search for finance, with only 49 per cent approaching more than two providers of finance. The range of potential sources approached is also limited. Approximately two-thirds of firms have approached their own bank plus private investors and about half have approached venture capital funds. However, fewer than half have approached other banks and less than one-quarter of firms have approached merchant banks or other companies.

In most cases the search for finance has been either unsuccessful or only partially successful. Twenty-six firms reported that they had received an acceptable offer for some or all of the finance that they sought, in some cases from more than one source, representing 37 per cent of firms that approached potential sources of finance. However, only five of these firms raised all of the finance that they sought. Firms had greatest success in raising finance from their own bank and from private investors. In contrast, approaches to other banks, merchant banks and venture capital funds were generally unsuccessful. The most common reasons why the clearing banks turned down requests for funding were associated with lack of personal security and the economic climate, while merchant banks and venture capital funds tended to turn down funding proposals either because the amount sought was too small or because of the economic climate.[4]

Just over two-thirds of firms registering with LINC were specifically looking for an investor who would play an active role in their business. Firms were mainly seeking investors with financial and marketing skills. There was a fairly good association between the skills sought by businesses and the areas of expertise of investors (Table 7.3).

Table 7.3 A comparison of skills sought by firms and management expertise of investors registered with LINC

Skills/expertise	Skills sought by firms (%)	Management expertise of investors (%)
Financial	79	44
Marketing	45	33
Sales	24	26
General management	24	19
Technical	13	14
Personnel	4	–
Other	11	–

Note: Both firms and investors could give more than one response.

Awareness of LINC

Both investors and businesses have become aware of LINC in a variety of ways (Table 7.4). The most important source of awareness for investors is the media. Such media coverage comprises editorial comment: LINC does not have the financial resources to undertake media advertising. Personal contacts (friends, business associates) and enterprise agencies were also important channels of information about LINC. Recommendations from informal and formal sources have been the most frequent source of awareness for businesses. Approximately half of the respondents had become aware of LINC through the small business support network – notably accountants, banks, enterprise agencies and chambers of commerce – while a further 19 per cent of firms had become aware of LINC through friends and business associates. In marked contrast to investors, few businesses have become aware of LINC as a result of media coverage.

Table 7.4 Sources of awareness of LINC

Information source	Investors (%)	Businesses (%)
Media	30.8	2.6
Enterprise agencies, chambers of commerce	15.3	19.2
Friends and business associates	13.5	19.2
Advertisement	7.7	7.7
Mailshot, circular	7.7	–
Professional adviser (e.g. bank, accountant)	13.5	29.5
Personal search	3.8	11.5
Other	7.6	10.3

The role of LINC as a source of deals for investors

Investors use LINC as just one of a number of sources of information on investment opportunities. Nevertheless, over three-quarters of respondents had seriously considered at least one investment opportunity from LINC during the previous three years (an average of two per investor). In aggregate, LINC was the source of 38 per cent of the investments that were seriously considered by investors. However, there is considerable variation between investors in the proportion of investment opportunities that they became aware of through LINC. At one extreme, nearly one-quarter of investors seriously considered investment opportunities that had exclusively come through LINC, while at the other extreme, 20 per cent of investors had not seriously considered any investment opportunities that had come through LINC (Table 7.5).

Most investors considered that the quality of the investment opportunities that they had received through LINC was only acceptable to fair. The quality of the entrepreneur attracted the most favourable assessment, while the management team, rate of return prospects and exit prospects were the attributes that received the lowest ratings (Table 7.6).

Just ten investors (19 per cent) have made investments in companies that they identified through LINC. The 11 investments that these investors made, involving a total investment of £545,000, represents just 14 per cent of all investments made by respondents, and accounts for only 11 per cent of the total amount that they have invested. However, setting this in the context of other information channels used by investors indicates that LINC is a relatively 'efficient' information source. The efficiency of an information channel can be expressed as the number referrals from a source which have resulted in investments, divided by the total number of referrals from that source. Informal referrals sources (i.e. friends and business associates) are the most efficient; however, LINC has the highest efficiency rate of all formal sources used by investors who responded to the survey, exceeding such informal sources as accountants, banks, stockbrokers, solicitors and business brokers.

Table 7.5 The proportion of investments seriously considered by investors identified through LINC

Proportion of investments seriously considered that were identified through LINC	% of investors
None	22
Less than 10%	2
10–24%	15
25–49%	15
50–99%	22
All	24

Table 7.6 Investors' views of the quality of investment opportunities received through LINC

Criteria	Excellent	Very good	Acceptable	Fair	Poor
			(% of respondents)		
Entrepreneur	3	24	27	32	14
Management team	–	6	35	38	21
Uniqueness/distinctiveness of firm's product/service	–	26	37	29	9
Growth potential of market	–	29	35	32	3
Extent of competition	3	17	30	40	10
Barriers to competition	–	14	29	43	14
Rate of return prospects	–	16	26	35	23
Equity share available	3	25	28	31	12
Cost of equity share	–	9	41	38	12
Exit prospects	3	13	17	23	43

Note: For various reasons (e.g. no introductions received, too early to tell, cannot generalise because each project varies), these options are based on about 60% of respondents.

The *Investment Bulletin* is the most effective part of the referral service that is provided by LINC. This can be indicated in various ways. First, nearly two-thirds of investors seriously considered one or more investment opportunities that appeared in the bulletin (median of two investment opportunities). This compares with just under one-quarter of respondents who seriously considered one or more investment opportunities arising from an investors' meeting. No investors reported that they had seriously considered any investment opportunities that had been brought to their attention through the investors' database. Second, the *Investment Bulletin* was the source of 80 per cent of the investment opportunities identified through LINC that were seriously considered by investors. A third measure of the effectiveness of the bulletin is that 12 per cent of investors made investments in companies that had been brought to their attention through the bulletin, compared with just 6 per cent who made investments in companies which made presentations at investors' meetings. Fourth, the *Investment Bulletin* was the source of two-thirds of the investments made in companies that were referred by LINC. These investments accounted for 79 per cent of the total amount invested in companies that investors identified through LINC.

The role of LINC in the entrepreneur's search for finance

Forty-six firms (59 per cent) had been introduced to potential investors through LINC. The number of investors ranged from one to eight (excluding investors' meetings), with a median of two. However, only six of these firms (13 per cent, but 7.7 per cent of all respondents) reported that their negotiations had led to an acceptable offer of finance being made. In a further three cases, negotiations were still in progress.

The amounts raised by these firms ranged from £3,500 to £135,000, with only two firms raising more than £25,000 through LINC investors. In three cases the finance that was raised from LINC investors was provided in the form of a combination of loans and ordinary shares, and in the other three cases the finance was in the form of a loan. Four of the six firms simultaneously raised finance from other sources.

The remaining 37 firms that had been introduced to potential investors through LINC reported that their negotiations had failed to lead to an acceptable offer of finance being made. These firms gave a variety of reasons why negotiations with potential investors had failed. However, four reasons stand out:

- The investor was unfamiliar with the market, product or technology.
- The investor was judged by the firm not to be serious.
- The individual to whom the firm was introduced turned out to be an intermediary rather than an investor.
- The investor was unhappy with the risk–reward ratio.

It is important to stress that we only have the entrepreneurs' views of the reasons why the negotiations failed. Clearly, the potential investors may have a different perspective to that of the entrepreneur on why they decided not to invest. The reasons most frequently cited by LINC investors for not investing were as follows:

- Lack of confidence in the entrepreneur.
- Lack of talent/expertise of management team.
- The business concept needed further development.
- Limited growth prospects of the business.

The majority of entrepreneurs were disappointed with the number of introductions that they had received. Of the entrepreneurs that had been put in touch with investors through LINC (46), only four (6.7 per cent) had been introduced to more investors than they had expected. In contrast, 29 firms (63 per cent) reported that the number of introductions to investors through LINC was less than expected. The balance of opinion among entrepreneurs concerning the quality of the investors to whom they had been introduced through LINC was also negative (Table 7.7).

Although firms register with LINC in the hope of being able to raise finance from a private investor, it is important to emphasise that firms can derive benefits even if they are unsuccessful in raising finance. Nearly half of the firms which had not raised finance through LINC at the time of the survey reported that they

Table 7.7 Entrepreneurs' views of the quality of the investors to whom they have been introduced through LINC

Assessment	Number of entrepreneurs	%
Excellent	1	2.3
Very good	9	20.5
Acceptable	14	31.8
Fair	7	15.9
Poor	13	29.5
(No response)	2	

had nevertheless derived useful benefits, notably in terms of feedback from discussion with investors. Thus, any evaluation of the impact of a business introduction service must take into account the benefits that many firms obtain, even if they are unsuccessful in raising finance.

Three-quarters of the entrepreneurs who responded to the survey were still seeking to raise finance. Most were searching quite widely. A high proportion were still seeking to raise finance from private investors, either as a result of their own search or through registration with LINC or another business referral service. Almost all of these firms were still registered with LINC at the time of the survey, but only 18 per cent were 'very' or 'quite' confident that they would be able to raise the finance that they required through this route.

Satisfaction with LINC: views of investors and entrepreneurs

The survey has tapped relatively little serious dissatisfaction with LINC among either investors or entrepreneurs, although it is important to emphasise that we have no way of knowing whether the respondents were biased towards the more satisfied users. With this caveat, it is clear that the majority of investors and entrepreneurs consider that LINC is providing an acceptable service, with just under one-third of investors and just over one-third of entrepreneurs judging LINC's service to be less than acceptable (Figure 7.3). Entrepreneurs' views are more polarised than those of investors: twice as many entrepreneurs as investors regarded LINC's service as being excellent or very good (33 per cent cf. 17 per cent); similarly, the proportion of entrepreneurs who regarded LINC's service as poor was nearly three times that of investors (17 per cent cf. 6 per cent). However, virtually identical proportions of firms and investors considered that the registration fee to join LINC was good value for money (65 per cent cf. 64 per cent).

The *Investment Bulletin* elicited few strong positive or negative opinions among either investors or entrepreneurs (Figure 7.4). In both cases the balance of views was towards the dissatisfied end of the spectrum, although the proportion of

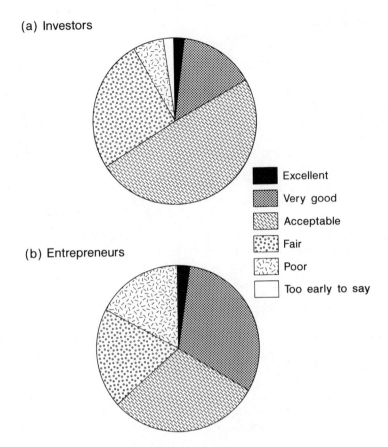

(a) Investors

(b) Entrepreneurs

Excellent
Very good
Acceptable
Fair
Poor
Too early to say

Figure 7.3 Opinions of LINC: (a) investors; (b) entrepreneurs.

respondents who considered the bulletin to be adequate was slightly higher among firms than investors: 62 per cent of firms considered that it was 'adequate', whereas 50 per cent of investors considered that it was 'acceptable'. Only 12 per cent of investors considered that the bulletin was either very good or excellent and only 8 per cent of entrepreneurs considered it to be more than adequate.

The key factors which an investor takes into account in making a judgement on the usefulness of an investment bulletin are the number of investment opportunities and the amount of information provided on each project. Exactly half of all investor respondents were satisfied with the number of investment opportunities contained in the *Investment Bulletin* and two-thirds were satisfied that the amount of information on each investment opportunity in the bulletin was sufficient for them to decide whether they wished to consider it in more detail. However, there were also a significant minority of investors who expressed

(a) Investors

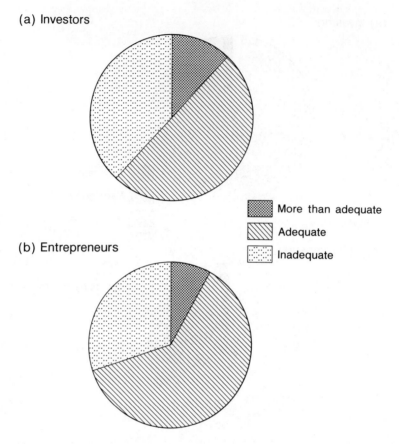

More than adequate

Adequate

Inadequate

(b) Entrepreneurs

Figure 7.4 Opinions of LINC's *Investment Bulletin*: (a) investors; (b) entrepreneurs.

dissatisfaction with these features: for example, over one-third wished to see more investment opportunities than the bulletin currently contains, and 15 per cent felt that bulletin entries had major omissions in the information provided.[5]

From the perspective of entrepreneurs, the key consideration is whether the bulletin provides sufficient scope to present their investment opportunity. Most entrepreneurs were satisfied that the brief entry in the *Investment Bulletin* provided sufficient opportunity for them to present their business adequately to potential investors. But here again there was a sizeable minority (30 per cent) who considered that the word limit was inadequate for this purpose.

The second service provided by LINC is to make a business plan summary available for any investment opportunities featured in the bulletin that an investor wishes to consider in more detail. Investors also automatically receive a business plan summary of any businesses that they are matched with in the database. The majority of investors were happy with the amount of additional information that the business plan summary contained; however, here again a significant minority of investors considered that important information was missing. Many of these investors commented that business plans were often poor and that the range and quality of information contents was variable, with financial data frequently missing or inadequate. In this context, it is pertinent to note that fewer than half of entrepreneurs (41 per cent) reported that they had received assistance in preparing the summary of their business plans. Half of these firms stated that this assistance had been provided by LINC. In all cases this assistance was judged to be helpful. Moreover, of the firms which did not receive assistance in the preparation of their business plan summaries, nearly half admitted that this would have been beneficial.

Most entrepreneurs were also satisfied that the two-page business plan provided a satisfactory opportunity to present their business adequately to potential investors. A small number of firms suggested that a longer or even a full business plan should be made available to investors (although one firm noted that it was a very good discipline to prepare a summary of the business plan). However, firms are at liberty to send additional information, such as a full business plan, to potential investors.

The third matching process provided by LINC is investors' meetings. At the time that the survey was undertaken, the only LINC agencies to operate investors' meetings on a regular basis were the London Enterprise Agency (LENTA) and the Staffordshire Development Association. Just under half of investors had attended one or more investors' meetings: all but one of these respondents had attended the meetings that were arranged by LENTA. For this reason it is not surprising to note that a much higher proportion of LINC investors living in the South East (including Greater London) had attended investors' meetings compared with members living elsewhere in the country (64 per cent compared with 27 per cent). LINC members who live in the South East were also more frequent attenders at investors' meetings, with 52 per cent having attended three or more meetings. Although the majority of investors were satisfied with the investors' meetings (57 per cent), there was a significant minority of investors (34 per cent) who were dissatisfied with the investors' meetings (Figure 7.5(a)).

One-third of firms (26) had made a presentation to an investors' meeting. Eleven firms (42 per cent) reported that they had received assistance in preparing their presentation. In most cases this assistance was provided by LINC, and in each case firms considered this assistance to be helpful. Exactly half of the firms that had made presentations to investors' meetings felt the format provided sufficient opportunity to present their business adequately to potential investors. However, more than one-third of firms felt that investors' meetings were inadequate (Figure 7.5(b)). Sources of dissatisfaction were varied. However, the main thrust of this dissatisfaction was that investors' meetings do not provide firms with an adequate opportunity to engage in a dialogue with potential

(a) Investors

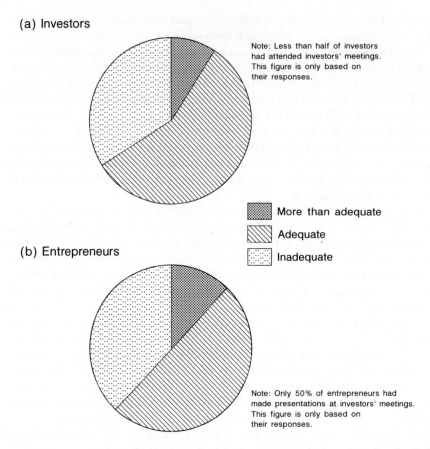

Note: Less than half of investors
had attended investors' meetings.
This figure is only based on
their responses.

☒ More than adequate

▨ Adequate

▦ Inadequate

(b) Entrepreneurs

Note: Only 50% of entrepreneurs had
made presentations at investors' meetings.
This figure is only based on
their responses.

Figure 7.5 Opinions of LINC's investors' meetings: (a) investors; (b) entrepreneurs.

investors. Some of the causes identified by entrepreneurs included the anonymity of investors (there was a suggestion that investors should be listed on the agenda), insufficient investors, the rapid disappearance of investors after the final presentation, and the atmosphere/setting,[6] which was not thought to be conducive to fostering dialogue with potential investors.

The final service provided by LINC is the investment database. However, this had not been available to LINC members for some time prior to this study on account of computer problems and the need to replace the original software, which proved unable to make sufficiently specific matches. Consequently, few of the respondents had any experience of the database.

Conclusion

Research on the informal venture capital market has indicated that most active business angels are unable to find sufficient investment opportunities and so have substantial amounts of uncommitted finance available for informal investments. In addition, the number of 'virgin' angels – people who share the same high net worth and business backgrounds as active angels but have never made any informal investments – considerably exceeds the number of active angels (Freear and Wetzel, 1992). The objective of business introduction services is to provide both active and virgin angels with a convenient means of identifying a range of investment opportunities that have been filtered to eliminate the 'lemons', thereby encouraging greater informal investment activity. Surprisingly, there have been very few attempts to assess how well business introduction services succeed in this objective. This case study of LINC is therefore one of the first attempts to undertake an objective evaluation of a business introduction service.

Our evaluation of LINC indicates that its impact on mobilising the large pool of uncommitted informal venture capital has been modest. Four statistics can be offered in support of this conclusion:

- Fewer than one in five investors registered with LINC have made any investments in companies that they identified through LINC. Furthermore, 86 per cent of these investors still have funds available – £100,000 per person on average – for informal investments, and in aggregate the amount that they have available for investment considerably exceeds the amount that they have invested during the three years prior to the survey.
- Less than 60 per cent of entrepreneurs have received any introductions to potential investors, and the majority of these entrepreneurs expected to receive a larger number of introductions.
- Fewer than one in ten businesses have raised finance through LINC.
- According to LINC's own statistics, just 49 deals were completed between 1989 and 1992 inclusive, involving a total investment of £2,460,000.

However, this conclusion needs to be qualified in a number of respects. First, the lack of comparative information on other business introduction services means that there is no yardstick against which to assess LINC's performance. A rough-and-ready comparison can be made with figures on *Venture Capital Report*'s performance (Chapter 8): in 1992, 14 per cent of business registered with LINC raised finance, which is not markedly dissimilar from VCR's performance.[7] Second, LINC is a relatively 'efficient' information source for investors: LINC's convertion rate (i.e. the number of investments resulting from the opportunities referred) is actually higher than every other formal information channel used by investors. Third, a significant proportion of firms which have been unsuccessful in raising finance through LINC nevertheless report deriving some benefit from registering with LINC, notably in terms of the free advice from LINC's business counsellors and the feedback from potential investors. Finally, LINC's performance in 1992 has been much more impressive than in previous years: according to LINC's own statistics, there were 27 deals in 1992 involving a total investment of £1.19 million, compared with 22 investments which raised £1.27 million during the three years from 1989 to 1991. While this is, in part, a result of growing awareness about the informal venture capital market – reflecting increasing media publicity – it is also associated with improvements in LINC's professionalism.

There are a number of reasons why LINC has not had a greater impact on the informal venture capital market. First, LINC's client base of firms and investors is too small. As a result, the probability of introductions and successful matches is reduced. Research and anecdotal information both indicate that awareness of LINC among investors, small businesses and professional intermediaries is low (for example, see Chapter 13). This reflects the limited financial and staff resources that LINC has available to promote the service both nationally and locally. Indeed, a number of LINC's member agencies – especially those which have recently dropped out – do not have a member of staff dedicated to promoting the service locally.

Because LINC has a limited marketing budget, it must find cost-effective ways of increasing its marketing effort. In effect, this means relying upon third parties to promote the service. Our evaluation of the DTI's informal investment demonstration projects (Chapter 14) indicates that a decline in marketing effort is quickly reflected in a drop-off in enquiries. Marketing effort must therefore be continuous, a point which has been recognised by *Venture Capital Report* (see Chapter 8). Our findings on awareness of LINC highlight the importance of achieving media coverage, particularly in attracting investors, and in networking with professional intermediaries and small business support organisations as the most effective ways of recruiting clients. Marketing of the service – for example, by brochures and editorials in relevant journals – should therefore be targeted at these important 'gatekeepers'. LINC should create more effective networking arrangements with intermediaries (banks, accountants, etc.) and other business support organisations (e.g. TECs) and become more fully integrated into the local business support structures. Referrals from friends and business associates are also a significant source of new members. Existing clients should therefore be encouraged to provide names and addresses of others who might be interested in joining, for LINC to follow up (for example, replicating the practice of Venture Capital Network (see Chapter 3) by including a recommendation form in its brochures and *Investment Bulletin*). In addition, it is important to follow up lapsed investors, since many have not made a conscious decision to leave LINC, but have simply let their subscription expire through forgetfulness or lethargy. LINC has recently addressed this problem by the simple expedient of providing a financial incentive to investors to pay their subscription by direct debit.

A second factor that has limited LINC's impact in stimulating informal venture capital relates to the quality of businesses and investors that have been recruited. A business introduction service risks losing its credibility if it is perceived to be providing poor-quality investment opportunities. While most investors have not been highly critical of the quality of investment opportunities that they have received through LINC, by the same token neither have they been particularly complimentary. Many investors consider that LINC should be more selective in the businesses that it accepts, in order to increase the quality of investment opportunities. This can be achieved by including 'minimum listing requirements' (see Chapter 4) and by more proactive marketing to recruit businesses with superior rate of return prospects. LINC should also respond to criticisms by entrepreneurs concerning the quality of investors. This is a much greater challenge: however, one appropriate strategy is to step up efforts to recruit investors with entrepreneurial business skills and expertise that they can contribute to investee businesses, in view of the demand by many firms for 'hands-on' investors to provide both finance and know-how.

Third, LINC's activities are too localised and geographically fragmented. Indeed, LINC's original rationale of providing a *nationwide* business introduction service is no longer tenable (if it ever was). LINC is represented in only a small – and diminishing – part of the UK, and its activities are weighted to an even smaller number of agencies which are responsible for recruiting a disproportionate share of investors and investment opportunities, and which are the most proactive in promoting introductions. Not surprisingly, these agencies also account for the majority of completed deals. This is a significant limitation for both businesses and investors. Businesses located in areas where there is not a LINC member agency are less likely to be aware of LINC, and the strong ties of LINC member agencies to specific geographical operating areas are likely to make them reluctant to accept non-local businesses. Although most investors prefer to invest in businesses located within 50–100 miles of home, and most matches are local,[8] there are a significant minority of investors who are willing to look much further afield. However, LINC provides these investors with a spatially constrained range of investment opportunities. LINC therefore needs to expand its geographical coverage.[9] One appropriate strategy is to seek to recruit TECs as member agencies, many of which are examining the feasibility of setting up their own business introduction services. Encouraging TECs to become LINC member agencies will increase LINC's efficiency and effectiveness by expanding its client base of investors and businesses, and creating a national pool of investors. Additionally, it will avoid the danger of fragmentation which Cary warns of in Chapter 8.

There are two further steps which LINC should take in order to increase its effectiveness. First, there is scope for improvements to the matching processes. The *Investment Bulletin* is the main source of information on deal flow for LINC investors. It may be appropriate to change its format in order to increase the amount of information provided on each investment opportunity.[10] Our preference is for 2–3 pages on each business seeking finance. Most of the entrepreneurs and investors who responded to our survey were satisfied with the short summary, combined with the availability of a business plan summary if requested. However, a significant minority of investors prefer more information to be published on each investment opportunity. There was also a demand by a number of investors for a standardised format for both bulletin entries and business plan summaries, to ensure that key information – for example, on sales and profits and the type of contribution required from an investor – is always provided.[11] Those LINC agencies which host investors' meetings claim that they are the single most effective matching mechanism. All LINC agencies should therefore host such meetings, and they should be actively promoted to encourage a high attendance by investors.

Second, LINC should play a more proactive role in the matching process, in order to try to increase the conversion rate of introductions into deals. A number of entrepreneurs were concerned about the lack of response and feedback from investors to whom they had been introduced. This suggests that there is a need for greater follow-up both of investors who receive summary business plans and also of those who meet entrepreneurs, in order to feed back their views to entrepreneurs. The survey evidence indicates that most entrepreneurs benefit from such feedback where it occurs. Another way in which LINC can play a more proactive role in the matching process is to prepare both investors and firms for the negotiating process. There is certainly a demand by many entrepreneurs for assistance in the preparation of their business plan, bulletin entry and investors' meeting presentation, but only a minority of entrepreneurs reported receiving such assistance. Most businesses which register with LINC are new or recent start-ups and are seeking to raise equity finance for the first time. Many investors are infrequent or virgin angels. LINC should therefore seek to educate both investors and entrepreneurs on various aspects of the informal venture capital market. Responses to the survey indicate that many investors and entrepreneurs would welcome training in various aspects of informal venture capital (e.g. pricing of investments, structure of deals, exit routes) and would be willing to pay a higher subscription for such services. The Venture Capital Network publishes guides to raising informal venture capital and organises training workshops (Chapter 3), practices which seem worthy of being replicated by LINC.

LINC has addressed a number of these criticisms by implementing some of our recommendations. Thus, in certain respects LINC has changed quite considerably in the period since our research was undertaken. Moreover, these changes have coincided with an improvement in LINC's performance in terms of numbers of investments and amount invested. However, the changes are largely confined to operational aspects. LINC's fundamental weaknesses of a lack of core financing – with its knock-on effects on marketing and promotion activity – the limited numbers of investors and businesses, and the patchy geographical coverage all remain. It seems inevitable that unless these can also be addressed LINC's impact on the informal venture capital market will remain modest.

Implications for practice

- Business angels who join business introduction services are distinctive: they are younger, with higher incomes and lower net worth, and invest larger amounts both in total and per deal.
- There is a high turnover of investors.
- Only a minority of investors who drop out do so because they are dissatisfied with the service.
- Most businesses that join a business introduction service are new and recent start-ups, seeking finance for product development and initial marketing.
- Only a minority of businesses have contacted LINC as a 'last resort'.
- Media coverage is the single most effective way of recruiting investors.
- Promotion via professional intermediaries and the small business support network are the most effective ways of recruiting businesses.
- LINC is a relatively 'efficient' information source for investors.
- Many firms which were unsuccessful in raising finance through LINC nevertheless reported that they had derived useful benefits.

Notes

1. We are grateful to LINC for enabling us to undertake this study and to Fiona Conoley, General Manager of LINC, for her comments on an earlier version of this chapter. However, the opinions expressed do not necessarily reflect those of LINC. The survey of LINC investors, which was undertaken in early 1991, was part of a research project entitled 'Informal Risk Capital in the UK', which was funded by the Economic and Social Research Council in conjunction with Barclays Bank, the Department of Employment, the Rural Development Commission and DG XXIII of the Commission of the European Communities (Ref. W108 25 1017). The survey of LINC businesses, undertaken in the final quarter of 1991, was funded by the Nuffield Foundation Social Sciences Small Grants Scheme. Any views expressed do not necessarily reflect those of the sponsoring organisations. We acknowledge the valuable contribution of Jennifer Chaloner, our research assistant, to this study. A more detailed account of the survey findings can be found in Mason *et al.* (1991) and Mason and Chaloner (1992).

2. The respondents to our survey are biased in favour of longer-established members (although as LINC's membership data is continually updated, it is not

possible to make an exact comparison). It seems probable that new members of LINC will have been less likely to respond to the questionnaire because they have had insufficient experience of the service to feel competent to answer many of the questions. Indeed, some investors who had only recently joined LINC and who did respond to the survey felt unable to answer some questions because it was 'too early to tell'.

3. One-third of entrepreneurs had sold one or more of their businesses and two entrepreneurs had obtained listings for their businesses on the Unlisted Securities Market.

4. The survey of businesses was undertaken during the depths of the recession in late 1991.

5. LINC has recently introduced a new format for the *Investment Bulletin* in which all entries follow the same structure for the first paragraph, thereby ensuring that key information that an investor is likely to require is always included.

6. As most entrepreneurs had given their presentations at LENTA, it seems probable that this final comment is likely to refer to the conference room at LENTA – a rather dingy basement with no natural light. Other LINC agencies hold their presentations in hotels. LENTA now holds its presentations at the premises of one of its sponsors.

7. For 1992, the number of businesses which raised finance through LINC was double that of VCR. However, it should be noted that these figures refer only to known investments and are based on each organisation's definition of what constitutes an investment.

8. 73 per cent of investments by LINC investors were made in businesses located within 100 miles of their home. Three of the five investments in the Mid-Scottish Consortium involved non-local investors, including two who were based in the English Midlands.

9. LINC is seeking to expand its membership. It is currently in negotiation with five enterprise agencies regarding membership and has invited the four remaining DTI informal investment demonstration projects (Chapter 14) to consider joining (TEChINVEST is already a member).

10. A redesigned *Investment Bulletin* was launched in June 1992. The major changes are, first, that it is now in loose-leaf format (with a file provided), and second, that entries now only appear in full for the first month; they will appear as a one-line entry for the next five months (with clear cross-reference to the issue in which they appeared in full). However, there has been no change in the length of each entry.

11. LINC has standardised the two-page executive summary of the business plan to overcome some of these comments.

References

Freear, J. and W. E. Wetzel Jr (1992) 'The informal venture capital market in the 1990s', in D. L. Sexton and J. D. Kasarada (eds.), *Entrepreneurship in the 1990s*, Boston, MA: PWS-Kent, pp. 462–86.

Mason, C. M. and J. Chaloner (1992) *The Operation and Effectiveness of LINC (Local*

Investment Networking Company). Part 2: Survey of businesses, Southampton: Urban Policy Research Unit, University of Southampton.

Mason, C. M. and R. T. Harrison (1994) 'The informal venture capital market in the UK', in A. Hughes and D. J. Storey (eds.), *Financing Small Firms*, London: Routledge, pp. 64–111.

Mason, C. M., R. T. Harrison and J. Chaloner (1991) 'Informal risk capital in the United Kingdom: a study of investor characteristics, investment preferences and decision making', Venture Finance Research Project, Working Paper No. 2, Southampton: Urban Policy Research Unit, University of Southampton.

CHAPTER 8

Venture Capital Report (VCR): achievements and lessons from an investment bulletin service

Lucius Cary

Origins

When I left university in 1972 I wanted to start my own business. I am an engineer, but I did not think that I would be able to raise enough money to start an engineering business. I therefore thought that I would raise money to start an American hamburger restaurant. The plan was that this restaurant would be the first of a chain and that within five years I would have five restaurants which I would then sell in order to start an engineering business. I wrote a business plan which showed that £27,000 was needed to start (equivalent to about £189,000 in today's prices). At the time I had an overdraft of £3,000, having borrowed to finance my education. I was thus in the classic position of the young entrepreneur. I had a business plan, but no money myself to carry it out, and the question was how to raise the necessary capital.

I first approached my bank, which offered £1,000 towards the venture by means of an increased overdraft facility. I next approached the only two venture capital companies in existence at the time – ICFC (now 3i) and the Small Business Capital Fund (now defunct). Both companies turned me down after a single short meeting. I next advertised in the *Financial Times,* and had 16 replies, of which six were trying to sell me more advertising, and one of these offered me £5,000 towards the business. Eventually, six months after I wrote the plan, and following another advertisement in the *Daily Telegraph,* I had raised the capital needed: my own contribution of £1,000 and £26,000 from four private investors – or business angels as they are sometimes known.

The first restaurant opened in 1973; the second, financed entirely from profits of the first, opened in 1976, and a third, financed entirely from the profits of the first two, opened in 1977. The business was profitable, the investors were repaid their initial stake, but still retained their 49 per cent shareholdings, and everyone was happy.

Thinking back to 1972, when I had only a business plan and an overdraft, it is apparent that I had been extremely lucky to raise any capital at all. The venture capital companies had turned me down, I had no rich relations and I only succeeded because there was one rich individual who shared my faith in the project among the ten who answered my tiny advertisement in the FT. What a slender thread on which to hang a business which five years later employed 50 people!

It seemed probable that there were many entrepreneurs with viable business plans who were not succeeding in raising capital, and that what was needed was a means of enabling these entrepreneurs to get their plans on to the desks of a large number of potential investors, rather than the ten who had answered my advertisement. It was with this objective that I started *Venture Capital Report* (VCR) in 1978.

How *Venture Capital Report* works

VCR was founded in order to create a forum in which entrepreneurs seeking venture capital could present their business plans in some detail to several hundred serious potential investors simultaneously. There was a problem at the start because of the 'chicken and egg' problem that without any investors it is difficult to get entrepreneurs to submit projects. But in the absence of any projects it is difficult to find potential investors to subscribe. In the event we found six entrepreneurs seeking capital to write about and 30 investors purchased the first issue. One of the projects was funded, showing that VCR could work, and this provided a solid basis on which to build.

The objective of VCR is to make matches between investors and entrepreneurs with the minimum amount of time wasted and the minimum expense for both parties. *Venture Capital Report* is published monthly. Each issue contains details of about ten businesses with about five pages (A4 size) devoted to each business. These articles are written by VCR after meeting the entrepreneur. VCR also publishes one-page advertisements written by the entrepreneur.

VCR receives about 1,200 enquiries a year from entrepreneurs seeking to raise capital. Of the 604 enquiries received between May and December 1991 which were logged on the computer, 260 came from an unknown source. Of the remainder:

- 36 per cent were referred to VCR.
- 36 per cent answered VCR advertisements.
- 12 per cent came from listings in directories.
- 4 per cent were approached by VCR.
- 12 per cent came by other routes (e.g. reading a newspaper article).

In addition to these enquiries from entrepreneurs which are logged on the computer, there are about half as many again from entrepreneurs who simply write in or telephone, and who get all the information they require from this contact.

To those enquiries which are logged on the computer, VCR sends an information pack and an invitation to send a business plan or, in the absence of a business plan, to complete a questionnaire. Some entrepreneurs already know about VCR, or have been referred to VCR, and simply send a business plan direct.

VCR currently receives about 30 business plans per month. Some of these are fully documented, professionally prepared plans. Others are brief outlines. Having read these plans, and usually followed them up with an initial discussion on the telephone, VCR then arranges to meet the entrepreneurs. At this meeting, which typically lasts for between three and five hours, VCR will go through the business plan in detail. Experience has shown that a flexible approach is needed to make the most of these meetings, since entrepreneurs are so varied. Some are timid and unsure of themselves. Some make wild claims about sales prospects, while others understate the potential of their idea. Some expect large salaries and a good life from the inception of the business, while others expect to struggle at the start. Many will have unrealistic expectations about the amount of equity they will need to surrender to stand a reasonable chance of attracting risk capital.

Some meetings will be between VCR and a lone entrepreneur, while others may involve VCR, an entrepreneurial team and their professional advisers. Whichever is the case, VCR's objective in the meeting is to try to get under the skin of the business plan and to establish whether the business could be viable given the right injection of resources, which can include both capital and non-financial resources such as management, marketing and production facilities. VCR will play devil's advocate, challenging the assumptions underlying the business plan and probing the project for weaknesses. We adopt this approach not to be unhelpful, but because it is important that entrepreneurs recognise the weaknesses in themselves and in their projects if they are to overcome them. VCR will also give guidance to entrepreneurs who request it about the appropriate methods of presenting a project and whether the financial structure is likely to attract investors. During or after the meeting, VCR will frequently talk to relevant people such as the entrepreneur's previous employer and existing customers to check facts and obtain additional information, and it may quote these references in the article. Nevertheless, the article will rely primarily upon information provided by the entrepreneur.

Provided that VCR is satisfied that the business is potentially viable, and that a financial structure which seems sensible to VCR and acceptable to the entrepreneur can be agreed, then VCR will prepare an article for publication. It is important to emphasise that the article is written by VCR and not by the entrepreneur, although it may sometimes quote from the business plan. This makes the article objective. VCR currently agrees to write articles for about two-thirds of the businesses that it meets. Typical reasons for rejection are that VCR considers that the business could never be viable, or that the entrepreneur has unrealistic expectations about the financial structure. The reasons for rejection will be clearly stated. Not infrequently, entrepreneurs return several months later, having made changes to their plans.

If everything is considered to be in order, VCR will write up an article for publication in *Venture Capital Report*. The objective of the article is to give investors all of the key facts about the business and the entrepreneur as concisely as possible, and to convey the entrepreneur's enthusiasm for the business. Thus, for example, a VCR article will always say if an entrepreneur has had a previous business which failed (even though such information is almost always omitted from business plans and sometimes even from prospectuses). The aim is to save time: some investors will be put off by such facts, other will not, and it is better to bring these facts out at the outset rather than after lengthy negotiations between entrepreneur and potential investor. In the same way and for the same reasons, the article will contain a balance sheet for an existing business, a photograph and full CV for the entrepreneur, and a precise suggested financial structure for the business. This is given not because it will necessarily be the final structure adopted, but because it gives an investor an indication about the entrepreneur's expectations. The statement that 33 per cent of the equity is available is much more meaningful than the vague statement that 'a substantial share' of the equity is available, since this may turn out to be anything from 10 to 80 per cent!

The article having been written, it is then sent to the entrepreneur and to his or her financial adviser (if he or she has one). The entrepreneur then returns the article with comments and with errors corrected. Occasionally there are major disagreements about the article, with the entrepreneur wishing to omit certain facts which VCR considers to be pertinent. Sometimes such disagreements cannot be resolved and the article is not published. Usually, however, agreement is straightforward and the article is published in the next issue of *Venture Capital Report*, which is mailed to subscribers on the first of each month.

Articles generally follow a fairly set pattern, usually beginning with a description of the product, an analysis of the market and competition, full CVs for the key entrepreneurs, with photographs, a history of the business, financial data including a balance sheet, profit and loss projection and cash flow, and a suggested financial structure. All articles end with the name, address and telephone number of the entrepreneur, so that investors can get directly in touch. This structure and content enables subscribers to use the article as a working document and to find the information they need as quickly as possible. Articles do not contain sufficient information to enable subscribers to make investments; rather, they contain enough information to enable subscribers to decide whether to pursue particular projects further.

VCR automatically follows up each article six weeks after publication to find out the response. Many entrepreneurs get in touch before then to let us know, and sometimes to ask if we know anything about a particular subscriber who has got in touch. Subscribers sometimes telephone about a particular project in which they are considering making an investment. However, VCR does not seek to get involved in detailed negotiations, although we are occasionally asked to do so, simply because we are not set up to do this and do not have the staff resources.

Since spring 1991 VCR has been preparing a computer database which lists the investment criteria and resources of VCR subscribers. When this is fully operational it will enable VCR to alert investors to projects which particularly suit them. VCR already does this on an *ad hoc* basis, and there is no doubt that it helps. Investors like to feel that they are receiving a personal service and most will at least agree to meet an entrepreneur if VCR suggests that it seems to be a good project and would appear to match their criteria.

Subscribers

The current annual subscription for investors is £350 per annum. The level is intended to be high enough to deter time-wasters, but not enough to deter serious investors with £100,000 or more to invest. As noted earlier, subscribers will receive details on about 100 investment opportunities over the course of a year.

VCR had over 630 subscribers in mid-1994, made up as follows:

- 54 per cent are wealthy individual investors. These individuals generally fall into two categories: first, individuals of high net worth who have either sold a business or inherited money, and often have over £1 million to invest; and second, individuals with between £50,000 and £150,000 to invest which they have received from a golden handshake, and who now seek a minority stake in a company with a view to being a part-time director.
- 28 per cent are managing directors of private companies. They subscribe to VCR primarily to help locate equity investment opportunities for themselves and their companies and to identify appropriate joint ventures.
- 4 per cent are quoted companies. Global companies have venture capital arms and intelligence units that are constantly seeking innovative products and ideas. 3M is one such quoted company subscribing to VCR. Its specific objective is both to investigate and assess companies as potential partners for joint ventures and acquisitions and to search for new product and technology opportunities outside 3M.
- 14 per cent are financial institutions and other organisations. This category primarily consists of specialist venture capital companies and merchant banks in the UK. These companies are seeking to make risk capital investments in excess of £250,000. Other organisations in this category include government and business school libraries.

Running costs

The VCR approach is relatively expensive on account of the time involved and the practical business experience required to undertake a proper investigation of the companies and then to prepare the articles. All VCR staff have degrees and those who write articles have MBAs or equivalent business degrees. Advertising and marketing costs to attract serious investors are also substantial. There is a constant need to attract new subscribers. Past subscribers will inevitably lapse on account of changes in their personal circumstances. For example, they may have made an investment or their business may be suffering, so they no longer have surplus capital available for informal investments. Experience shows that there is a need to spend £3,000 a month to attract ten new subscribers. This includes the cost of advertising, mailshots, printing brochures, case studies, etc. In addition, there is a need to spend on advertising and marketing in order to market the service to entrepreneurs. VCR receives no grant, subsidy or support of any kind, and must survive as a purely commercial organisation.

VCR estimates that the marginal cost of producing an article (meeting, writing, word processing, discussing and agreeing, typesetting, publishing, mailing and following up) is about £700. VCR currently charges entrepreneurs an up-front fee of £350 + VAT (i.e. half of its costs). This fee may be waived, reduced or deferred if an entrepreneur is genuinely poor, but has a good idea. VCR believes that this represents good value for the evaluation process which an entrepreneur experiences during the meeting with VCR. Almost all entrepreneurs say that they find this meeting to be useful, and in many cases it leads to modifications in their business plan or its presentation. Entrepreneurs use the meeting as a 'dry run' for a meeting with a real investor. Many entrepreneurs subsequently use the VCR article as a mini business plan with which to approach other potential investors. VCR also charges entrepreneurs a fee if they are successful in raising finance. This success fee is calculated as £1,000 plus 2.5 per cent of the funds raised via VCR[1] (and not more than 5 per cent of the total).

Achievements

VCR is successful to the extent that it achieves matches and has survived as a business since 1978. In the period that VCR has been operating, at least a dozen competitors have been established, none of them taking the same degree of trouble as VCR to vet the investment propositions, and with the exception of LINC (which is subsidised) none have survived for long. Nevertheless, VCR has not so far fulfilled my hopes for it.

VCR believes that statistics produced by business introduction services about the number of matches achieved should be supported by names and addresses of the companies concerned in order to be treated seriously. VCR makes this information available on a regular basis. VCR's record on making matches is as follows. Between December 1978 and September 1992 VCR featured 1,455 projects, of which we have received feedback from 1,291 (89 per cent).[2] Of these:

- 188 (15 per cent) received an offer for all of the money they sought from a VCR subscriber.
- 141 (11 per cent) received an offer for all of the money they sought, but not from a VCR subscriber.
- 137 (11 per cent) received an offer for some of the money they sought.
- 72 (6 per cent) received something positive (e.g. TV coverage or sales).
- 749 (58 per cent) had no success in raising funds.

Although there is an absence of comparable audited information, VCR nevertheless suspects that its success rate is higher than that achieved by other business introduction services.

Private individuals have been the most frequent backers of projects featured in *Venture Capital Report*, investing in a total of 136 projects, followed by private companies, which invested in 82 projects. The clearing banks supported 30 projects (many under the Loan Guarantee Scheme), while merchant banks backed 7 projects. Venture capital firms invested in 20 projects while a further 25 raised finance from public companies. Eight businesses raised finance from government agencies and through grants. The remaining 21 businesses were funded from other sources. Many of the entrepreneurs who have raised finance from sources other than VCR subscribers have nevertheless said the VCR article was a help.

Analysis of the 185 projects featured between 1990 and 1992 are shown in Table 8.1. Even though the number of subscribers fell by just under 100 over this period, the proportion of projects which raised all of the finance they sought from VCR subscribers remained constant at 15 per cent.

Between July 1992 and August 1994 a total of £2.83 million was invested by VCR subscribers in a total of 34 projects (Table 8.2). The amounts invested ranged from £6,000 to £350,000 (median of £55,000). It is likely that the eventual total will be significantly higher than this, since deals often take many months to finalise. In addition to this, VCR subscribers have made a number of offers to invest in businesses which, for various reasons, were not accepted. In some cases, the offer may have helped the business to raise finance from other sources. VCR

Table 8.1 Outcomes of projects featured in *Venture Capital Report*, 1990–2

	Number	%
Articles published	185	
Feedback received	164	89
Raised all of the finance sought from VCR subscriber	24	15
Raised all of the finance sought from another source	25	15
Raised some of the finance that they sought	28	17
Received some positive benefit	16	10
No success in raising finance	71	43

Table 8.2 Projects featured in *Venture Capital Report* in 1992 which have raised finance from VCR subscribers

Yoghurt manufacture	£30,000 was sought from one or more investors under the Business Expansion Scheme (BES). A VCR investor who had recently moved into the area invested £15,000, and friends of the founder invested the balance.
Uni-mailer	£100,000 was sought to launch a new mailing machine which mails a single piece of standard paper. The machine folds, glues and perforates, and offers large savings to a large mailer. At the time of the article, the first prototype was being built. The company received one offer from a subscriber, but did not like the terms. In the end Seed Capital invested £55,000.
Signalbus	£100,000 was sought to enable this company to negotiate with licensees from a position of greater strength. Signalbus is an analogue as opposed to a digital bus, and was targeted at the automotive industry. A VCR subscriber provided an initial investment of £6,000, and other investors similar sums, to enable the company to continue. Chrysler has now completed a detailed technical review and is intending to recommend the system as the new standard for Ford, General Motors and Chrysler for C3 communications networks.
Enviropure	A small team of entrepreneurs had conducted a very successful sales trial in the Middle East for an environmentally friendly cleaning fluid manufactured in Germany. The German company had been impressed and had given them exclusive rights to the UK market. Capital was sought to set up a UK sales operation. The company received offers of £75,000 from VCR subscribers, and complicated legal negotiations are now in progress with the Germans about the precise terms of the licence, etc.
World design classics	An entrepreneur sought £150,000 for her business, Wealth of Nations, which manufactures classic garments in their country of origin (e.g. Mexican shirts made in Mexico) and markets them through a catalogue. She received several offers of funds from subscribers and finally accepted all £150,000 from an individual subscriber.
Organic fertiliser	A private investor provided £44,000 to help establish a factory to produce a slow-release organic fertiliser for golf courses.
Scottish mohair spinning	An individual whose family had been in spinning and who had owned angora goats herself invested £50,000 (£40,000 of this under the BES) to relocate and modify a Victorian mill in Scotland to produce 100% mohair yarn, a hitherto impossible task due to the very short length of mohair fibres.
Tool hire	An individual invested £50,000 as part of a total investment package of £150,000 to enable a tool hire company in Cornwall to purchase a competitor and to increase stock.
Golf travel video	A VCR subscriber was one of six individuals who invested £15,000 each to produce a series of video guides for the touring golfer.
Marine salvage	A VCR subscriber invested £350,000 to enable the business to purchase a boat from which to salvage copper and other largely non-ferrous metal cargoes from a database of 450 marine wrecks.

is aware of 11 businesses featured during 1992, including some which received offers of finance from VCR subscribers, which raised finance from other sources. Again, if past experience is a guide, the number of projects which eventually find funds from other sources will also increase over time.[3]

Improving the success

When VCR started in 1978 its target was to obtain funding for 10 per cent of the projects featured. Its record of 15 per cent is therefore encouraging, especially when the high-risk nature of many of the projects featured is considered. Nevertheless VCR could achieve greater success if a number of conditions were met.

If there were more subscribers. Currently VCR has about 630 subscribers where, ideally, there should be 4,000. At its peak in 1985 VCR had 975 subscribers.[4] In particular, I would like to see more companies subscribe to VCR. There are 17,000 companies in the UK which make profits of over £250,000 and I believe that most of them would benefit over a ten-year period from seeing VCR. The great merit of companies is that they can provide very valuable non-financial resources to an entrepreneur, often at very little cost to themselves. For example, a large company which is already marketing toys can quite easily test-market a new toy on behalf of a new company: such a test might be worth much more than a financial investment to do the same thing independently. VCR gives as much detail about projects as it does precisely in order to try to appeal to busy business people, investors and company executives who do not have time to waste pursuing vague leads.

If entrepreneurs could present their projects directly to investors. There is no substitute for a face-to-face meeting at which an entrepreneur can convey his or her enthusiasm and belief in the project. VCR would like to be able to arrange regional meetings, like LINC (Chapter 7), at which entrepreneurs can present their ideas to several potential investors.

If there were less southern bias in the projects featured in VCR. Although not deliberate, there is a regional bias in the projects featured in *Venture Capital Report* towards London, the South East and the Thames Valley. This reflects the location of VCR's head office, which was originally in Bristol and is now in Henley-on-Thames. A network of regional offices could overcome this problem.

If VCR could do more personal follow-up. VCR will sometimes telephone investors and recommend that they meet a particular entrepreneur, if VCR happens to be aware of the investment criteria and personal needs of particular investors. There is no doubt that this has a very positive effect in achieving successful matches. The technology now exists to do this intelligently on a wider scale. VCR has taken some steps in this direction and is compiling a database of subscribers' interests, resources and expertise, and the resources and preferences of investors. I believe that a really efficient database which enabled a matchmaker to alert investors to suitable opportunities by means of a personal telephone call would greatly increase the number of matches. More resources devoted to this activity would therefore increase the number of matches.

If there were greater co-operation between VCR and other business introduction services. From a national perspective, there is a major problem in having so many organisations engaged in match-making, mostly at a local level. This can be illustrated by the following hypothetical example. Consider an entrepreneur seeking £50,000 to start a new business. Let us suppose that there are five individuals in the UK who would be able and prepared to back this project if it were properly presented to them. The problem for the entrepreneur is how to find these individuals. At the moment, the entrepreneur can try VCR, LINC, some Training and Enterprise Councils (TECs), advertising, accountancy firms and personal contacts. Each of these will take time, and each will charge the entrepreneur a registration fee. Even if all the methods are used, the entrepreneur's chances of getting to one of the five investors are quite remote. Consequently, there seems to be a strong case for co-operation between the various match-making organisations if the interests of entrepreneurs and investors are to be best served. What is needed to make the greatest impact on stimulating informal investment in the UK is maximum co-operation between VCR, LINC and the TECs, drawing on the strengths of each, but without compromising VCR's quality standards.

Conclusion

There have been many attempts over the years to close the equity gap by means of business referral services, and despite the best intentions and often with considerable expenditure, none – including VCR – has made much of an impact. Most have ceased after a few months or a few years unless they have received some form of financial support. Although VCR receives no financial support, it has survived, but only by undertaking other related activities, such as publishing the *VCR Guide to Venture Capital in the UK Europe*.[5] However, VCR is not genuinely profitable, in the sense that it pays salaries below the market rate and cannot afford to open regional offices, which had been an intention when VCR was started. I therefore conclude that match-making at the equity-gap end of the spectrum cannot be profitable by itself. It is possible that it can be profitable if it is done as an ancillary service by a company which is already providing other services. For example, most firms of accountants do some match-making and hope to make a profit by charging for other services such as writing the business plan, and if the matchmaking is successful, by auditing the accounts and providing other consultancy services to the business (see Chapter 11).

VCR believes that the only way to run an effective business introduction service is to undertake a detailed investigation of each project to verify material facts, obtain customer references and so on, and to reject those projects that do not come up to standard.[6] Only by this means can serious investors be retained as subscribers. If investors are persuaded to meet entrepreneurs who turn out to be poor quality, they will cancel their subscriptions, to the detriment of good-quality entrepreneurs of the future.

VCR has been successful in achieving matches. However, it would achieve more matches if it had more subscribers (investors) and if it had more regional offices. It would also achieve more matches if it were able to organise presentations by entrepreneurs to investors. And while the VCR format works quite well, there is little doubt that it works better if accompanied by some direct contact with investors, based on a knowledge of what they are looking for.

A further crucial requirement is for a single nationwide forum to enable entrepreneurs to present their ideas to as many business angels as possible. At present there are many separate schemes aimed at reaching local groups of business angels. However, it is apparent from VCR projects that have been funded that investors do not always come from the same geographical area as the entrepreneur, and entrepreneurs therefore need access to both local and non-local angels. At the moment the entrepreneur must register with the various locally focused match-making services in order to reach a sufficiently wide circle of angels: each approach takes time and costs money. VCR believes that the best interests of entrepreneurs are not served by the current situation, in which many organisations – all with good intentions – provide business introduction services which overlap. It is for this reason that VCR regards the Department of Trade and Industry's informal investment demonstration projects, involving the funding of five TECs to launch local business introduction services, to be misguided (although well meaning). Encouraging the establishment of another five 'ports of call' for the entrepreneur seeking a business angel simply compounds the problem and further fragments an already small market.

If the logic for a single nationwide business angel network is accepted, the question becomes one of what form it should take. I believe that the best approach involves co-operation between VCR, LINC and the TEC demonstration projects, drawing on the strengths of each. Not surprisingly, I believe that the format and methodology used by VCR is the most appropriate, having stood the test of time. However, I also believe that the LINC marriage bureau meetings at which entrepreneurs present to investors are excellent and should also be used. Finally, I believe that the TECs can provide support, training and counselling in their areas, and can provide a focus for business angels, entrepreneurs and entrepreneurial activity.

The optimum solution would be for VCR to combine with LINC and the TECs to produce a monthly publication like *Venture Capital Report*, containing articles in the VCR format which had been prepared by VCR, TECs and LINC members who had met and vetted the entrepreneurs and their businesses. The publication would be mailed to VCR subscribers, LINC subscribers and business angels whom the TECs would find in their local areas. Ideally the circulation would be several thousand, and the price might be less than VCR's current price of £350.

Ideally, also, more companies might be encouraged to subscribe. At the end of each article, in addition to the contact name and address would be an announcement saying that the entrepreneur would be presenting his or her project at the local TEC on a particular date. Investors would be encouraged to come, and someone at the local TEC would be designated as a contact point to stimulate activity and to encourage investors to attend. Providing that the quality of the projects and articles was adequate, such a system could achieve the necessary critical mass to make a real impact. Entrepreneurs would soon come to know that an article in such a publication, followed by a presentation, gave them the best chance of raising capital, and as the quality of the projects rose, word would spread to investors, and a virtuous circle would be established.

At a seminar in January 1992 for representatives of the five TECs that had been selected under the DTI's informal investment demonstration projects, a specific proposal for co-operation with VCR was proposed. The details were as follows:

- VCR would send 25 copies of *Venture Capital Report* each month to each of these TECs.
- The TECs would mail these to business angels in their area.
- TECs would publish articles about entrepreneurs in their area in *Venture Capital Report*, so giving these entrepreneurs access to a larger group of investors (VCR would provide training to TEC counsellors).
- TECs would hold marriage bureau-type meetings for entrepreneurs in their area.

VCR believed that this arrangement would benefit all of the parties involved. The TECs would get their demonstration projects off to a flying start with interesting and well-presented projects to send to their local business angels from the outset, and could draw on VCR's experience. Entrepreneurs approaching TECs would benefit by gaining access to VCR subscribers as well as to local business angels.

However, only two demonstration projects – TEChINVEST, which is operated by South and East Cheshire TEC in collaboration with NORMID TEC and CEWTEC, and Trevint, which manages the Devon and Cornwall Business Angels Scheme on behalf of Devon and Cornwall TEC – have recognised the merit of this proposal. The arrangement with TEChINVEST is that entrepreneurs located in Cheshire seeking informal venture capital have their projects published in *Venture Capital Report*, and VCR is mailed to TEChINVEST's investors, who are predominantly located in Cheshire. VCR controls the quality by insisting that articles meet a certain minimum standard before publication. To this end VCR has had several day-long sessions to train TEChINVEST counsellors in how to assess and prepare articles, using live examples. Where necessary, VCR polishes the articles prepared by TEChINVEST's business counsellors. This collaborative arrangement means that, for one meeting and one fee,[7] the entrepreneurs in Cheshire reach VCR's 600+ subscribers throughout the UK – far more than can be found in Cheshire alone – as well as the Cheshire-based business angels who have registered with TEChINVEST; these investors, in turn, receive a larger number of projects than are available in Cheshire alone. Thus, everyone – and especially the entrepreneur – benefits. TEChINVEST has a similar co-operative arrangement with LINC. This arrangement between VCR and TEChINVEST seems to be working well and everyone appears to be benefiting. During the first half of 1994 two businesses registered with TEChINVEST and featured in *Venture Capital Report* were successful in raising finance from VCR subscribers. Trevint's co-operative agreement with VCR operates in a similar fashion.

Implications for practice

- 15 per cent of businesses featured in VCR have raised finance from VCR subscribers: this provides a useful benchmark for other business introduction services.
- Business introduction services are unlikely to be genuinely profitable: private sector services are therefore likely to require support from ancillary services.
- Too many business introduction services is unlikely to be in the interests of entrepreneurs or business angels.
- There is logic in seeking to integrate existing business introduction services into a single national framework; the challenge is in getting the various participants to agree to dilute their independence and to agree to common operating procedures.
- The arrangement between VCR, TEChINVEST and LINC provides a good model of collaboration between independent organisations which combines the strengths of a locally based business introduction service with those of a national service.

Notes

1. VCR's fees were raised to these levels from the beginning of 1993. Part of the reason was to compensate for lost subscribers in the recession. However, the decision was also prompted by an entrepreneur who had successfully raised finance from other sources and who raised £350,000 via VCR in November 1992. He rang to thank VCR and said that VCR's fees were very low and he would have been happy to pay at least twice as much for such a good service. The previous fees were an up-front fee of £200 and a success fee which equated to £1,000 plus 1 per cent for sums over £50,000.

2. Not receiving feedback is not necessarily an indication that there has been no match, especially since a fee is due on a successful match. For example, one afternoon a VCR subscriber came into the VCR office to buy a copy of the *VCR Guide to Venture Capital*. In the course of our brief conversation he mentioned that he had invested in a project which we had published two years earlier and that it had gone very well. This was the first that we had heard of the investment, not having been able to contact the entrepreneur concerned.

3. More specific information for the period June 1992 to June 1993 indicates that 12 ventures have received all funds sought from VCR subscribers (£946,000), a further 15 featured ventures still in negotiation or received firm offers of funds from VCR subscribers (£6,880,000, including two projects seeking £4.8 million in total). A further 14 ventures featured in VCR during this period are known to have received all funds from non-VCR subscribers (£1,420,000).

4. Of these perhaps only 600 were real business angels and the remainder were dreamers acquired by advertising which used to make me blush!

5. Cary, L. (1993) *The Venture Capital Guide to Venture Capital in the UK and Europe*, 6th edn, London: Pitman.

6. A criticism sometimes made of VCR by its subscribers is that VCR publishes only three 'good' projects each year. However, if ten subscribers are asked to list their three 'good' projects then the resultant list is likely to contain 30 projects! What one investor perceives as an exciting project, another will consider to be too risky or of poor quality.

7. TEChINVEST operates on the same fee scale as VCR (see note 1).

CHAPTER 9

Creating an informal investor syndicate: personal experiences of a seasoned informal investor

Andrew Blair

Introduction

I retired in my mid-fifties from a very active business career in media communications, which ranged from public relations to publishing and from advertising to film production. During a visit to Florida, I had a fortuitous encounter with an American attorney actively involved in private venture capital networks. I was fascinated with the concept and on my return to the UK I decided to devote my time and energy to forming a syndicate of business angels. In the following account I describe my experiences of forming two syndicates of business angels in London between 1986 and 1991.

The first syndicate of angels: Metrogroup

My first task was to seek out other like-minded angels. Having considered a variety of media in which to advertise for angels, I decided to take a small box advertisement in the *Financial Times* 'Business Opportunities' column, on the grounds that its readership seemed most appropriate for this purpose. An advertisement headed 'Entrepreneurs' was inserted on two separate occasions (Figure 9.1) and produced in the order of 60 replies. I regarded this as a most encouraging response.

My next step was to meet everyone who had replied in order to gain an insight into the motivation and mentality of those responding to this type of advertisement, and to try to devise a rational system for eliminating those whom I felt were unsuitable to take part in an eventual syndicate. I adopted as my base the Institute of Directors in Pall Mall (where I had been a Fellow for some considerable time), using its elegant facilities for meetings and interviews.

FINANCIAL TIMES

Business Opportunities

Copyright © Enterprise Research Foundation 1994

Figure 9.1 The Metrogroup (first syndicate) advertisement.

Respondents to my advertisement fell into three main categories:

- Redundant executives, with their 'golden' (or 'silver') handshakes, seeking a new place for themselves and their money.
- Intermediaries – generally accountants or similar advisers – seeking new clients and potential deals.
- Successful businesspeople on the lookout for greener pastures.

Clearly, it was the latter group on which I would be concentrating. Unfortunately, they proved to be the most elusive of all respondents!

The first informal meeting would last about one hour on average. I followed this up with a telephone call to all those whom I had decided to short-list as potential partners. These respondents also received a document which set out detailed proposals of what I described as an investment 'clearing house' or private investor partnership. I hoped this would give them an insight into what structure I had envisaged when I placed the advertisements. The net result of this process – which had taken some three months (working consistently for two or three days a week) – was that I had recruited 26 potentially suitable applicants at the end.

The next stage was to invite 15 of these applicants to a small informal reception to talk about the business angel proposal, to meet one another and to give me the opportunity of appraising why – and if so, how seriously – they were interested in the syndicate concept. It was on the basis of their contributions that I decided which applicants to eliminate. In making this decision, I considered the following key factors:

- Compatibility of personality.
- Experience of the *small business* world.
- A commitment to the private investor syndication concept.
- Adequate time available for the venture.
- Negative overriding motives: full-time job, networking for consultancy assignments, social meetings.

Interestingly, I discovered that the majority of respondents were not clear about their true motives – indeed, it seemed that most had simply come for the wine and little else!

Nevertheless, I was not disheartened by the result. In fact, I repeated the advertisement and, having learnt a great deal from the previous experience, decided to spend less time interviewing in order to eliminate the more obvious time-wasters. Even though the process had been speeded up considerably as a result, it was still a further two months before I was in a position finally to select 11 individuals (all of whom had met one another on several occasions) to become the founder members of my first informal investor syndicate. We called it Metrogroup to reflect the Metropolitan London nature of the grouping. The members – all men – included two property developers, three chartered accountants and four successful businessmen who had sold their concerns and were now looking for new business interests.

The syndicate was incorporated as a limited company and each member invested in its ordinary share capital. There was no lower level for this investment, but an upper limit was set in order not to create an imbalance in favour of any single dominant shareholder. A total of £120,000 of money was thus raised from the founder shareholders. A business plan was soon prepared setting out the overall strategy to be adopted by Metrogroup in utilising shareholders' funds. These funds were essentially to be allocated for working capital, aimed at potential deals, plus the funding of overheads – chiefly premises and administrative/secretarial staff. A stockbroker with whom I had struck up a friendship offered the syndicate a very elegant self-contained office suite and a part-time secretary at cost.

Operationally, I felt that it was essential that the syndicate functioned as a well-organised team of private investors with a board of directors, so I proposed that a chairman be appointed. I felt that I should not take on this role myself because of what I considered might be seen by some to be a vested interest and an unfair advantage (in retrospect, this was a serious error of judgement!). The founder members eventually nominated and elected another member – one of the highly successful businessmen – as chair. It was also considered essential to have a detailed set of rules devised and accepted by all members before the actual business of investment selection and appraisal was finally put in motion.

It was at this stage that I first began to be concerned about the way in which the syndicate seemed to be operating. The creation of the 'Rule Book' took about ten weeks to finalise because of the endless meetings called to amend it. But having handed over the reins, I felt that it was only proper for me to go along with the majority view. Furthermore, it is only fair to acknowledge that it was essential to have a set of rules which were accepted by *all* members before the actual business of the syndicate became fully operational. Had this not been done, and with the benefit of hindsight, I believe that there would have been either anarchy or a complete breakdown in systems.

Deal generation

So, having finally established the ground rules and the operation of the syndicate, it was now a question of locating potential deals. Bearing in mind the fact that there were no syndicate members who could claim to have had previous first-hand experience as business angels, it fell upon all of us, collectively, to learn the requisite techniques and exchange that knowledge the hard way.

The first area of learning was in the area of selecting investment propositions. There was a general consensus by the syndicate not to concentrate on any particular industry sector and the size of any investment would also be left fairly loose. It was similarly felt that the equity/loan structure would be left open to discussion, that the majority/minority control issue would similarly not be predetermined, and that any hands-on participation in the investee company would be left for the selection committee to decide at a later date. All in all, a fairly liberal regime, with few, if any, restrictions!

With the help of an extremely competent young business graduate – a skilled project analyst who was appointed co-ordinator and general manager – an impressive set of forms was devised to enable participants to appraise companies which had been 'inspected' (Figure 9.2(a), (b), (c)). In this way, it was thought that any syndicate member could report back to colleagues succinctly and with a view to preparing a suitable summary and recommendations. Armed with the requisite analysis forms and other documentation, members went out to seek investment opportunities that had come into the office for consideration. The procedure was quite simple: members would visit the company (generally accompanied by one other colleague), meet the management, report to the weekly project meeting and present their recommendations to other members.

However, looking back at the experience, the theory that syndicate members – simply because they had previously been in some form of business activity themselves – would be in a 'natural' position to appraise a new proposition in a satisfactory way, communicate it clearly to colleagues and arrive at a considered opinion on its financial viability was totally unrealistic.

It quickly became clear to us that, contrary to common belief, there was no shortage of deals available for consideration. I had made it my personal responsibility to concentrate on deal generation because I felt that it lay at the heart of the syndicate's activity – and I was certainly enjoying it!

GB ☐ MM ☐	DATE RECEIVED	SOURCE (TICK APPROPRIATE BOX) DIRECT MAIL ☐ METROGROUP ADVERTISING ☐ PRESS RELEASE ☐ RESPONSE TO AD ☐ LEAFLET ☐ BROKER ☐	NAME OF CONTACT	**M1** REF

COMPANY NAME			TELEPHONE NUMBER

COMPANY ADDRESS (FOR NON-DIRECT MAIL ONLY)

	TOWN	POSTCODE

DESCRIPTION

ATTACH CONTINUATION SHEET IF REQUIRED

ACTION:

Meeting arranged for	Directors attending	Requested from Company	Send out standard letter & brochure	Microfiche required	Newsletter input date
		Sales Lit ☐ Accounts ☐			

Ask your secretary to process this immediately

Ask Co. Researcher to add this to company search list

Figure 9.2 (a) An example of a Metrogroup project appraisal form.

FINANCIALS			
	Y/E	Y/E	Y/E
PAST TRADING RECORD	£'000	£'000	£'000
SALES			
GROSS PROFIT			
GROSS PROFIT %			
PROFIT BEFORE TAX			
OTHER			
AUDITED (TICK)	☐	☐	☐

	£'000	£'000
FIXED ASSETS	☐	
Current assets		
Stocks	☐	
Debtors	☐	
Cash	☐	
Deduct creditors	☐	
NET CURRENT ASSETS (LIABILITIES)		☐
REPRESENTED BY		
ISSUED SHARE CAPITAL	☐	
SHARE PREMIUM ACCOUNT	☐	
PROFIT & LOSS ACCOUNT	☐	
TOTAL		☐

FUTURE PROJECTIONS	Y/E £'000	Y/E £'000	Y/E £'000
SALES			
GROSS PROFIT			
PROFIT BEFORE TAX			
OTHER			

AMOUNT REQUIRED	USE OF FINANCE		

ACTION	DATE	ACTION	DATE
M1 Initial investigation		M3 Funding Proposal	
M2 Detailed investigation		M4 Share Applications	

Figure 9.2 (a) continued.

M3 FUNDING PROPOSAL

REF	COMPANY NAME	**M3**

NET ASSET VALUE	Book value of assets as per latest balance sheet	£
	Estimated market value of assets on realisation	£

COMPANY VALUATION: EARNINGS BASIS	Maintainable post-tax profits	£
	Price earnings ratio for sector	X
	Price earnings ratio discounted for non-marketability etc	
		=
	Estimated capitalisation of company	£

FUNDING PROPOSAL	Amount of finance required by company	£	
	Estimated issue expenses	£	
	Total amount of finance required		£
	Satisfied by investment in Ordinary Shares	£	
	Satisfied by investment in Redeemable Preference Shares	£	
	Other class of shares	£	
	Loan capital from investors	£	
	Loan capital from bank	£	
	TOTAL		£

		Investors	Management	Metrogroup	
EQUITY PROFILE	At outset	%	%	%	= 100%
	On achievement of profit target	%	%	%	= 100%
	Details of Equity ratchet				

TERMS OF ISSUE	Sponsors Placing Fee		£
	Financial Advisory Fee	£	
	Equity Option	£	
	Estimated Accountancy Fees		£
	Estimated Legal Fees		£
	Estimated Printing Costs		£
	Estimated Advertising and Marketing Costs		£
	Other Costs		£
	TOTAL ISSUE EXPENSES		£

AUTHORISATION	This Funding Proposal was vetted and approved by the undersigned
	on ....
	Executive Director Project Director
	....

Figure 9.2 (b) An example of a Metrogroup project appraisal form.

M2 INVESTIGATION CHECKLIST

1. FULL NAME OF COMPANY

2. TRADING ADDRESS OF COMPANY

3. DIRECTORS AND ADVISERS

   - Full listing of Directors
   - Secretary and Registered Offices
   - Company's Auditors/Address
   - Company's Solicitors/Address
   - Company's Bankers/Address

4. KEY INFORMATION[*]

   - Brief description of the company and its marketplace
   - Highlights of financial projections
   - Amount of finance required
   - Use of proceeds

5. MARKET BACKGROUND

   A. Description and outlook

   - Description of industry
   - Current size of market
   - Major customers and users
   - What target market segments are to be penetrated
   - Location (regional, national, international)
   - What is projected growth rate of market
   - Critical product characteristics (performance, reliability,
     durability, price, etc)

   B. The Competition

   - Identity of current competitors
   - Size and potential of current competitors
   - Comparison of products/services with current competitors

6. THE BUSINESS

   A. History and Description of Business

   - Date of incorporation
   - Brief summary of progress since incorporation

   B. Description

   - Products or services
   - Markets
   - Applications
   - Competitive edge

   C. Current Technology

   - Essential features (e.g. similarities/differences from
     competitors)
   - Status (e.g. development, prototype, pre-production, etc.)
   - Intellectual property (e.g. patents applied for, etc.)

Figure 9.2 (c) An example of a Metrogroup appraisal form.

D. Future Development

- Need for replacement products
- Research and development, objectives, new products, resources required

E. Sources of Supply

- Significant dependence on key materials, skilled labour, etc.

F. Manufacturing

- In-house capability/use of sub-contractors
- Nature of productive process
- Importance of plan and machinery

H. Marketing

- Market positioning - how will products/services be positioned in relation to competitors (in terms of quality, price, customer service, image, etc)
- Pricing policy (cost-based or demand-based, volume discounts, etc.)
- Promotion and advertising

I. Sales

- Distribution channels: agents, franchising, in-house sales force, exports)
- Size and geographical coverage of sales force
- Anticipated productivity of sales force (e.g. calls per sales person, sales per call, average order size)
- Sales force compensation policy (commission structure, salary/commission mix)

J. Interest shown by prospective customers

- Extent (enquiries, orders, contacts signed, etc.)
- Basis (were they given prototypes, demonstration models, etc.)

7. TRADING RECORD

- Details of Company's past trading record
- Full audited accounts for past five years (if applicable)

8. REASONS FOR INVESTMENT AND USE OF PROCEEDS

- Timing and use of funds required

9. ILLUSTRATIVE FINANCIAL PROJECTIONS

- Profit projections for three years of future trading from date of investment

- Commentary on forecasts

- profit and loss
  trend of sales and product contribution
  fixed cost patterns (e.g. R&D marketing expenses)
  impact on profitability

Figure 9.2 (c) continued.

    - cash flow
      peak cash requirement
      impact of capital expenditure/working capital investment on
      cash generation

10. PRO FORMA BALANCE SHEET[*]

    - Projected Balance Sheet assuming that total funds are raised

11. ACCOUNTANTS' LETTER

    - Letter from Reporting Accountants confirming that assumptions
      on which financial projections have been based have been
      verified and are consistent with company's normal accounting
      policies

12. DIRECTORS AND STAFF

    A. Owners/Directors

      - Experience and role of executive and non-executive directors

    B. Line Management

      - Summary of planned staff numbers (broken down by key
        function)
      - Brief details of experience and expertise of key management
      - Future recruitment plans (if strengthening of management team
        is required)
      - Strategies to develop and retain staff (e.g. share option
        schemes, etc.)

13. MANAGEMENT INCENTIVES[*]

    - Details of any performance-related incentives relating to
      Directors/Managers

14. WORKING CAPITAL[*]

    - Statement that following investment the Company will have
      adequate working capital to satisfy its immediate requirements

15. DIVIDEND POLICY

    - Statement of Company's proposed dividend policy

16. RISK FACTORS

    - Risks and how management plans to minimize them
    - Potential problems (e.g. operational difficulties, development
      of markets, etc.)

17. FUTURE PROSPECTS

    - Short-term trading objectives and targets

18. REALISATION OF INVESTMENT[*]

    - Long-term strategy and potential exit routes for investors:
      Public offering (Stock Exchange listing, USM, Third Market)
      Take-over by third party
      Purchase by the company of investors shareholding

Figure 9.2 (c) continued.

```
  19. APPENDICES*

    - Appendix I  - Accountant's report
    - Appendix II - Statutory and General Information

  20. PROCEDURE FOR APPLICATIONS*

    - Procedure for applications in shares
    - Closing date of placing


  *
    To be completed by Head Office
```

Figure 9.2 (c) continued.

Our concerted efforts had confirmed the fact that there was no shortage of deal sources from the following places:

- Business opportunity columns in national newspapers such as the *Financial Times* and *Sunday Times*.
- Specialist magazines such as *Venture Capital Report*, which devoted their entire contents to reviewing a number of well-researched projects every month (see Chapter 8).
- Business brokers and accountants who offered an intermediary 'marriage bureau' service linking investors to investee companies of all sizes.
- Direct mail list suppliers who had sophisticated computer databases of a large number of companies, carefully analysed by various criteria.
- Network clubs (such as LINC – see Chapter 7) and investor clubs run by accountants; these provided opportunities for investors to see presentations and be introduced to selected entrepreneurs on a regular basis.
- Market research documents such as the 'Business Ratio' reports, which cover an industry in surprising detail and identify all the players by turnover, profitability, region, etc.

Armed with this extraordinary array of source material, it was not long before we began to be approached with business propositions from other entrepreneurs.

The selection procedure which we eventually developed was quite sophisticated. The syndicate co-ordinator (or project manager) would initially eliminate any proposal that did not look financially viable. This accounted for about 80 per cent of all the deal flow. The co-ordinator then circulated brief details of the remaining 20 per cent of businesses of interest to syndicate members for their first appraisal. These would be followed up with a longer, well-illustrated report (which we entitled 'Metroventure'), containing the key elements of the proposal for consideration by syndicate members (Appendix 9.1). At its peak 'Metro-venture' reports were produced weekly with an average of six to ten projects featured each month. The next step consisted of the appointment of a project leader, selected for his knowledge of the industry under review. The project leader, in turn, would invite two syndicate members to join him in the in-depth investigation and appraisal process. This project team would then arrange to visit the investee company armed with the various checklists to enable them to carry out an in-depth assessment of the company's requirements, personnel, marketplace, etc.

Finally, the team would distil the project and convey their conclusions to a full syndicate meeting usually held once a week. When a selected project was considered commercially viable, a formal offer letter would be submitted to the target company. At the same time, the team who had researched the project might recommend how to structure and to apportion an investment proposition and which syndicate member might participate in the hands-on management function within the investee company. However, any *actual* investment would ultimately have to be agreed by a consensus decision of the entire syndicate.

The critical post-mortem

The Metrogroup informal investor syndicate remained in operation for nearly two years. During that period, out of 150 projects that had been received, some 15 had been analysed and reported in depth, while two were invested into by three individual syndicate members. The syndicate was dissolved in early 1988 having utilised the majority of its founders' capital, the bulk of its funds having been expended on overheads, market research and the development of systems. Incidentally, the two investments that were eventually effected were funded by *individual* members and not from any common syndicate funds.

So why did this syndicate of business angels fail?

There seem to have been a number of interrelated causes. First, the Metrogroup syndicate was exclusively comprised of *virgin* angels. I discovered that, by their very nature, virgin angels (unlike professional venture capitalists) are unfamiliar with the highly intricate techniques of investing in smaller businesses. Virgin angels certainly seemed to have cash, time and motivation, but they generally lacked professionalism. To use the parallel of theatrical angels, the business aspect here is left to a syndicate manager who is responsible not only for raising the funds, but also for managing these funds without constant reference to the investors. However, in the case of Metrogroup, we had virgins leading other virgins; there was no truly experienced, professional sponsor or promoter to direct the syndicate – with a minimum interference. Of course, that may have been the very attribute which made Metrogroup attractive to its founder members.

A second major problem was that the syndicate did not manage to attract sufficient *proactive* members. None of its founders had realised the full extent of the commitment that was essential, or the number of hours that was realistically required to create a successful informal investor syndicate. In retrospect, most of those who had founded Metrogroup never really expected to have to work hard to find the elusive 'golden egg'. Instead, they expected to find it ready and on a plate! The consequence was that, at the end, enquiries from target companies were flowing in, but the syndicate was unable to process, effectively enough, sufficient of these proposals. The fact of the matter was that the in-depth research required for each project, before it was sufficiently advanced to recommend an investment, required anything up to 200 hours of appraisal time. The group had been formed on the assumption – obviously false in retrospect – that each of the founders (who had invested up to £15,000) would protect his money by doing some in-depth appraisal and analysis. In the event, only myself and the greatly overworked syndicate manager were able to put in sufficient time for these vital tasks.

Third, Metrogroup operated loosely as a number of *separate* individuals; never as a corporate entity. Selfish motives? Perhaps. Unclear vision? Lack of real entrepreneurial skills? I believe that all of these factors played a role in the outcome. Above all, however, I believe that it was predominantly the lack of one highly structured, tightly managed investment vehicle, or 'captive fund', which was responsible for the demise of the experiment.

Fourth, none of the founders of the original Metrogroup syndicate seemed to have found it essential to make the venture a success; they appeared to become involved simply because it was 'a good idea' and provided a friendly club for 'lone wolf' private investors. I often wonder whether perhaps the reason for its demise lay in my own hands as the promoter and originator of the concept. I recall my ambition: to mould a group of entrepreneurial investors into an amalgam. I had not realised how it needed to be carefully bonded if it was to succeed. I chose not to demonstrate my 'missionary zeal' sufficiently, but to hand over the reins – quite democratically – to a titular leader and to allow him to create a cumbersome bureaucratic framework. This taught me another lesson: that democracy does not work efficiently in such situations.

A final factor was that there did not seem to be any deadline set on the period for investigations and negotiations. Nor was the valuation process for a target company established, or the stage of business development which we were seeking. Yet it is undoubtedly important for the investor to know, from the very outset, precisely what he is really seeking and, equally, what he is willing to pay.

The second experience: the Private Investor Consortium (PIC)

The two years I spent creating the Metrogroup syndicate had provided me with a wealth of experience. I was no longer a virgin angel and had made innumerable contacts which would hold me in good stead as a more seasoned business angel in years to come. The experience of working closely with ten other colleagues, the frustrations of trying to obtain consensus opinions at every juncture and the lack of knowledge (and experience) that was so abundantly evident among the majority of colleagues had all taken their toll. Nevertheless, I was determined that, after a well-earned rest, I would come back to the informal venture capital marketplace with renewed determination.

When I returned from the long vacation that I badly needed, I decided that I would form a second group of business angels, which I would call PIC – Private Investor Consortium – and which would be shaped to a large extent by the lessons that I had learnt from the Metrogroup experience.

My initial step was to record, for the sake of all concerned, all the principal functions which I considered were required in the day-to-day activities of a consortium of private investors:

- Initial approval of incoming business plans.
- Meeting management teams and visiting their premises.
- Agreeing outline investment terms and company structures.
- Detailing in-house appraisals of companies and verifying data with customers, suppliers, competitors, etc.
- Obtaining independent reports from accountants, lawyers and advisers.
- Formulating investment strategy and finalising 'financial engineering'.

I also decided to produce a second list covering the appraisal process itself – all the steps that are involved for the benefit of anyone seriously interested in the project. The key areas for investigation were likely to include the following:

- Track record of the entrepreneur and supporting management team.
- Technical performance assumptions relating to the product, process or service.
- Detailed assumptions of the market size, growth and penetration (i.e. market share and distribution effectiveness).
- Price/cost analysis, particularly with regard to the principal competition.
- Human resource assumptions, with special attention to the present mix, source and cost of essential skills.
- Overall timescale and important milestones along the business's projected development.

Finally, I drew up two further charts. The first, which I labelled 'The games private investors play', demonstrated some of the facts of life for anyone seriously thinking of becoming a business angel (Figure 9.3). The second chart demonstrated how long it took, on average, from start to finish to enable a project to be properly appraised, analysed and verified, and for an investment to be made. The total, to my amazement, came to 162 hours (Figure 9.4). It was then that I appreciated how this type of chart was essential to convey to all potential investors the magnitude of what was really involved in being a *professional* – as opposed to a virgin (or amateur) angel. If I could achieve this, I would be confident of my

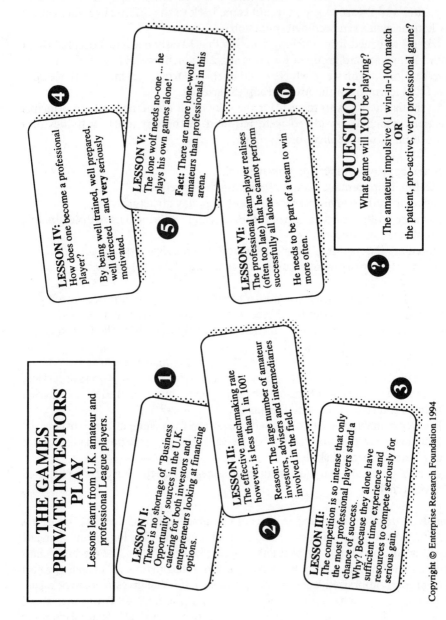

THE GAMES PRIVATE INVESTORS PLAY

Lessons learnt from U.K. amateur and professional League players.

① LESSON I:
There is no shortage of "Business Opportunity" sources in the U.K. catering for both investors and entrepreneurs looking at financing options.

② LESSON II:
The effective matchmaking rate however, is less than 1 in 100!

Reason: The large number of amateur investors, advisers and intermediaries involved in the field.

③ LESSON III:
The competition is so intense that only the most professional players stand a chance of success.

Why? Because they alone have sufficient time, experience and resources to compete seriously for serious gain.

④ LESSON IV:
How does one become a professional player?

By being well trained, well prepared, well directed ... and **very** seriously motivated.

⑤ LESSON V:
The lone wolf needs no-one ... he plays his own games alone!

Fact: There are more lone-wolf amateurs than professionals in this arena.

⑥ LESSON VI:
The professional team-player realises (often too late) that he cannot perform successfully all alone.

He needs to be part of a team to win more often.

? QUESTION:
What game will YOU be playing?

The amateur, impulsive (1 win-in-100) match
OR
the patient, pro-active, very professional game?

Figure 9.3 The games private investors play.

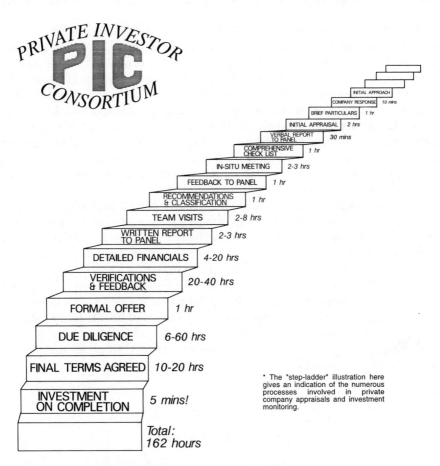

PRIVATE INVESTOR PIC CONSORTIUM

INITIAL APPROACH	
COMPANY RESPONSE	10 mins
BRIEF PARTICULARS	1 hr
INITIAL APPRAISAL	2 hrs
VERBAL REPORT TO PANEL	30 mins
COMPREHENSIVE CHECK LIST	1 hr
IN-SITU MEETING	2-3 hrs
FEEDBACK TO PANEL	1 hr
RECOMMENDATIONS & CLASSIFICATION	1 hr
TEAM VISITS	2-8 hrs
WRITTEN REPORT TO PANEL	2-3 hrs
DETAILED FINANCIALS	4-20 hrs
VERIFICATIONS & FEEDBACK	20-40 hrs
FORMAL OFFER	1 hr
DUE DILIGENCE	6-60 hrs
FINAL TERMS AGREED	10-20 hrs
INVESTMENT ON COMPLETION	5 mins!
	Total: 162 hours

* The "step-ladder" illustration here gives an indication of the numerous processes involved in private company appraisals and investment monitoring.

How "Business Angels" help Entrepreneurs

Entrepreneurs in smaller companies generally require a great deal of business counselling which they are unable (or unwilling) to obtain from their usual professional advisers ... either because it is unavailable or considered too costly.

One thing which they invariably need, in any event, is a sounding board for their own business problems and the company's strategic plans. Answers to questions on how best to expand, where to obtain finance or, quite simply, who to go to for a sympathetic ear.

No wonder they come to the conclusion that it is extremely lonely up there at the top!

Because a Private Investor Consortium is made up of seasoned businessmen with varying (but complementary) experiences and skills, the advisory functions can readily be shared between the relevant members ... and the target company benefits from up to five different sets of inputs, covering most aspects of their business.

It is this hands-on (some even call it hand-holding) role that provides a great deal of satisfaction - quite apart from the financial considerations - to both sides during the lengthy negotiation period leading to an investment.

The business appraisal process is, of necessity, laborious and tedious* but it is essentially the very special, close-knit relationship which makes "business angels" in a Private Investor Consortium something quite unique.

But, it is only for those who are genuinely committed to the concept and sufficiently motivated for their clearly defined, personal reasons.

Figure 9.4 The project appraisal process.

ability to form the right team to participate in a second – presumably more successful – consortium.

Essentially, the key conceptual difference between PIC and Metrogroup was that, whereas Metrogroup never intended to have a captive fund at its disposal, PIC would ensure that its founder members actually deposited sizeable sums of their own money into a bank account as part of a captive investment fund. The second big difference was that, whereas Metrogroup had ten participants, PIC would have a maximum of five members for ease of management, and the strategy would be substantially different. There would be nothing amateurish: no one other than the most professional private investor would be considered and the procedure for eliminating marginal applicants would be extremely stringent from the outset. In other words, the most rigorous, business-like techniques would be adopted in setting the style of this new (PIC) venture.

An advertisement headed 'Millionaire' (which proved intriguing while also being directed at those with substantial funds) was inserted in the *Financial Times* in January 1990 (Figure 9.5) and respondents were invited to write to a box number. A total of 74 people responded. Each was then sent a copy of a concise report which I had produced, setting out the proposal for a private investor fund (Figure 9.6). Respondents were requested to fill in a detailed four-page application covering personal, business and investor profiles and investment history (Appendix 9.2). This was followed by a series of further forms covering everything from meetings, systematised procedures, discussions with solicitors and bank mandates. Figure 9.7 contains extracts from a selection of questionnaires returned in order to illustrate the reasons for participation.

MILLIONAIRE

...YET? Wouldn't it be fun if five entrepreneurs with energy, integrity, experience & ambition each put £100,000 into a pool to purchase, build up & eventually float a company on the Stock Market.
"Corporate Adventurers" with good contacts and the desire & flexibility to act in concert, write to:

Box F9434, Financial Times,
One Southwark Bridge,
London SE1 9HL

Copyright © Enterprise Research Foundation 1994

Figure 9.5 The Private Investor Consortium (second syndicate) advertisement.

A PROPOSAL FOR A
CORPORATE INVESTMENT FUND

The basic concept is for an independent consortium of five private investors to be formed, with a £500,000 fund held in trust by a reputable firm of Solicitors or Financial Advisers in a high interest-bearing account. The Consortium would have negligible operational overheads and would meet on a regular basis to discuss business opportunities brought to the table by each of the partners via business brokers, advertisements, direct mail and other sources. The objective is to identify and acquire one or more profitable private companies within the first 6 to 12 months.

A number of the partners would then assist in the strategic management and expansion of the target company until such time as it reaches a position whereby investors can realise their shareholdings at a significant profit. The investment window would be 2-3 years with the most likely exit routes being through a profitable trade sale, a placing of shares on a quoted Market or a buy-back by the management.

How does this proposal have any advantages over the more informal "Marriage Bureau" or Investors Club scenario?

1. Although shareholdings in a target company would be registered in each individual member's name (to avoid double-taxation), the Consortium's capital would be in position in a bank account and in advance of any investment being made. The relatively high entry commitment would eliminate intermediaries, amateurs and other time-wasters, enabling the group to speak as Principal. Essentially, it speeds up the otherwise lengthy and laborious time-scale for deal assessment and completion. In the event that no suitable investment is identified, the group's capital would simply be refunded to each of its constituent members together with any interest accrued to date. There is therefore no significant downside and a very strong upside.

2. The group would be concerned either with outright acquisitions or, at the very least, a strategic holding (together with an earn-out arrangement) with the vendors. Unlike some of the conventional Investor Clubs - or, for that matter, professional venture capital firms - the consortium would only consider sizeable stakes in target companies.

3. Again, in contrast to other Investor Clubs, where membership is open-ended, it is recommended that a ceiling of five members is imposed in the Consortium. This is because, at £500,000, it is felt that most deals will be within the grasp of the Consortium particularly if further institutional gearing were used to increase the total amount of finance available. Another important factor is that decision-making tends to become harder (and slower) in direct proportion to the number of investors in the group.

Figure 9.6 The proposal for a private investor consortium.

Clearly, a lot more can be accomplished by fusing the financial and managerial resources of <u>five individual entrepreneurs into one cohesive unit</u> as opposed to acting independently. Additionally, there are clear benefits attached to having one of the team act as Project Leader to spur the proposition along, dynamise and motivate his colleagues and, above all, avoid natural complacency setting in.

However, before considering the concept further, <u>potential members should ask themselves four important questions</u>:

    (1) Do you have adequate time to visit target companies and investigate potential deals ... seriously and professionally?

    (2) Do you have funds of £100,000 readily available which you are prepared to lock into a suitable target company for up to 3 years?

    (3) Do you prefer acting in concert with others as opposed to being a "lone wolf" (i.e. wholly-independent) investor?

    (4) Do you have reasonable business contacts and a flow of deals which you could bring to the table for consideration by your fellow partners?

If you can honestly reply "YES" to most of the above, then you may appreciate the advantages of joining a Private Investor Consortium along these lines. In the event - <u>and only if you are absolutely</u> convinced of <u>your own motives</u> - you may well benefit by exploring this route further.

For further information, please contact Andrew Blair at:

Figure 9.6 continued.

The final stage of the selection, or membership, process comprised two eliminator meetings held (as in the case of Metrogroup) at the Institute of Directors. This time, they were held in a much more formal manner and were thus distinctly different to the Metrogroup procedure where wines and food were on offer. The various philosophies and aims of PIC were outlined to those attending and a set of tasks prepared which formed a series of further filters. These led to a final 'Director's Enquiry' form being completed for due diligence purposes.

Following this intensive filtering process – spanning some four months, during which the original 74 respondents had been contacted in writing or personally interviewed – seven individuals were selected to form the PIC founders, of whom five ultimately agreed to participate. Each member actually contributed £100,000 in cash to the fund, and PIC thus began with what was in effect a 'captive fund' of £500,000 in its bank deposit account. This contrasted radically with Metrogroup, where members had been required to make only a financial

No. 1: An investment analyst

I receive a great number of proposals through accountants, merchant banks, brokers, etc. 95% of these are NOT suitable for investment because of poor management, the absence of real sales ability or the lack of any perceived exit route within the short to medium term.

My solution to these problems has been to approach only profitable, well-managed target companies and establish a face-to-face dialogue with the principal director/shareholder.

Typically, these companies have 2 or 3 years of profits of around £100,000 to £150,000. At this stage, they often need additional capital either for increased production or acquisitions. They also tend to need someone to help plan the future of the company while they are busy 'looking after the shop'.

My personal ambition is to acquire a sizeable equity stake in a viable business with a view to taking the company public within 12 to 18 months. It makes a lot of commercial sense for me to leverage my capital (a zero interest!) by means of a consortium of private investors.

No. 2: A stockbroker

I have enjoyed a very rapid and successful City career to date. Although this is likely to continue to be my main focus, I have become increasingly drawn to seek business opportunities elsewhere. Firstly, because of the evident possibilities to make money in Thatcherite Britain, but also because the City remains a much more difficult place in which to prosper after Big Bang.

What could I bring to the party? No direct experience of running a small business, but certainly a keen analytical mind. My experience in the City, especially in the recent 'bear' market, plus a natural intelligence and determination, would make me an ideal partner for others with more direct, 'hands-on' experience.

No. 3: Factory manager

I prefer the idea of a small group of private investors, not merely from the viewpoint of their complementary skills, but from a more common goal and sense of purpose, linked with the comfort of knowing one another before embarking on an investment.

I have a very flexible and open-minded attitude to business opportunities and strategies and would look forward to exploring this in some depth with other members of a team.

No. 4: Estate agent

I have up to now, been busy building up my estate agency network and have had little time to do other things.

Now that the business is successful, well established and with a substantial capital base, I wish to use some of our accumulated funds to increase profitability over and above the bank interest we earn. I would be particularly interested in such sectors as laser technology.

Figure 9.7 A selection of comments by respondents to the PIC questionnaire.

No. 5: Chartered engineer

My main objective is to make a substantial investment – with active participants – in one private company, either by outright purchase or through an MBI.

I have researched the market for about six months, unfortunately without success. A wider contact network, and like-minds with similar aims, would be most useful to me. My philosophies are similar – established company (no start-ups), low tech or services (customer driven) with high growth potential. Turnover up to £1m, low asset base, high goodwill, needing new management or refinancing to unlock potential.

No. 6: Entrepreneur

Having enjoyed six years of successfully building up a business in which I had significant shareholding through a well-planned strategy, I am now just three months down the road to establishing or reinforcing business contacts for my next entrepreneurial phase.

A Consortium of five like-minded individuals – provided the chemistry works – should enhance the effort by a factor greater than five!

Although I am interested in a wide variety of sectors and am open-minded on this issue, I do believe that 'UK Limited' must retain a manufacturing base.

No. 7: Chartered accountant

I am interested in being part of a small group of investors with different business talents, with a view to spreading my financial risk and management responsibilities. The objective must be to make money by promoting and assisting the growth of a private company to Stock Exchange status.

Any type of strategy could be considered but an on-going situation is preferred, particularly if the group is itself interested in trying to obtain quoted status.

Any dealings involving property, land or building would be of particular interest to me as this would assist in the gearing of the business by institutional borrowings.

No. 8: Marketing consultant

While the main appeal of a Consortium is its ability to gather together a meaningful sum of money, the skills of its members must be complementary if it is to be most successful.

My own business strategy would be to build up a company (together with my partners) and sell it for a capital gain. I am a restless person by nature and like new challenges once a problem has been solved.

No. 9: Author and publisher

Having disposed of my last 'start-up' company, I decided that I wished to acquire a business in sectors in which I had personal empathy (publishing, media, etc.) with the object of building up

Figure 9.7 continued.

the company for sale or flotation within a few years. The difficulty has been to date in locating target vehicles with both the potential and infrastructure to fulfil these objectives.

My personal preference is for 'hands-on' participation in the target company as I am not particularly keen on passive investments in unquoted companies.

I am most interested in joining a small, like-minded Consortium as it would enable me to spread my personal risk and enlarge the investment window while obtaining the benefits of complementary skills.

No. 10: High street retailer*

Although I have already had success at an early stage in life (I am only 26), I know where my strengths and weaknesses lie in terms of both investment opportunity and practical experience.

I believe that becoming part of a group of investors will generate many more leads than I could do on my own. It will also provide many more skills than I possess, and would still allow me to input my own expertise and enthusiasm.

No. 11: Investment adviser*

I have worked alone for 15 years, but I realise that I cannot develop further without joining a Consortium which is able to invest larger amounts of money cumulatively. My contacts are not all that good at present but my experience is rich.

I have never been frightened of risking money as long as I know the bottom line. I spent a year as Director/Consultant for an Advertising Agency recently looking at over 30 merger/takeover propositions and I have been involved in the buying/selling of three businesses. I am at present negotiating an exit from a Nursing Home partnership where I have trebled my investment in three years (these are the joys and risks of joint gearing!).

My personal objective would be to grow one or more private companies to the stage when one of them could go public. This is probably best achieved through a new joint-holding vehicle with capital gains made on realisation of investments being reinvested rather than distributed.

No. 12: Ex-food distributor*

My working life – from 21 to retirement at 49 – has been spent in our family business, growing from two brothers and one secretary to a multi-million pound operation in 26 years.

Essentially, I am a broad-thinking entrepreneurial type of person used to being leader of a top-class team of managers, who supply the professional expertise. Essentially a team player used to rolling up my sleeves.

My weakness is an understanding of high finance – beyond knowing how to make a profit! That is why the consortium concept appeals to me.

Figure 9.7 continued.

No. 13: Pension fund manager*

Worked in the USA in the '70s, then business school. Then worked for a venture capital firm in New York followed by three years as a partner in an entrepreneurial investment/consulting group. Joined fast-growing computer firm in 1976 and headed the leasing division – initially covering Far East and eventually the corporate-wide operations. Then, off to Geneva (European HQ) with a variety of financial management positions. In 1983 I moved to the UK to head the finance function in a multinational computer operation where I soon created a fund management position for all their pension assets, reporting to Corporate Treasurer in the US.

This current position gives me scope to carve out several hours per week to pursue my personal investment interests. I started reviewing opportunities a year ago and very much like the idea of working with others similarly inclined.

No. 14: Entrepreneur*

After two years establishing business opportunity contacts and developing lead techniques, I find myself now generating more high-grade propositions than I could possibly invest in on my own.

Forming a small Consortium of private investors appeals to me for these reasons:

(a) spreading financial risk (and management) responsibilities;
(b) target company would benefit from complementary skills – so essential to smaller businesses;
(c) multiplying the 'hands-on' function results in closer monitoring of a wider range of companies;
(d) privately funded equity capital at the outset can be speedily geared up through bank/ institutional sources.

---

* A member of the Consortium.

Figure 9.7 continued.

commitment, writing a cheque only when a deal was found. Clearly, the lack of a captive fund had reduced the speed at which Metrogroup could move to take advantage of the daily investment opportunities.

An immediate priority was to resolve the question of a corporate framework for the PIC consortium, for tax mitigation purposes. Should the business be set up offshore or be based in the UK? The debate took account of the majority view of consortium members. Because of the sophisticated nature of the investors involved this time, and following advice from a tax accountant, it was decided to set up the consortium as an offshore 'feeder' fund.

PIC was therefore established as an exempt company, registered in the Channel Islands. A small unit in a service office centre in the West End of London was used by the consortium and a secretary/PA – responsible to me as the nominated co-ordinator – was employed part time. It was hoped that all PIC overheads would be adequately covered from the accumulated bank interest. Once again a comprehensive 'Rule Book' was created to cover the fundamentals of how the consortium would operate, the relationship between members and a multitude of policy matters which, it was generally agreed, would be codified.

The PIC consortium became effectively operational in March 1990. During its first few months the consortium met an average of twice a month. This time was devoted to a fairly intensive learning process whereby members were given 'study' material covering such issues as company valuation and appraisal techniques, and other techniques for checking the viability of projects. Particular reference was made to the importance of sufficient time being allocated to the inevitably laborious investigation process. The pitfalls and experiences of other 'fallen' angels as well as other active business angels were also examined. This enabled the PIC consortium to remain at all times pragmatic and scientific in its approach to deal generation and project appraisal. This was in marked contrast to the more emotive approach of the Metrogroup syndicate, who were essentially virgin angels, as opposed to PIC members, who were more seasoned businessmen approaching the task much more clinically. Indeed, they all appreciated the importance of *learning from outside experts*: for example, I recall being sent, on behalf of my colleagues, to a seminar by a leading firm of company acquisition specialists on how successful deals are structured.

The deal generation process

The PIC consortium adopted the following techniques to identify investment propositions:

- Newspaper advertising under business opportunities.
- Network 'clubs' (such as LINC), where potential investment projects were presented live to investors.
- Intermediaries, including business brokers and accountants.
- Direct response based on advanced databases and list-building and mailing techniques.
- All important word-of-mouth recommendations.

It was discovered, after various experiments, that the most successful form of response was generated from well-planned direct-mail campaigns. These were being targeted specifically at sectors in which a member had a particular expertise. For example, a mailshot targeted at 900 named executives (costing £1.60 per name) generated a response in the order of 3 per cent – producing some 25 company contacts. These were eventually whittled down to six that were worthy of further examination.

Other examples of identifying deals included a targeted mailshot of selected companies in Greater London with an annual turnover of £1 million or more and with profits of at least £200,000. PIC also made use of letters to accountants in the Home Counties; follow-ups to advertisers seeking business finance; placing of advertisements in selected trade journals; and following up companies in receivership.

However, the latter proved to be difficult for the consortium because of the need to move quickly, inherent problems of valuation, lack of essential information and the possibility that no senior staff would effectively be available to manage a turnaround. Frequently, the management team of insolvent companies were themselves competitors in reconstruction situations of this type.

Based on my earlier Metrogroup experiences – spanning over 150 company investigations – the following strategy now emerged:

- Select a specific market sector in which one or more syndicate members had practical experience and/or 'hands-on' involvement.
- Obtain detailed (published) company statistics and overviews relating to a selected market sector.
- Review and abstract, from predetermined geographical/financial parameters, a short-list of 50 companies to be targeted – comprising the 'hit list'.
- Direct mail personalised letters to named chief executives of the hit-list companies, using a proven standard format and direct response technique (Figure 9.8).
- Establish telephone response and call-back procedures based on a well-researched 'tele-script' and brief checklist (Figure 9.9).
- Allocate a 'project director' who would be personally responsible for follow-ups in accordance with agreed routines.
- Filter respondents through an established elimination process prior to any site visits being arranged.
- Visit target companies only if they have satisfied the earlier filter, and implement the first phase of the appraisal using the longer checklist.
- Prepare a project summary (not exceeding two or three pages) for submission by the project director to all consortium members for selection on to the approved list.
- Obtain more detailed research data covering the overall market (e.g. specialist published reports) once the decision was made to proceed with further investigative work.
- Prepare a target company appraisal for each approved project and circulate to all members.
- Arrange a group visit to the target company – under the direction of the project director and at least one other member – to proceed with an in-depth assessment using appropriate checklists.
- Convene a project meeting of all members to determine whether to proceed with the investment and, if so, the broad terms and conditions of the formal offer.
- Schedule a timetable of events including accountant's report, service contracts, due diligence, etc.

6 Cork Street Mayfair London W1X 1PB Telephone: 01-437 0483

June 1990   <u>STRICTLY CONFIDENTIAL</u>

I would like to get straight to the point!

You are running a profitable company.

I, and some colleagues, are looking to buy into a business
such as yours where we can use our substantial finance, energy
and management expertise to help make more profits and provide
expansion capital.

We are <u>not</u> competitors or brokers ... simply a group of
private investors with £500K on deposit looking for a good
home!

Can we do business together?

If so, give me a ring on the above number.

Yours sincerely

<u>Andrew Blair</u>
CO-ORDINATOR

P.S. Just in case you're wondering why I chose <u>your</u> company.
We have spent some time researching your industry and we
believe there are excellent growth prospects --- particularly
in the light of EC trade potential.

Figure 9.8 A letter used in company mailshots.

The project appraisal process

Based on the experiences gained, it was clear that appraisal procedures would
continue to be of paramount importance. In the case of Metrogroup, it had been
decided to use an in-house analyst (a function which the general manager had

<u>TELE-SCRIPT</u>

We are a group of five successful businessmen with a great deal of energy and experience in a variety of fields -- ranging from finance through admin/systems to sales and marketing.

We have come together to pool our skills and extensive contacts with our own substantial financial resources so as to form what is effectively a 5-man private investor consortium.

In a nutshell, we aim to provide to a target company not only expansion funds but, what is more important, a dynamic "hands-on", Board-level management team, comprising anything between one and five people, dependent on a target company's requirements.

In return, we seek a sizeable equity stake in a business which we feel could go to the Market or become part of a larger group in which ALL the shareholders' stakes could be worth considerably more than what they are at present.

What we normally do, before taking discussions much further, is simply this:-

(1) We first ask the M.D. a number of relevant questions on the phone.

(2) We then ask to receive in strict confidence, of course, as much written information as can practically be provided: sales literature, press cuttings, audited and management accounts, etc., etc.

(3) Following that, we arrange a meeting at the company's premises where one or more of us meet the senior management and we begin to get the "feel" of the business.

(4) Following that phase and, subject to the chemistry being right, we then carry out our own business appraisal and, eventually, involve our respective financial advisers for the purpose of ironing our various details and agreeing a negotiating strategy leading, we hope, to a formal offer being made by us.

To achieve all this we have to invest a great deal of our time in sound companies with good growth potential. <u>Provided</u> you are genuinely serious and prepared to do the same in what is quite a lengthy exploratory process, we believe it would be worth taking things further.

- Now, how does this strike you?

    REPLY ....

- Shall we start the ball rolling?

    REPLY ....

    If positive, "Checklist" comes into operation at this stage.

    If doubtful, suggest a phone follow—up or leave your name with respondent to call back office (or home, if preferred).

Figure 9.9 The Private Investor Consortium tele-script.

undertaken). However, in the case of other syndicates which had been examined in this connection, it was common for professional outside consultants to be utilised full time or part time. The typical fee for appraisal work of this nature appeared to be up to £150 per hour. As the average time required for a comprehensive assessment was estimated to be in the order of seven to ten hours, the cost of utilising outside consultants would therefore equate to between £1,000 and £1,500 *per project*, plus VAT and expenses. Clearly, very few groups of business angels could afford many externally handled assessments at this rate! In the circumstances, therefore, PIC members decided, because of their own business background and professional abilities, that they would undertake to carry out at least one assignment per member per month.

Additionally, there was little doubt that, armed with a range of new tools (which Metrogroup had not possessed), PIC members were now better equipped to perform most of these functions. The consortium had developed an 'Investigation Checklist' (Figure 9.2b), for example, containing some 80 essential questions to answer during each investigation. Nonetheless, in actual practice, most members cut corners and unknowingly avoided many of the essential points listed.

Consortium members were at liberty to present their findings in any manner that they chose, provided these contained the minimum elements of information set out in the standard checklists. This resulted in a variety of material being presented. The full appraisal on each of the selected projects was discussed at one of the periodic selection meetings, and a decision was taken by a simple majority of those attending as to whether the project would be short-listed.

Further developments

The members of the syndicate had agreed at the outset that the venture would be given 12 months to succeed or be reconstituted. This again was a marked departure from the less stringent, *laissez-faire* approach adopted by the Metrogroup syndicate, which had no specific targets or performance deadline, from its inception.

Of the 20 or so projects that had been short-listed by PIC for further investigation, two had been identified as potential investments. Gro-Plastics was a Lincoln-based manufacturer of PVC sheeting used in the packaging industry. Mantax was based in Essex and produced a highly specialised range of mechanical tools for use in a particular trade where there was little competition. Both companies were trading extremely profitably and had indicated to PIC that they were willing to dispose of the majority of their equity at a price to be negotiated. However, the consortium had not realised that the valuation of private companies was every bit as complex as the appraisal of their management, products and markets. We sought, and obtained, as much professional input as possible for this important aspect and supplemented it by reading as much as we could on the subject of small company valuations. Nevertheless, in both cases, we were outbid by trade competitors who were prepared to pay up to 30 per cent more for what would effectively be a bolt-on acquisition.

As our first anniversary approached, the PIC consortium met to discuss whether to renew its original mandate or exercise individuals' right to withdraw. One member wished to depart, having found a partner to form a twosome closer to his home. A second member, pressurised by domestic considerations, decided to withdraw and reinvest his funds separately into a company in receivership which had just been offered personally to him. The attraction to him was that within a matter of weeks he would have found not only a home for his money but also a full-time job together with an attractive salary. This left three remaining members: the youngest had already expressed a desire to fly alone and did not feel himself suitably matched with his two older colleagues; I then felt that a consortium of only two was hardly worth the effort involved in running a syndicate. In any event, my own motivation was to create a *group* of private investors rather than to locate a single partner.

Lessons learnt from Metrogroup and PIC

I believe that one thing is striking from my own personal experiences of both Metrogroup and PIC: that the potential for business angels is still truly untapped, particularly since traditional venture capital funds are becoming little more than risk-taking merchant bankers. This appears to be leaving the field wide open, especially in the smaller investment (or equity gap) area where the entrepreneur is not only looking for funds, but is seeking a meaningful management input from a hands-on investor. It was this very type of entrepreneur who reported being consistently disillusioned with the formal venture capital market – staffed by MBAs, FCAs, corporate financiers and other out-of-touch executives who, by and large, do not appreciate his needs.

To conclude, I offer some thoughts, based on the lessons of creating and operating private investor syndicates – involving some 15 business angels, over three years. I trust that these may be of value to all those seeking to emulate these business angels.

One of the most crucial lessons learnt over that period was *how to source a deal effectively*. There is today, at the disposal of business angels, a vast arsenal of sophisticated computers that can churn, at the push of a button, thousands of good business opportunity sources for investment. I learnt, too, that *professional direct response* is one of the most powerful tools available for this purpose. I also discovered that *newspapers and magazine advertisements* could result in a response rate of between two and ten proposals per week. *Intermediaries and brokers* provided a further one and two propositions per week, and direct mail approaches were producing between two and five conversions.

The net result seemed to be that one could generate anything up to 50 business leads each week given sufficient funds to expend in proven media. Another key lesson was that deal quality is unquestionably more important than deal quantity. I discovered that there is no shortage of deals to be found; the problem seemed to be identifying the *quality ones to pursue*. There were also many deal conversion techniques to learn in order to enable a professional angel to use the well-worn methods of the professional salesperson.

Second, identifying at the outset, with precision, the specific areas of business in which the business angel group was interested remains of vital significance. Third, I realised the importance of the human element in all business negotiations. This is undoubtedly the key to success for any professional business angel. Fourth, because of the chemistry involved in all human relations, establishing precise role models, participation by investors as hands-on project planners, their declared expectations and those of the entrepreneur, and, equally important, deal conversion techniques *all have to be taught and learnt if virgin angels are to graduate to professional angels*.

Time management throughout the process is crucial. I found that it was so easy to spend more time than was really necessary in locating a proposition and then researching and appraising it. Good business angels must know how to limit the time they spend with a potential investee. They must have trained themselves early to establish whether the target company's management are serious players. Sadly, eight out of ten are not.

Yet another lesson learnt was the fact that small business entrepreneurs do not hesitate to use the business angel as a convenient sounding board or *free business counsellor*. Here again, it is essential for the angel to identify his or her own role precisely: is the angel primarily an investor seeking a good match or happy just to provide free advice? Certainly a mixture of the two is often necessary, but the secret seems to be how to establish the correct proportion.

I have come to realise, from my salutary experiences as a seasoned business angel, that it is not necessary to have significant overheads in order to become a professional angel . . . or even to operate a private investor syndicate. The PIC syndicate had no office premises, no payroll staff, no fixed overheads to speak of. All it required was purchased on an *ad hoc* basis. In contrast, Metrogroup *did* run from elegant offices with competent staff – secretary, accountant and analyst/ manager – to administer the day-to-day business of a syndicate of ten virgin angels. Looking back, it was essentially those costs which sank what could have been an enviable ship.

Finally, in this retrospective, there are many valuable lessons to be found relating to the importance of correct structuring. These covered strategic issues like the investment aims of the business angel. Questions like: was the intention to achieve annual profits or to build up capital value for the longer term? Questions too of human resourcing: how involved would the business angel wish to become in the investee company and how involved did the entrepreneur *want* the angel to become? Were they naturally compatible or were financial considerations overriding human ones?

Then, there were lessons learnt from the intricacies of negotiating a deal. Often there had been no clear exit route available to the investor. The fact, for example, that there was no efficient company marketplace (such as a stock exchange) meant that any exit route for a private investor still remained of paramount importance if he chose not to be locked into the investment indefinitely. There were also lessons to be learnt about 'corporate engineering' techniques: understanding terms such as debt and equity ratios, short-term aims and gains, strategic planning for profit growth and incentives, warranties, covenants, buybacks and trade exits, to mention but a few.

But above all else, the main conclusions that emerged were these:

- Informal investment is essentially about *people*. It is not about financials or business plans or projections: it is about people and how people think and relate.
- Informal investment is about *skills on both sides*: investor and investee.
- Informal investment is about *professionalism on all sides*: the entrepreneur, the investor, the counsellor, the marriage broker, the local authority and the trainers.

The greatest lesson of all is that there are essentially two types of business angel: *virgin angels* – untrained, innocent and unsuspecting – who wish to enjoy the benefits of corporate life and yet be out of touch with its reality; and *professional angels*, who really mean business as sophisticated private investors. Incidentally, a professional angel is not a contradiction in terms. The professional angel knows that, in order to succeed, he or she has to compete with other professionals in the venture capital field – with brokers, accountants and other advisers – who have to act very professionally in order to survive. Professional business angels are the ones who are nearest to being *formal* investors: fund managers, corporate finance advisers, merchant banks and stockbrokers. Of course, street-wise entrepreneurs know the difference between a virgin and a professional angel. Guess who *they* would prefer to deal with?

Becoming a business angel

But how does one become a professional angel? Are they born or are they made? My experience indicates that they are both born and made. In the same manner that academics debate whether entrepreneurs are born or must be trained, I contend that the professional angel has to retain the attributes of the professional entrepreneur – natural intuition, resourcefulness, enterprise and ruthlessness. The business angel will also have to learn much that he or she has not discovered – and which others have documented – about being a professional angel. No, it is not sufficient to have been a successful captain of industry in order to become a successful angel. The serious business angel needs certain analytic (even investigative) skills not commonly found in the average businessperson. These are skills more often associated with the management consultant. Neither would the average businessperson have the counselling skills which today's brand of business counsellor is being trained to dispense.

The lesson is therefore clear: do not expect an average business angel (and certainly not your virgin angel) to be *automatically* equipped for investing without any prior training. Unless they are specifically trained for the task, they will generally be doomed to failure as angels. Of course, they may have had considerable fun and spent much surplus time playing the 'Angel Game'. However, it is highly irresponsible, if not immoral, for them to waste the time of unsuspecting business entrepreneurs, their accountants and the numerous others who mistakenly assume that the average business angel is skilled enough to be a professional player. In fact, entrepreneurs need to be advised on how to vet potential investors who approach them with offers of help. A typical cautionary note is provided in some of the documentation produced by the Venture Capital Network (see Chapter 3):

> Entrepreneurs are advised to think of fund raising as a process of 'buying capital' rather than of 'selling stock'. The difference is subtle but important. Equity capital is a commodity that is available from a variety of sources on a variety of terms. For every venture, some combination of sources and terms will be more appropriate than others, and will exert a powerful influence on the future performance of the venture. Besides the price, such factors as exit expectations, the availability of future growth funds, the quality of management assistance from investors, and investors' experience in dealing with illiquid, high risk situations, will all influence the choice of sources. The final deal should be a partnership of professionals with complementary resources and shared goals.

Clearly, the time is fast approaching when informal investors (and their professional advisers) will have to take seriously the question of specialist training if they are to attempt to compete for the better deals with the more formal venture capital organisations.

Implications for practice

- A private investor syndicate is unlikely to succeed if all members are 'virgin' angels.
- All members must recognise the considerable time input that is required and be willing to put in an amount of effort.
- A syndicate should avoid having overelaborate rules and operating procedures.

- There are benefits of having a captive fund at the disposal of the syndicate rather than relying on members to write a cheque when a deal is found.
- There is no shortage of deals available for consideration: the challenge is in identifying the quality opportunities to pursue.
- Time management is essential: the syndicate must know how to limit the time spent on locating, researching and appraising deals.
- There is no room for amateurism: a syndicate must develop rigorous and professional procedures for identifying and evaluating deals to be able to compete with the professional players in the venture capital field.
- There is a need for the development of specialist training for business angels to enable them to compete with the professionals for the better deals.

Appendix 9.1 An example of a 'Metroventure' report

METROVENTURE
METROGROUP PROJECT UPDATE

DATE: 19th May 1987   NUMBER 4

COMPANY NAME	TOWN	SOURCE	REFERENCE
HIGHWAY LOCATION LTD	EASTLEIGH, HANTS	BROKER	P63

DESCRIPTION

Highway Location Ltd (HLL) has been formed for the specific purpose of providing a bureau service for the electronic monitoring of vehicle locations. It is considered that such a service will be of use to most forms of commercial and private transport, such as emergency services, haulage contractors, security companies and service engineer operations.

Considerable experience of this new technology has been gained in the United States using a combination of location techniques coupled with radio communications to base. In the UK, the existing Decca navigation system will be used together with an installed cellular telephone network to provide regularly updated digital location information stored on a central computer.

The information can be displayed on a visual display unit as a point of light superimposed on normal Ordnance Survey maps. Failure of the vehicle to make a regular pre-programmed transmission of location data automatically initiates alarm procedures, a useful feature in crime prevention.

Whereas major users may be expected in due course to install their own dedicated system, most smaller users are expected to opt for a central bureau operation. Highway Location Ltd has the sole UK rights to operate such a system using software licensed by the CAP Group PLC. There are believed to be no comparable systems available at this time in Europe.

The Decca based vehicle tracking system in this concept is integrated with a vehicular cellular telephone. The vehicle system consists of a Decca receiver with an interface which automatically dials the host computer at the bureau centre using the cellular telephone in the vehicle, transfers the vehicle position information, and hangs up. This event can be accomplished without interfering with the normal voice operation of the telephone and automatically without any driver intervention.

A Decca marine navigation receiver is used to provide longitude and latitude readings, signal quality indicators and time (in digital form). Vehicle status and identification information can be entered via the front panel of the receiver and is also included in the data message which is sent every three seconds.

RELATIONSHIP WITH CAP GROUP PLC

The CAP Group has licensed Highway Location Ltd to operate the first national bureau tracking service in the UK with the AutoTrac Vehicle Tracking software program.

The system is already in operation in the United States in Chicago, Washington and New York in a variety of applications including monitoring of security vehicles, high value vehicle fleets, Government vehicles and service fleets.

CAP will provide the hardware and software to support the base station bureau operation, and will develop and enhance the facilities of the system in conjunction with the bureau on an on-going basis.

In addition, CAP will assist in the establishment of Highway Location bureaux in other countries, as detailed in the marketing plan.

MARKET/MARKETING

There is a potential bureau user market within the cellular telephone system market because the carrier signal uses the cellular network: a prerequisite to using the service is a cellular telephone installed in the vehicle. Figures produced by the two operating networks, Cellnet and Vodafone, show a user base by the end of 1987 of some 200,000 subscribers and a user base by 1990 of over 500,000 subscribers. HLL would need to capture less than 1% of the cellular market place to achieve the projected total bureau subscriber base by the end of the third year of operation.

There will of course be new bureau users who are not yet equipped with cellular telephones.

The insurance underwriting market have indicated that they would be prepared to offer discounts of up to 50% on goods in transit insurance for vehicles equipped with vehicle tracking and in some cases would also insure goods previously held to be uninsurable.

An invitation has also been received from one of the underwriters specialising in goods in transit insurance at Lloyd's, to make a presentation at Lloyd's on the system during 1987.

The company has also spoken with a company which handles goods in transit insurance for the Road Haulage Association, and they have indicated that they would consider premium reductions in cases where the system was in use.

The introduction of subscribers to the bureau will be undertaken by three methods:

a) via introduction through CAP
b) through dealers
c) from HLL's own sales staff

It has been agreed with CAP that the Company will offer the bureau service to CAP customers who wish to examine the possibility of buying their own in-house system, but who wish to run a small trial initially, without committing themselves to purchasing a full system.

The cellular telephone networks currently have some 150,000 subscribers who are potential customers of the bureau. These subscribers are managed by some 40 Airtime Retailers/Service providers whom the company will appoint as dealers and who will receive an introductory commission payment for bureau customers.

HLL Accounts Manager and Sales Team will themselves generate direct contact with end users, whilst promoting the service through the dealer network.

ADVERTISING AND PRODUCT PROMOTION

Lead generation is obtained through three main areas:

a) Telesales
b) Mailshots
c) Exhibitions

Telesales

It is intended to operate a small Telesales facility in Eastleigh to support the dealer operation.

Mailshots

Centralised mailshots to specific business user types will be sent out on a regular basis from Eastleigh.

Exhibitions

HLL will in conjunction with CAP exhibit at various exhibitions throughout 1987/88 to promote the bureau service and the AutoTrac system generally.

FINANCIALS

Future Projections

	Year 1	Year 2	Year 3
Turnover (£)	245,625	776,250	1,410,750
PBT (£)	(208,333)	220,520	652,862

AMOUNT REQUIRED

On the basis of the financial projections the maximum cash requirement is £426,000.

OPINION

It would appear that the concept of automated vehicle tracking is just beginning to appeal to large fleet operators. Before cellular technology, two-way communications required either conventional mobile telephones or a dedicated mobile radio system. The former is frequently complicated by long waiting times for service and channel access whereas the latter requires costly base stations and often a long wait for frequency allocation.

At present, there are no commercially available vehicle tracking systems in Europe. Securicor are currently setting up a system using their own in-house system to establish a tracking facility in 3 major areas - London, Birmingham and Manchester.

The research and development phase of the company is now complete and there would seem to be a clear market opportunity for the company's product.

ACTION

Please contact Giles Blair for further information.

Appendix 9.2 Questionnaire sent to respondents to the advertisement

Investor
Insight

Please handwrite all replies. Delete or tick as many items as are applicable

CONFIDENTIAL

A - PERSONAL PROFILE

(1) Name ....

Address ....

....

Tel No .... (Day) .... (Evg)

┌ ─ ─ ─ ─ ─ ─ ┐
│
│
│
│
│   **RECENT**
│   **PHOTOGRAPH**
│
└ ─ ─ ─ ─ ─ ─ ┘

Age .....

(2) Single/Married .... yrs/Separated/Divorced

No. of Children ...... Ages: ....

(3) Have you attended Advanced Study courses for:

University/Polytechnic exams ☐

Post-graduate or professional exams ☐

(4) Foreign Language proficiency:-

Language(s) ....

....

(Please enter relevant letter in brackets)

(G) Good (A) Average (P) Passable

(5) Past or present membership of:-

Professional Bodies ....

....

Clubs ....

Voluntary Organisations ....

....

(6) Hobbies/Sport/Leisure activities

....

B - BUSINESS PROFILE

(1) Current business activities

....

....

....

Full Time	Part Time	Non Exec	Consult.
☐	☐	☐	☐
☐	☐	☐	☐
☐	☐	☐	☐

(2) Summary of business experience to date:-

Sector	Country	No. of Years	Role/Position reached
....	....	....	....
....	....	....	....
....	....	....	....
....	....	....	....
....	....	....	....

(3) Is your network of contacts among private investors:-

Good ☐ Average ☐ Poor ☐

Is your network of contacts among Professional Advisers:-

Good ☐ Average ☐ Poor ☐

C - INVESTOR PROFILE

(1) Would you prefer to invest as an individual ☐ (private investor)

on behalf of a company ☐ (UK/offshore)

as a Consortium member ☐ (in private company)

as a Consortium member ☐ (in quoted company)

(2) In which geographic areas would you wish to become involved as an investor:

South/S.E.	☐	Wales and S. West	☐	Scotland	☐
London and Home Counties	☐	North	☐		
Midlands	☐	N. Ireland	☐	Nationwide	☐

(3) Which types of ventures are of most interest to you:

	Type of Company	Characteristics
☐	A. Start-up firm	A venture in the idea stage or in the process of being organised
☐	B. Early stage	A venture that has been organised and operating less than two years
☐	C. Young firm	A venture that has been in existence for two to five years
☐	D. Established £1m T/O	A venture that is over five years old and needs capital to maintain growth
☐	E. Established £2m T/O	A venture that is over five years old and in need of turn-around assistance
☐	F. Established £3m T/O +	A venture that is for sale

(4) Which business industry categories are of interest to you?

☐	A. Agriculture/Fishing/Forestry	☐	I. Manufacturing - Consumer Products
☐	B. Communications	☐	J. Medical/Health Care
☐	C. Computers and Related Services	☐	K. Real Estate
☐	D. Education/Training	☐	L. Recreation/Tourism
☐	E. Energy/Natural Resources	☐	M. Retail Trade
☐	F. Finance and Insurance	☐	N. Service - Technology Related
☐	G. Manufacturing - Hi-Tech Products	☐	O. Service - Other
☐	H. Manufacturing - Industrial and Commercial Products	☐	P. Transportation
		☐	Q. Wholesale Distribution

(5) What is the maximum amount you would consider investing in any one venture:-

			In Total
☐ under £20K	☐ £50K - £100K		£ ....
☐ £20K - £30K	☐ over £100K		for investment in a maximum
☐ £30K - £50K			of .... companies

C - INVESTOR PROFILE CONT.

(6) Are you willing to join an investor consortium where the amount exceeds maximum indicated in (5) ?

YES/NO

(7) Please indicate a company's minimum annual sale turnover/pre-tax profit you consider of interest.

Turnover: £ _____   Profits: £ _____

(8) Are you qualified and willing to provide management assistance in any of the following areas?

☐ A. Marketing   ☐ D. Research & Development   ☐ G. Strategic Planning   ☐ J. Manufacturing

☐ B. Production   ☐ E. Personnel   ☐ H. Retail   ☐ K. Service

☐ C. Finance   ☐ F. General Management   ☐ I. Wholesale   ☐ L. Other _____

(9) To what extent do you normally expect to become involved with a risk capital portfolio company?

☐ A. No involvement other than reviewing periodic reports and attending management meetings

☐ B. Representation on the Board

☐ C. Provide consulting help as needed

☐ D. Work part-time in the Company

☐ E. Work full-time in the Company

D - INVESTMENT HISTORY

(1) Do you belong to any Investor Consortium/Partnership:- YES/NO

If so, state name (s) _____.

(2) In the last 12 months:-

(a) How many **detailed** investment propositions from mature companies have you examined _____.

(b) How many Business Plans have you received from entrepreneurs seeking finance _____

(c) How many different investments have you actually made _____ Average invested £ _____

(d) How much time have you spent in **actively** researching/examining projects:

_____ hours _____ days _____ months

(e) Have you found the time spent generally useful/wasteful _____

(f) How many **serious** investment propositions are you currently investigating _____

(g) Were the majority of rejected proposals eliminated because of:-

Poor management	☐	Start-up/early stage	☐
Inadequate information	☐	Insufficient funds	☐
Unattractive sector	☐	Requiring considerable personal involvement	☐
Over-priced	☐		
Turnover/profits too low	☐	Other reasons _____	

E - OTHER RELEVANT INFORMATION

Enter here any personal views, experiences or philosophies which could assist any potential consortium partner(s) in establishing areas of common interest. Please attach c.v. if available

Pick the symbol which best reflects your personality. Choose quickly - it's your first impression that counts.
Now pick again.

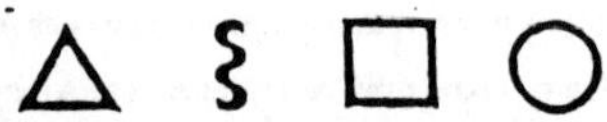

Your first choice reveals the most dominant aspect of your personality. The second symbol indicates a less powerful but still influential part of your character.

WHEN COMPLETED, PLEASE POST TO:
ANDREW BLAIR, METROGROUP, 6 CORK STREET, LONDON W1X 1PB
MARKED "CONFIDENTIAL"

FOR REFERENCE ONLY

To be completed at later stage

Bankers --

Personal references --

Authorised to circulate details --

Copyright © Enterprise Research Foundation 1994

CHAPTER 10

The role and potential of a formal investor syndicate: Priory Investments Limited

Edward Knighton

Introduction

In one sense Priory Investments should no longer feature in a book about informal investor syndicates, since it now operates very definitely as an investment banking business which happens to be owned by private individuals. However, during the first three years of its existence it was operated as an investment syndicate, with all important decisions being taken by the board of seven director-shareholders. During that period we do seem to have learned some useful lessons about the role that such syndicates have to play in the funding of small companies.

When successful entrepreneurs sell out of their main life's work, there are often many temptations on offer – invitations to join the ranks of the great and the good by involvement in civic affairs or charitable endeavour, or perhaps merely the lure of early retirement. But it is more than likely that the post bag will also start to bulge with business plans from aspiring entrepreneurs, offering a nonexecutive directorship in exchange for advice on the concept and access to sources of finance.

Tim Waterstone, founder of the Waterstone's booksellers chain, received one such start-up plan for a London publishing company in April 1990, shortly after the sale of his business to W. H. Smith. The institutional funds were secure, but one last tranche of equity investment was required – too large to be filled by any one private individual. Waterstone had the idea of forming a private investment company together with other entrepreneurs interested in the proposal, which would fill that last slot and then go on to make other investments in unquoted small companies.

Three years later, Priory Investments had seven directors/shareholders, including Tim Waterstone's fellow founders Maurice Pinto (an Affiliated Professor at the London Business School and originally a co-founder of Sea Containers), David Astor (farmer and professional investor) and Brian Brolly (formerly Managing Director of The Really Useful Group plc). A more recent

197

addition to the team was Shaun Lawson, a stockbroker and fund manager with many years' experience of unquoted investment (see Appendix 10.1).

The first seven investments completed had a strong media bias, reflecting the enthusiasms of the directors, but in the very broadest sense – they ranged from a publisher of scientific software packages, to the London radio station Jazz FM and a management buyout of the Hutchinson Encyclopaedia business from Random House (see Appendices 10.2 and 10.3).

Previous experience of small business life should be a good start for the provision of advice and investment to new ventures. The ability to recognise an impending cash-flow crisis, a shortage of new products or an attempt to massage profits through overoptimistic accounting polices will come naturally. However, all of Priory's directors would acknowledge that investment is a very different skill from running one's own business. All the more reason that initially such 'business angels' should wish to pool their knowledge and resources in a syndicate common enough in the USA, but as yet very rare in the UK.

Informal investor syndicates: roles and limitations

Informal investor syndicates naturally fill the 'equity gap' – the provision of capital at the level of £100,000–£250,000. Priory's initial capital was £1.7 million, so it was natural for us to invest at this level in order to spread our risk over a reasonable number of opportunities.

In the 1980s the equity gap in the UK was filled principally by Business Expansion Scheme (BES) funds. They had two weaknesses:

- There was some pressure on the managers to invest the total capital raised within a specific time period, with the result that the ability to perform the necessary due diligence in a large number of different sectors was severely stretched.
- The five-year time scale for tax relief inevitably favoured investment in companies where a clear exit was envisaged, encouraging some short-termism and a desire to see an eventual capital gain rather than income generation.

With the cessation of the BES in 1993 and in the absence of any other 'institutional' mechanism of significance, the equity gap in the 1990s could well be partially filled by informal investor syndicates. They have two principal advantages over the individual private investor:

- The pooled resources allow scope for the establishment of a small office with at least one full-time investment manager. This in turn provides an unstoppable momentum which is healthy for the business. There should be opportunities to cover most of one's operating costs by generating consultancy fee income, and it ensures a full-time presence when an individual company requires hands-on assistance.

● They are able to cover a wide geographical area. We will look at any investment opportunity in the UK so long as it is feasible and cost-effective to visit at least once a month.

Informal syndicates are considered useful fellow investors by venture capital funds, who are comforted by the presence on the board of an experienced executive who can provide strategic thrust and access to new opportunities.

The limitations centre on two areas – the management of the fund and the ability to raise new capital once the initial investors' contributions are fully invested.

The management of the fund will initially be conducted by the full-time manager, with all important decisions referred to a monthly board meeting. However, at some point the complexion of the fund will change from being a type of 'club' to being a 'business'. This is an important transition and will necessarily result in an enhanced management team with more autonomy from the board.

The question of funding the company beyond the initial round of finance occupied much of our time during the first three years.

Obviously the end objective is to generate sufficient income to cover three requirements:

● Operating costs.
● An adequate return to shareholders.
● Cash to be reinvested in further investments.

In Priory's case the initial round of finance was enough to fund three years of investment and associated operating costs. I will return to the question of how to provide an adequate return to shareholders at the end of this chapter.

Tax incentives and the private investor

It is important to note that, unlike private investors in the BES, the Priory investors received no tax incentives to join this initiative in unquoted investment. Such incentives are bound to be accompanied by restrictions which, I suspect, most Priory shareholders would have found unacceptable and a disincentive to an unbiased investment decision. The attraction of an early investment in Priory had much more to do with the spread of risk, the ability to get involved in larger transactions, the sheer fun in joining a collegiate decision-making process, and the chemistry and opportunities to be obtained by working alongside investors with complementary industrial experience.

Sources of deals

Another common feature of the first seven investments is that the proposals all came from personal contacts of the directors. This is not coincidental, but equally well should not be taken as indicative of innate conservatism; rather the Priory directors have learnt by experience that these personal contacts will act as an initial sifting mechanism and that time will be better spent on this sort of deal rather than on the many unsolicited deals that come through the post. It also is a reflection of the fact that providers of deal flow, be they accountants, intermediaries or company corporate disposal directors, need assurance that investors have the resources, experience and initiative to complete deals in which they show interest. The best way of providing this confidence to deal providers is obviously to establish a track record over time through successfully completed deals.

Our experience was also that marriage broking services for private investors were unlikely to be a valuable source of deals for Priory. This is not to say that they do not provide a much needed service in offering small firms an alternative source of finance to the banks and smaller venture capital funds; however, the size of the average deal (£50,000 to £100,000) is more suitable for the wealthy private individual operating on his or her own, who has the enthusiasm and resources to invest but, unlike Priory, no network of contacts to provide regular deals.

The due diligence process

I suspect our due diligence processes are little different from the average small venture capital fund. However, Priory probably puts less emphasis on evaluating the strict IRR of a particular proposal and more weight on using industry contacts and personal experience to gauge the quality of the business and its management.

Generally my input will have a strong accounting angle; an investigation into the accuracy of the historic results and the assumptions underlying the forward projections. The director responsible for the investment will focus more on the quality of the opportunity and the negotiation of the deal structure.

Priory's future

Priory's history has revealed many of the advantages and limitations of operating an informal investor syndicate. Broadly speaking, the advantages lie in the wealth of personal experience and contacts, and the value of a collegiate decision-making process. The disadvantages centre upon the difficulties in funding the business up to the point at which it will be self-financing and generating an adequate return for shareholders.

Priory's strategy has always been very much for the long term – it will be at least two or three years before income will be received from several of our current investments, and probably longer before any capital gains will be realised.

Investments in unquoted companies can often be highly illiquid, and any syndicate of individuals faces a difficult choice of how to attract new funds once the founder's subscriptions have been fully utilised by the first round of investments. In autumn 1992 the board considered several options:

- A rights issue to raise funds solely from the existing shareholders.
- Becoming the corporate venturing arm of a holding company interested in unquoted investment, by selling, say, 20 per cent of the equity.
- Introducing new private individuals as subscribers up to the point at which Priory becomes self-financing.

The final decision involved a wholesale change in the way in which Priory operates. Until then, Priory operated with a full-time manager reporting to a group of non-executive directors at a monthly board meeting. The change has been to increase the size and autonomy of the management team; the board meets only when required to approve major investment decisions or changes of strategy. Priory has changed from being a syndicate of informal investors into an investment banking business funded by private capital.

The expansion of the management team was achieved by the following means: the two directors with the most experience of unquoted investment, Maurice Pinto and Shaun Lawson, agreed to operate their personal consultancy businesses from within the Priory umbrella. This immeasurably strengthens Priory's management resources, and the additional overhead will be entirely covered by consultancy fees chargeable to clients both within and without the Priory portfolio. Thus an experienced management team is available to Priory for due diligence work on new investments when required, but is otherwise gainfully employed on fee-generating activities.

In conjunction with this augmentation of the management team, the board approved an issue of £3 million unsecured loan stock, convertible at the holder's option into ordinary shares at the current share price. Approximately two-thirds of the issue was taken up by existing shareholders with the balance being offered to new private individuals. It was important to ensure that new subscribers were well known to at least one director, understood fully not only the risks involved but also our strategy and investment style, and lastly had some tangible experience to contribute to the Priory team.

I mentioned above the need to hold out a prospect of an adequate return on investment. The preference of all Priory subscribers is for long-term capital gain, but the new issue of convertible loan stock carries a modest coupon; this has the advantage that the management bear in mind the need to fund a running yield and to structure investments accordingly.

Another consequence of the shift in strategy for Priory will be in the type of opportunities that will be pursued. We now invest at the level of £250,000 to £1 million – increasingly as a deal leader in transactions with a total value of between £1 million and £5 million.

These deals will commonly be management buyouts for the following reasons:

- Our management team has considerable experience in identifying value and assessing risk in this area of the market.
- There is very much less competition from the major buyout funds and merchant banks for smaller deals, because they do not have the human resources to invest the large sums they control in a great many investments, which means they must seek larger deals.
- In the current environment the major corporations are actively rationalising their portfolio of businesses towards core activities, and this frequently involves the disposal of smaller business units. Some large corporations are known as 'expensive sellers' and these are generally to be avoided. Others are more concerned with strategic issues or head office directives, and these are often prepared to offer attractive terms to an acceptable buyer who is prepared to move expeditiously.

To whom will we syndicate our deals? Small and medium-sized venture/development capital funds, high-net-worth individuals and overseas – principally US – investors. Priory hopes to establish special relationships with certain of these, whose investment criteria are similar to Priory's; they will be given the first opportunity to invest in Priory deals and, for their part, will be prepared to undertake to review the proposals rapidly and, in principle, sympathetically.

Future sector bias

Although there is a media slant both in the experience of the Priory directors and in the profile of the current portfolio, the management team feels reasonably comfortable in assessing companies from a number of different sectors and would not want to be bound by any hard and fast rules about which sectors should be targeted or avoided.

We will therefore continue to be opportunistic in terms of the industries in which we invest, our decision tending to be driven by the merits of the particular opportunity on offer in terms of value versus price and risk profile. However, Priory will clearly continue to be exposed through the networking of its individual directors to more opportunities in some sectors (particularly retail, media and telecommunications) than others.

In short, the new Priory retains many of the characteristics of the original syndicate, but with an increased exploitation of the networking skills of its management and directors. One issue which the business plan for this round of investment deliberately did not address was the question of where Priory will be in five or ten years' time. I believe that this should be taken as an indication that there is a determination to grow the business at a very rapid pace indeed.

Implications for practice

- For an entrepreneur, becoming a business angel involves different skills to those required to create a successful business.
- There is a spectrum of private investor syndicates ranging from 'clubs' to 'businesses'.
- The major source of deal flow is likely to be the personal contacts of the syndicate members.
- Private investor syndicates that are towards the 'business' end of the spectrum are likely to be looking for deals in traditional venture capital fund territory: deals of over £500,000 and management buyouts.

Appendix 10.1 Priory Investments Limited: directors and management

Timothy Waterstone

In 1982 Tim Waterstone founded and chaired Waterstone's Booksellers Limited. In 1989 the company had reached a turnover of over £50 million, and was acquired by W. H. Smith in a £42 million transaction. Tim Waterstone remained Chief Executive of Waterstone's until 1993, and is Chairman of Priory Investments.

David Astor

David Astor is a farmer and private investor. In 1977, together with his cousin Michael Astor, he became involved with the Advent Corporation in Boston, which resulted in a number of successful venture capital investments. In 1985, again with Michael Astor, he founded Jupiter Asset Management, which is now a quoted financial services company under the name of Jupiter Tyndall plc.

Michael Astor

As noted above, Michael Astor was the founder and remains a director of Jupiter Asset Management (now Jupiter Tyndall plc). Throughout his career, he has also managed his family's interests in agriculture and investment.

Avie Bennett

Avie Bennett is the sole owner and Chairman of McClelland & Stewart Inc., the respected Canadian publishing house. His business background involves 40 years of real estate development, primarily in shopping centres and, to a lesser extent, office buildings.

Brian Brolly

Brian Brolly, who was Managing Director of the Really Useful Group until 1988, has had over 30 years' experience in the fields of theatre, records, music, television, film, publishing and cultural management. In 1991 he was a founder shareholder in the new national commercial radio station Classic FM.

Shaun Lawson

Shaun Lawson acts as a consultant to a number of companies of which he is also a non-executive director. His job in most cases is to monitor their progress on behalf of their investors and to add value to these companies by helping with the development of new products and/or new markets, by identifying add-on acquisitions with industrial logic and by devising and executing creative financing schemes.

Maurice Pinto

Maurice Pinto co-founded Sea Containers Group in 1965 and was a director until he sold his interest in 1986. Over the past ten years he has initiated and/or participated in various venture and development capital opportunities in the United States and Europe as a private investor. He is an Affiliated Professor of Entrepreneurship at the London Business School.

Edward Knighton

Edward Knighton joined Priory Investments in early 1991. He trained as a chartered accountant with Coopers and Lybrand; the majority of his five years there were spent in the Business Services Department, but also included a few months in the firm's Istanbul office. On leaving the profession he gained three years' commercial experience, first with Waterstone's Booksellers Limited (a period straddling the company's takeover by W. H. Smith) and subsequently with House of Fraser.

Appendix 10.2   Investment portfolio: August 1993

Cherwell Scientific Publishing Ltd (CSP)

CSP is an Oxford-based publisher of scientific software founded in 1990. Adam Hodgkin, the managing director, started and spent five years building Oxford University Press's electronic publishing business before leaving to found CSP. Priory took a 10 per cent stake for £100,000 in May 1990 and has supported the company with two non-executive directors (David Astor and Maurice Pinto). Maurice Pinto has an interest in a further 30 per cent of the company through Coldharbour Ventures Ltd. CSP is at an early stage of its development, but is already performing ahead of its budget. The company has signed up a German distributor which will serve as a model for CSP's future representation in the European market, and has also set up a small office in Boston, USA. CSP is projected to break even for the year ending 31 December 1993, in accordance with the original business plan.

Golden Rose Communications plc (GRC)

GRC is an unquoted public company set up in November 1991 to acquire loss-making commercial radio stations in key towns and cities, utilising mangement skills to achieve an early and lasting transformation of the acquired companies' profit-earning capabilities. The management team is led by David Maker, one of the most experienced radio executives in the UK, who was previously Chief Executive of the Red Rose Group (now Transworld Communications plc). The Group acquired a 90 per cent stake in London Jazz Radio plc (Jazz FM) in November 1991. In 1993, GRC renewed its Jazz FM licence in London and also won a new licence to broadcast the same format in the North West of England. Priory originally conceived the opportunity for GRC, and was actively involved in securing its initial funding. Priory holds a 12 per cent stake in GRC at a cost of £363,000. We are represented on the board by David Astor.

Helicon Publishing Ltd

Priory invested £75,000 in March 1992 in a management buyout of this division of the Random House Group. Random House sold the division, which publishes the *Hutchinson Encyclopaedia* and a wealth of other spin-off products from its database, in exchange for a 20 per cent stake and a three-year sales and distribution agreement in addition to the purchase price. The business plan envisaged that around 20 per cent of turnover would arise from electronic publishing; the company has already been involved in producing software for use with the Commodore CD-ROM and the Sony Discman.

Lamancha Productions Ltd (LPL)

LPL is an Edinburgh-based production company in the sell-through video market. Its speciality is the acquisition and skilled editing of archive material, particularly in the field of military history. The resultant programmes are of television standard quality and have been sold as such to stations in the USA and Europe as well as to customers such as W. H. Smith and Woolworth in the UK in a video format. Priory took a 23 per cent stake for £250,000 in October 1991 and is represented on the board by Maurice Pinto. In 1993 we increased our interest by funding the production of seven programmes on a joint venture basis at a total advance of £175,000.

SDX Business Systems Ltd (SDX)

Priory's investment in SDX Business Systems Limited represents a typical example of our current strategy. This was a management buyout of the Business Systems Division of Northern Telecom led by a Priory director (Maurice Pinto) and a three-strong management team in November 1991. With 1992 sales of £10 million and operating profits approaching £500,000, SDX is one of the UK's leading suppliers of customer premises telecommunications equipment to small and medium-sized businesses. The opportunity came to Maurice Pinto through a social contact with the Northern Telecom Corporate Disposals director. NT was interested in selling SDX (which formed part of its 1990 acquisition of STC) because of the conflict of interest between SDX products and those produced by BT – an important NT customer. Priory holds a 5 per cent stake in SDX at a cost of £100,000. We are represented on the board by Maurice Pinto (chairman) whose family partnership invested £300,000 and syndicated the rest of the investor group's contribution of £1 million to friends, relations and Priory. The deal has given Priory a valuable foothold in the fast-expanding telecommunications software area and is expected to lead to a number of follow-on investments in the near future.

Westfield Medical Limited (WML)

In August 1993 Priory completed the management buyout of the Westfield Medical business (trading as Welton Medical) from Bowater plc. Bowater had given the Office of Fair Trading an undertaking to sell WML following its acquisition of DRG in 1992, as it competed directly with a DRG division.

The company is involved in the manufacture of medical pouches, bags and rollstock for sale to the NHS, and to industrial and hospital customers in the UK and many other countries. The business has been consistently profitable for some years and was already trading ahead of the business plan at the time of the buyout.

The deal structure was a new departure for Priory – we took a controlling 74 per cent share of the equity for a total investment of £895,000, with the management team holding the balance. Thus Westfield is our first trading subsidiary and will contribute substantially to the Priory group's profitability.

Appendix 10.3 Priory Investments Limited: investment history to August 1993

Name	Date	At cost	Description	Outcome
Sinclair-Stevenson Holdings Ltd	April 1990	550	Book publishing	Management unable to control start-up losses – sold in trade sale to Reed International Books for £110k
Cherwell Scientific Publishing Limited	May 1990	100	Software publishing	Now profitable and exceeding forecasts in original plan
Coldstream Winemakers Limited	October 1990	70	Wine production	Producer of high-quality Australian table wine – sold in 1993 to new investor at £33k
Antiques Roadshow Collection Part 1	July 1990	75	Partwork based around BBC TV series	Joint venture investment realised profit of £49k in June 1991
Antiques Roadshow Collection Part 2	June 1991	110	Second partwork series	Joint venture investment realised profit of £33k in November 1992
Lamancha Productions Limited	October 1991 July 1993	250 45	Video production	Supplier of military history videos to retailers including W. H. Smith
SDX Business Systems Limited	November 1991	100	Telephone system marketing	MBO of division of Northern Telecom – significantly profitable since the buy-out
Golden Rose Communications plc	November 1991 July 1992 May 1993	250 62 51	Radio holding company	The subsidiary Jazz FM has won a significant share of the London market.
Helicon Publishing Limited	March 1992	75	Reference book publishing	MBO of the reference division of the publishers Random House – projected to break even in second year of operations
Westfield Medical Limited	August 1993	895	Medical packaging	MBO of medical packaging division of Bowater plc
Total value of investments		2,633		

Note

This is an expanded and updated version of an article that originally appeared in the August 1992 edition of *Venture Capital Report*.

CHAPTER 11

Operating a business introduction service on a for-profit basis: Blackstone Franks Corporate Finance

Richard Coon

Introduction

Blackstone Franks was founded in 1975, initially specialising in corporate finance, but subsequently developing into a full practice. The Blackstone Franks Group comprises six companies employing a total of 100 staff:

- Blackstone Franks Chartered Accountants, providing audit, accounts, tax and other services to small companies.
- Blackstone Franks Corporate Finance, dealing with management buyouts and buyins, the buying and selling of businesses and fund raising (for amounts in excess of £50,000).
- Blackstone Franks Financial Management, providing independent financial tax planning and pensions advice (registered with FIMBRA).
- Blackstone Franks Investment Management, which manages £45m of funds on behalf of private clients, trustees and pension funds in quoted securities.
- Blackstone Franks Mortgage Services, which is a mortgage broking service.
- Blackstone Franks International, which provides financial and investment advice to expatriates (with offices in France, Spain and Portugal).

The main services of Blackstone Franks Corporate Finance are raising capital, acquisitions and disposals. The original objective was to look for the larger deals. However, the decision to include business referral services was made in 1990 because many excellent deals were smaller ones in which venture capital funds were not interested purely because of size. As a result, Blackstone Franks is one of the few corporate finance institutions still prepared to look at smaller deals in spite of the difficulties of making money on them.

Blackstone Franks acts on behalf of the company seeking to raise funds. It does not work for the investors, and does not hold itself liable for investor failure. However, as a corporate finance practice, it is not offering a pure business introduction service; rather, it looks to take a deal through to completion. Thus Blackstone Franks Corporate Finance offers a range of services to business clients: these include help in the preparation of their business plans; valuation of the business (entrepreneurs tend to overvalue their business, whereas investors tend to undervalue the business); structuring the deal (which rarely involves straight equity alone); and investigative-type work. These services are charged for either on the basis of time or for a fixed fee. Other services available include the provision of a quasi-finance director (on a monthly retainer) and consultancy services. Blackstone Franks is also able to provide a range of financial products to its clients for which it receives commissions: these include tax planning, minority protection, keyman cover, cross-shareholder protection, investigation/audit and the use of pension funds to raise further finance. By offering a full range of products and services, it becomes possible to make small deals pay, particularly if a long-term relationship is established with the client business.

In order to establish credibility with entrepreneurs, the match-making team needs both practical and technical experience. It therefore involves senior staff and has little scope for delegation. As a result, in addition to a wide range of corporate finance experience in financial management, control and capital raising with large companies, many of the key personnel involved in the introduction service have practical experience in founding and growing entrepreneurial ventures and in capital raising in the unquoted companies sector.

With companies as the client, Blackstone Franks Corporate Finance operates only on an exclusive basis on a retained deal. Clients are liable to pay a monthly retainer based on the anticipated workload, but at a much reduced hourly rate – typically this will range between £500 and £2,000. For such retained deals Blackstone Franks Corporate Finance will prepare all necessary documentation with appropriate disclaimers, and will, therefore, include in the service considerable due diligence work to meet obligations under the Financial Services Act (see chapter 12) and under the Investment Business Regulations of the Institute of Chartered Accountants in England and Wales. In addition to the retainer, Blackstone Franks Corporate Finance charges a success fee which can be geared to the amount raised or simply topping up to their normal charge-out rate. The Lehman scale is used: 5 per cent on the first £1.0 million (subject to a minimum of £10,000), 4 per cent on the second £1.0 million, 3 per cent on the third £1.0 million, 2 per cent on the fourth £1.0 million, and 1 per cent thereafter.

Deal flow

A mixture of deal sizes is essential for the profitability of the service. Small deals are more demanding in terms of management time relative to their size, and therefore more expensive to do. Some large deals are therefore necessary in view of the size of the success fees they generate (for example, a £5 million investment will generate advisers' fees of £150,000; a retained deal of £100,000 will generate a success fee of £10,000 (minimum fee) in addition to the monthly retainer).

The key to a successful deal flow is a well-developed network. Blackstone Franks initially used brokers to develop a client base of businesses which could then be used to attract investors. However, the quality of business opportunities coming from this source is relatively low and it proved essential quickly to develop a network of sources to refer deals. Blackstone Franks Corporate Finance has used the following sources of investment opportunities:

- Solicitors – these have proved to be a particularly good source of deal flow, generating higher-quality opportunities than many other sources, reflecting the fact that they do not see Blackstone Franks as a competitor.
- Business brokers – they may refer on deals which do not fit their specialisms.
- Advertising – this has proved effective in generating quality opportunities and leads either through company-specific advertising on behalf of clients seeking investors, which also attracts other firms, or, less effectively, through more speculative general advertising for businesses; equally, responding to advertisements placed by other firms and/or indicating businesses for sale or in receivership has proved effective.
- Accountants – although this source is limited because of potential competitive conflicts of interest, some opportunities are referred to Blackstone Franks through merger and acquisition activities.
- Banks – it is possible to get opportunity referrals that the banks cannot help and that are too small to interest their captive venture capital funds; however, this source of deal flow is a function of the relationship with bank personnel, and more usually does not produce high-quality deals, which are retained in-house.
- Venture capitalists – the relationship between Blackstone Franks and venture capital houses can involve a two-way flow of deals and referrals, depending on the size of deal, and good relationships have been built up with a number of venture capitalists which are still active at the lower end of the market; this is an area in which Blackstone Franks would like to see more activity and referrals, and in which there is still potential for greater collaboration in providing a 'ladder' of equity financing opportunities to business ventures (see also Chapter 14, which discusses venture capital links in the context of the DTI TEC demonstration projects in the UK).
- Consultants, including those who have been working under the DTI Enterprise Initiative, have provided access to opportunities, although this has not been a major source.
- Investors on occasion bring to Blackstone Franks companies which are seeking more capital than they themselves can provide, and for which Blackstone Franks becomes the surrogate for the type of informal investment deal syndication which is more common in the United States (see Chapter 3 and 5).

- A general mailshot of companies and investors yielded a 3 per cent response rate, but the overall quality of opportunities so identified was low.
- General PR activity, including press coverage, publications and seminars (including seminars arranged jointly with solicitors), usefully supplements more specific advertising in raising the profile of the service and generating opportunities and deal flow.
- Finally, but by no means least, personal contacts and networking remain important, and underlie the effectiveness of many of the other sources of deal flow identified above.

These sources generate an average of 20 to 30 enquiries per week, although the number has tended to fall recently as the practice has become more selective of the opportunities considered, and has concentrated more on merger and acquisition activity in a market in which private companies have been available on a price/earnings ratio of around 6, compared with a p/e of 16–17 for small public companies. These opportunities are filtered on the basis of the viability of the product or service, the strength of the management team and the reasonableness of the entrepreneur's expectations regarding valuation and the percentage of the equity given up: Blackstone Franks seeks to concentrate on the better prospects and turn away companies that do not look promising. In addition, companies filter themselves out if they seek less than £50,000 (where the minimum success fee represents at least 20 per cent of the capital sought). Based on these two sets of filters, imposed by Blackstone Franks or self-imposed by the companies themselves, around 90 per cent of opportunities are eliminated, and only 10 per cent, representing around 10–12 potential deals per month, are progressed. Clients are then entered on to a database in which they are coded according to their quality and prospects of attracting finance. This enables Blackstone Franks to prioritise opportunities and avoid spending too much time on the poorer prospects. Regular status reports are produced on each client.

Investors

Blackstone Franks has identified and deals with three distinct groups of investors, each of which has particular investment preferences. First, there are a number of institutional investors seeking to invest sums in excess of £200,000. Second, there are companies seeking joint ventures and corporate venturing activities. Third, there are private investors, with the capability of making investments in the range £50,000 to £200,000. Blackstone Franks has made contact with 600 private investors since launching the service. They are an extremely diverse group, ranging from 25 to 75 years in age, with between £50,000 and £15 million available for investment, and predominantly based in the South East. The majority of private investors are cash-out entrepreneurs or have a senior management background. Many have institutional venture capital, or private fund capital, backing available for co-investment with their own funds. In some cases, private investors present small teams or informal syndicates offering investments, although experience has shown that these are generally one-investment cases only. Unlike the normal pattern of informal investment in both the UK and North America, where minority shareholding is the norm, many of these private investors are looking for effective ownership and control of the businesses in which they invest, and in some cases this reflects a primary motivation to, in effect, buy a job through effectively a management buyin. Almost without exception these investors intend to be active rather than passive.

Private investors have been attracted to the service by a variety of means. The single most important source has been referrals by other investors, and all investors are sent a referral form. This has been supplemented by general public relations activities, personal contacts, referrals of clients of other parts of the practice, advertising and mailshots, such as those to BES investors in non-tenancy issues. In addition, solicitors, accountants and stockbrokers have been the source of some referrals. Investors pay no fee for the service: this register is maintained as part of the service to Blackstone Franks' client companies.

Matching processes

Blackstone Franks believes that investors in general know what they do *not* want to invest in, but because of their varied interests, do not necessarily know what they *do* want to invest in until they see it. Hence, investors are given the opportunity to examine all the investment opportunities available. Investors are introduced to investment opportunities by means of an investment opportunities list. In addition, Blackstone Franks undertakes proactive matching by telephone contact with selected investors to inform them of the details of deals which are known to fall within their interests. One of the objectives is to build up a rapport with the investors so that they will be more likely to follow up opportunities put to them.

The investor population broadly conforms to a 20:40:20 rule: 20 per cent are known to have a high probability of investing, 40 per cent might invest and 20 per cent are unlikely to invest – the status of the remainder is indeterminate. The assessment of the investor's likelihood of investing is based on face-to-face meetings, a sense of their determination to invest (possibly in connection with an investor's desire for employment) and their prior track record. In order to build personal relationships with the investor base, and hence be in a position to offer a better return to client companies through effective matching, investors are allocated to members of the corporate finance team. To maximise the efficiency of this process as the number of investors has grown, only the 'top' 10 per cent of investors are now allocated to team members, who will normally have five to seven investors each in their portfolios, in the belief that this more targeted approach will be reflected in greater returns and improved efficiency from the client company's perspective.

The investment opportunities list goes to all investors: of the 600 or so who receive it, between 50 and 100 will respond. This response is not, however, consistent from list to list, nor is it consistent with respect to successful listing of the same opportunity, which may receive enquiries on one listing but not on the previous listing. Furthermore, some investors will respond positively to opportunities following a telephone call, but will not do so in response to the list entry itself, emphasising the importance of personal matching based on detailed knowledge of the investor base and the high degree of inertia among informal investors registered with a business introduction service.

Investment deals

As noted above, Blackstone Franks has a systematic filtering process before accepting clients, and only around 10 per cent of the potential deals which it looks at are taken on. Of these, 15–20 per cent will be successful in raising finance from investors. This effective success rate, which may rise slightly as potential deals still under negotiation come to fruition, is relatively high. Business referral services that have little or no filtering must, therefore, expect to have a much lower success rate. However, the combined effects of Blackstone Franks' filtering to exclude all but the most attractive potential deals, and the investors' filtering out from within that very much reduced list, suggest that only around 1 in 50 of potential deals initially identified will be successful in raising finance in this way, a ratio not unlike that conventionally quoted for the UK institutional venture capital industry. The overall implication of this experience is that a business referral service must attract sufficient deals and avoid spending too much time on deals that have a low probability of attracting investment: ·as experience elsewhere in the UK has shown (see Chapter 14), the poor quality of deal flow is often the primary restriction on the successful operation of locally based business introduction services.

Blackstone Franks has been doing around one deal per month, which is less than at the start of the service. However, these deals are tending to be larger than some of the very small deals which initially came through the company. In part this can be attributed to the persistence of the equity gap, as venture capital providers move further away from the small end of the market: there are now more deals in the £200,000 to £500,000 range which cannot attract the interest of venture capitalists and are turning to private investor sources such as Blackstone Franks instead. Although smaller deals are harder to do, technically and from an efficiency standpoint, there is a sufficient spread of deal size to make the operation profitable overall. There are also two additional benefits from maintaining the private investor network service: the first is that it represents a valuable marketing and promotional channel for the practice; the second is that, in building client company and investor relationships, it provides an opportunity to develop fee-earning opportunities for other parts of the practice (which, as in the case of many seed capital providers in the UK, is often necessary to ensure the overall profitability of this type of service). Finally, in order to keep costs and revenues in balance in the private investor network activity, the Blackstone Franks team works essentially on a results-only basis.

Developments

Blackstone Franks has continued to explore potential future developments and enhancements of the business introduction service. Fundamental to this are the twin desires, first, to maintain the deal flow but improve the quality by reinforcing existing efficient and productive sources of good-quality potential deals; and second, to expand the investor base without losing the degree of personal contact with and knowledge of the serious or committed investors which is central to the matching and deal-making process.

In an attempt to overcome the strong bias in the investor base to the South East of England, an attempt has been made to develop associates in the North. However, experience has shown that this is very difficult to apply in practice, due largely to the lack of effective control over both the process and the economies of the operation. To some extent, the growing importance of merger and acquisition activity in the unquoted sector has in part compensated for this southern bias, as such opportunities have arisen on a wider regional basis.

Based on the shifting focus of institutional venture capital funds away from small- or relatively small-scale investments, Blackstone Franks explored the possibility of launching a £5 million venture capital fund which would co-invest alongside private investors in businesses that required more finance than a private investor was able to provide. This fund experienced difficulty in attracting finance, especially from institutional sources, reflecting the general problems experienced by the venture capital industry in raising new funds. In addition, there was very limited interest on the part of private investors in investing through a fund jointly with venture capital, which is compounded by the practical and legal difficulties of setting up and running such a composite fund. In response to this experience, Blackstone Franks is considering a 'catalyst' fund as a quasi-syndication device to increase the funding available to clients. Although only a relatively small proportion of registered investors (around 10 per cent) have expressed positive interest in the catalyst fund idea, looking at syndication for an investment of £10,000 to £50,000 each, a potential fund of £0.5 million could be created. As these would be pledged funds, the private investors would retain a say in the investments to be made, unlike (for example) a pooled BES fund where the investor has no say in investment policy and practice. Although it is still too early to determine the effectiveness of this particular initiative, the catalyst fund idea does appear to offer one possible way round the relatively low reliance on syndication of informal investments in the UK compared with the situation in North America, where syndication is the norm.

Making a profit

If business referral services are to operate at a profit they must have a number of key attributes:

- A mixture of small and large deals, with the capability of thereby cross-subsiding the non-cost-effective smaller deal.
- Ruthless and systematic filtering of businesses that have little prospect of attracting an investor.
- A fee structure that includes both retainers and minimum fees for success fees.
- Exclusivity, to ensure that the service receives a return on its activities on behalf of a client.
- A charge to clients for assistance in writing their business plans.
- The establishment of long-term relationships with clients.
- The offering of a range of additional services that can be sold to clients.
- Maintenance of a low overhead base – in Blackstone Franks' case this is achieved through sharing the practice infrastructure, paying on a result-only reward basis and making the maximum use of personal and business networks.
- Knowledge of the investors, as a business introduction service cannot rely on impersonal matching processes for investors who often know what they do not want rather than what they do want, and who show a high degree of inertia in the face of circulated information.

If it is to be successful, a business referral service must address the following key issues at the outset. First, is it to be (or can it be) actively involved in making introductions, seeing deals through to completion and securing the business as a long-term client, or will it simply operate as a 'mailbox'? Second, is the entrepreneur or the investor the client? Third, how do you ensure that the service generates deal quality rather than just deal quantity? Fourth, can the service provide the necessary additional services to sell to clients? Fifth, are there in place carefully thought-out strategies to make the service pay? The Blackstone Franks experience has been that a business referral service can operate on a for-profit basis, not as a free-standing activity, but as part of a wider infrastructure and package of services which support client development and growth.

Implications for practice

- A for-profit business introduction service best operates as a service for companies seeking to raise funds.
- A for-profit business introduction service best operates as part of a portfolio of corporate finance services which take a deal through to completion.

- Because of the fixed costs of due diligence, evaluation and monitoring, for-profit services are unlikely to operate successfully at the bottom end of the investment range (i.e. below £50,000 deal size).
- A mix of deal sizes is important to ensure profitability.
- Business which have little prospect of attracting an investor must be systematically filtered out.
- Deal flow can be generated from a wide range of sources, and personal contacts and networking underlie the effectiveness of these sources.
- Investors often find it easier to specify what they do not want to invest in, and it is important not to filter out opportunities presented to them.

CHAPTER 12

Business introduction services in the United Kingdom and the Financial Services Act 1986

Jim Clarke

The Financial Services Act 1986: basic structure

The Financial Services Act 1986 (FSA) is a major statute. Its main provisions came into effect on 29 April 1988 replacing and substantially increasing the scope of the Prevention of Fraud (Investments) Act 1958. The FSA confers various powers on HM Treasury and on the Secretary of State for Trade and Industry.[1] Broadly speaking, HM Treasury is granted powers relating to the authorisation and regulation of persons who carry on investment business as well as powers to exempt persons from requiting authorisation and from the restrictions which the FSA places on investment advertising. The Secretary of State is granted enforcement powers relating to such matters as investigation and prosecution.

The FSA also provides for certain of these powers to be delegated, either in their entirety or on a shared basis, to a designated agency. The designated agency under the FSA for the time being is the Securities and Investments Board (SIB). The powers delegated to the SIB include those of authorisation and others relating to enforcement matters. The power to exempt persons from the need for authorisation is, however, retained by HM Treasury.

The FSA also empowers the designated agency to recognise self-regulating organisations or SROs (of which there are currently four – LAUTRO, FIMBRA, IMRO and the Securities and Futures Authority) and professional bodies or RPBs (such as the Law Societies and the Institutes of Chartered Accountants). Although it exercises statutory powers, the SIB is a private body. The SROs and RPBs are also private bodies, but their powers are derived from the contract between them and their members rather than under statute. The costs which the SIB and the SROs and RPBs incur in carrying out their regulatory functions under the FSA are ultimately borne by the financial services industry itself and not from government.

The authorisation requirement: investment business

Under Section 3 of the FSA, any person who carries on investment business in the United Kingdom must be authorised or exempted from the need for authorisation. Authorisation may be obtained direct from the SIB itself, through membership of an SRO or through certification by an RPB. In addition, certain persons have authorisation conferred on them directly under the FSA itself (for example, authorised life insurance companies and registered friendly societies).

A person is carrying on investment business in the United Kingdom if, by way of business, he or she engages in any of the activities listed in Part II of Schedule 1 to the FSA unless any of the exclusions provided in Part III or IV of Schedule 1 are available to that person. The activities which involve investment business comprise the following:

- Dealing in investments as principal or agent (paragraph 12, Schedule 1).
- Arranging deals in investments (paragraph 13, Schedule 1).
- Managing investments (paragraph 14, Schedule 1).
- Giving investment advice (paragraph 15, Schedule 1).
- Establishing, operating or winding up a collective investment scheme (paragraph 16, Schedule 1).

The FSA also contains a definition of 'investments' in Part I of Schedule 1. Broadly speaking, FSA 'investments' include shares and debt securities, warrants, futures and options, unit trusts and other collective investment schemes, and most long-term insurance contracts having any form of investment element. The FSA does not, however, apply to other forms of investment such as direct, non-collective, individual investment in real property, commodities, works of art or racehorses. Neither does it apply to deposits, mortgages or ordinary bank lending.

The definition of investments and of the activities comprising investment business and exclusions thereto may all be, and have on a number of occasions already been, changed by way of secondary legislation.

Business introduction services

It can be seen from the above that much of the FSA has no bearing on business introduction services, but there are certain possible implications of which the providers of such services will need to be aware. It is presumed for the purposes of this chapter that business introduction services are concerned solely with the process whereby businesses which are in need of external funding or 'venture capital' are put in contact with possible sources of such funding.

Where such businesses take the form of bodies corporate, and where the type of funding envisaged will involve the issue or disposal of shares or other investments, it will be necessary for the provider of business introduction services to consider whether or not his or her activities would constitute one or more of the following areas of investment business:

1. *Dealing in investments.* This covers situations where persons enter into investment transactions either for their own account or as agent for another person. Generally speaking, this would be unlikely to apply to the provider of business introduction services if he or she has no role to play in negotiations subsequent to an introduction.

2. *Arranging deals in investments.* This is defined as making arrangements with a view either to persons buying, selling, subscribing for or underwriting a particular investment, or to persons who participate in the arrangements of buying, selling, subscribing for or underwriting investments generally. This definition is potentially very wide and seems capable of applying to many arrangements which a person may make and which contemplate an investment transaction taking place to which other persons will be party. Typical arrangements which the providers of business introduction service may make and which seem capable of falling within this definition include:

(a) the operation of a register either of business investment opportunities or of prospective investors or both, whether or not combined with any form of system for matching prospective partners;

(b) the regular publication of details either of potential business investment opportunities offered to prospective investors or vice versa, for instance through the medium of a subscriber-only journal or other publication, and

(c) the active seeking out of prospective partners by personal communications or through seminars or in similar circumstances.

3. *Giving investment advice.* Investment advice is defined as advice given to persons in their capacity as investors or potential investors on the merits of their buying, selling, subscribing for or underwriting an investment (or exercising rights conferred by an investment to do any such thing). In this respect, businesses which are looking for external funding are not investors or potential investors and hence any advice offered to them as regards the merits of their obtaining or seeking to obtain funds through the issue of securities is unlikely to amount to investment advice. However, the providers of business introduction services will have to consider whether any advice they may give to prospective investors will amount to investment advice. Whether or not such advice will be caught by the definition will depend on whether it may be viewed as the provision of neutral or factual information, as opposed to it amounting to a recommendation or other form of comment on the merits of the opportunity as an investor. The SIB has published formal guidance which deals with this area in more detail.[2]

A provider of business introduction services who engages in one or more of these activities by way of business will normally require to be authorised or exempted under the FSA.

The FSA does not seek to define the circumstances in which a person is to be viewed as carrying on business. Generally speaking, if there is a commercial benefit to be derived by the provider of the service, that fact would point towards the carrying on of a business. Beyond that, in SIB's view, the presence or absence of a commercial benefit or motive is not necessarily the sole determining factor. Other factors will need to be taken into account, such as the frequency with which the activity is carried on and the extent to which a person holds him or herself out as willing to provide the services in question. A contrast may thus be drawn between a person who might simply respond to an occasional request from a client by referring him or her to potential sources of venture capital with whom he or she has no special relationship, and a person who offers to make introductions for reward on a systematic basis.

Exemption under Section 46 of the FSA

As referred to above, there is power under the FSA for HM Treasury to exempt persons from the need for authorisation either completely or to a specified extent. In this respect, the government, when enacting the FSA, decided to grant such a limited exemption for certain providers of business introduction services in specified circumstances. The terms of the Exemption Order (which is reproduced in the appendix to this chapter) require the following:

- that the person be a body corporate;
- that its principal object or one of its principal objects is the promotion or encouragement of industrial or commercial activity in the UK or the dissemination of information in that respect; and
- that it has no pecuniary interest in the arrangements other than such as to enable it to recover the cost of providing the service.

It should be noted that the exemption applies *only* to the arranging of deals. It does not exempt a person who deals in investments or a person who gives investment advice.

The first two conditions referred to above will be matters of fact. As regards the third, the essential point is whether any fees or charges which the provider of the service may levy are reasonably to be regarded as necessary only to recover the costs of making the arrangements. There is no specific requirement that the charges must take the form of a flat fee. Hence it is open to the provider of a business introduction service to levy charges in whatever manner he or she chooses (including, for example, by basing them on the successful outcome of introductions made), provided that they remain reasonably to be regarded as necessary to meet the costs involved. It follows that, provided any charges levelled meet the statutory criteria, the fact that, in the event, there may be an excess of income over the costs of making the arrangements will not necessarily negate the availability of the exemption. On the other hand, were the provider of a service systematically to charge more than may prove necessary to cover the costs of making the arrangements, the continuing availability of the exemption might be called into question.

Investment advertising

Section 57 of the FSA prohibits, subject to certain exemptions contained in Section 58, an unauthorised person from issuing or causing the issue of an investment advertisement unless its contents have been approved by an authorised person (such as many solicitors or accountants, stockbrokers, merchant banks, etc.). An investment advertisement includes any form of advertising which contains information calculated directly or indirectly to lead to persons entering or offering or agreeing to enter into an investment agreement (such as an agreement for the acquisition of shares or debentures). Breach of Section 57 is a criminal offence.

Hence, any promotional material which business introduction services may distribute or make available to potential investors as to the business investment opportunities available, or vice versa, is likely to be an investment advertisement. In this respect, however, Section 58(1)(b) of the FSA provides a specific exemption from the requirement to have the contents of an advertisement approved by an authorised person where it has been issued by a person who is exempted under, *inter alia*, Section 46. This exemption applies only to the extent that the advertisement in question relates to matters in respect of which its issuer is an exempted person and does not impose any specific requirements as to its contents.

Any provider of business introduction services who is not to be treated as an exempted person under Section 46 – for instance, because he or she is not carrying on the business of making arrangements – may be able to take advantage of another specific exemption granted pursuant to Section 58(3) of the FSA. This exemption (which is reproduced in the appendix) provides that any person who meets the stipulated requirements can issue an investment advertisement without its contents having been approved by an authorised person. It should be noted that such investment advertisements are required to carry a prominent 'wealth warning' in the manner prescribed in the exemption. Providers of business introduction services who are able to take advantage of the advertising exemption in Section 58(1)(b) of the FSA, as referred to above, may wish to consider including a warning on similar lines in any advertisements they may issue.

Cold calling

Section 56 of the FSA prohibits any person from entering into investment agreements in the course of or as a consequence of an unsolicited call made on a person in the UK (or made from the UK on a person elsewhere), or from procuring or endeavouring to procure that person to enter into an investment agreement except so far as permitted by regulations made by the SIB (the Common Unsolicited Calls Regulations) or, in the case of a person regulated by a recognised professional body, the rules of that body.

An unsolicited call is defined as a personal visit or oral communication made without express invitation.

The Common Unsolicited Calls Regulations provide for unsolicited calls to be made on non-private investors (as defined) and on private investors in certain circumstances. Generally speaking, the providers of business introduction services will be able to make unsolicited calls on prospective investors if they are government departments, local or public authorities, or large companies or partnerships (as defined). The extent to which they will be able to make unsolicited calls on others is beyond the scope of this chapter. It should be noted that investment agreements concluded in consequence of calls made in breach of Section 56 of the FSA are, prima facie, unenforceable against investors.

Summary

The providers of business introduction services may be likely to carry on investment business. If a provider's business constitutes dealing in investments or giving investment advice then he or she is likely to require to be authorised (for instance, by obtaining membership of an SRO such as the Securities and Futures Authority or direct from SIB). If, however, the only investment business activity to be carried on is that of arranging deals in investments, the provider of the service may be able to avail him or herself of the exemption granted under Section 46 of the FSA. Generally speaking, essentially non-profit-making bodies such as local enterprise agencies, chambers of commerce or Training and Enterprise Councils would be likely to qualify for the exemption provided they could satisfy the 'pecuniary interest' test.

It must be borne in mind that the views expressed in this chapter are those of the SIB and, as such, they are not conclusive and will not bind in a court of law. The interpretation of the FSA remains a matter for the courts to determine, and persons who remain uncertain of their position under the FSA would be well advised to seek independent legal advice.

Implications for practice

- Business introduction services need to be aware of the implications of the Financial Services Act 1986 (FSA).
- Business introduction services need to consider whether their activities fall within the definition of an 'investment business' under the terms of the Act; if so, they will normally require to be authorised or exempted under the FSA.
- Whether or not a business introduction service is seeking a commercial benefit is not necessarily the only factor determining whether it requires to be authorised under the FSA.
- Some types of business introduction service may fall within an Exemption Order which removes the need for authorisation.
- Business introduction services are also affected by FSA rules regarding investment advertising; however, business introduction services may also be able to take advantage of another specific exemption.
- Organisations which intend to set up a business introduction service should seek independent legal advice to establish their position under the FSA.

Appendix 12.1 Financial Services Act 1986: principal provisions likely to be relevant to the operators of business introduction services

Section 3   Need for persons who carry on investment business to be authorised or exempted.

Section 4   Offence caused by breach of Section 3.

Section 5   Contracts entered into in breach of Section 3 may be unenforceable against the investor, who may be entitled to compensation for any loss suffered.

Section 46   Provision for the granting by means of a Statutory Instrument of miscellaneous exemptions from the need to be authorised in order to carry on investment business in the UK.

Section 47   Offence to make false, misleading or deceptive statements for the purpose of inducing persons to buy or sell investments.

Section 56   Restrictions on cold calling and power to make regulations. Contracts entered into as a result of a breach of Section 56 may be unenforceable against the investor, who may be entitled to compensation for any loss suffered.

Section 57   Prohibition on unauthorised persons issuing investment advertisements unless contents approved by an authorised person.

Section 58(1)(b) Advertisements exempted from scope of Section 57 if issued by an exempted person in the course of his or her exempted business.

Section 58(3)   Power to exempt advertisements from scope of Section 57 by means of a Statutory Instrument.

Schedule 1

Part I   Paragraphs 1 to 11   Definition of 'investments'

Part II   Paragraphs 12 to 16   Activities constituting investment business

            Paragraph 12   Dealing in investments
            Paragraph 13   Arranging deals in investments
            Paragraph 15   Investment advice

Part III   Paragraphs 17 to 25B   Excluded activities

Relevant Statutory Instruments

SI 1988 No. 723 – The Financial Services Act 1986 (Miscellaneous Exemptions) (No. 2) Order 1988. Paragraph 8 of Schedule 2.

Any body corporate which has as its principal object or one of its principal objects the promotion or encouragement of industrial or commercial activity or enterprise in the United Kingdom or in any particular area of it or the dissemination of information concerning persons engaged in such activity or enterprise or requiring capital to become so engaged being a body corporate which has no direct or indirect pecuniary interest in the arrangements or in any investment agreement which may be entered into by persons participating in them except any such interest as may arise from the receipt of such sums as may reasonably be regarded as necessary to meet the costs of making the arrangements is an exempted person as respects any arrangements it makes which fall within paragraph 13 of Schedule 1 to the Financial Services Act 1986.

SI 1988 No. 716 – The Financial Services Act 1986 (Investment Advertisements) (Exemptions) (No. 2) Order 1988. Article 3.

3. (1) Section 57 of the Act shall not apply to an investment advertisement issued

or caused to be issued by a body corporate of the kind described in paragraph (2) below which:

(a) relates to shares in or debentures of a private company;

(b) contains no invitation or information which would make it an investment advertisement other than an invitation or information which it is reasonable to expect a person engaged in an activity of the kind described in that paragraph to give in the course of engaging in that activity; and

(c) complies with the requirements of paragraph (3) of this article.

(2) A body corporate falls within this paragraph if:

(a) it is a body corporate which has as its principal object or one of its principal objects the promotion or encouragement of industrial or commercial activity or enterprise in the United Kingdom or in any particular area of it or the dissemination of information concerning persons engaged in such activity or enterprise or requiring capital to become so engaged; and

(b) it has no direct or indirect pecuniary interest in any matters which are the subject of any investment advertisement it issues which is exempt by virtue of this article or in any investment agreement which may be entered into following such an advertisement.

(3) The requirements referred to in paragraph (1)(c) of this article are that the advertisement should contain the following statements presented in a manner which, depending upon the medium through which the advertisement is issued, are calculated to bring the contents of the statements prominently to the attention of recipients of the advertisement:

"Investment in new business carries high risks, as well as the possibility of high rewards. It is highly speculative and potential investors should be aware that no established market exists for the trading of shares in private companies. Before investing in a project about which information is given, potential investors are strongly advised to take advice from a person authorised under the Financial Services Act 1986 who specialises in advising on investments of this kind.

The persons to whose order this advertisement has been issued have taken reasonable steps to ensure that the information it contains is neither inaccurate nor misleading."

Notes

1. The powers in question were originally conferred solely on the Secretary of State for Trade and Industry, but subsequently were in large part transferred to HM Treasury – Statutory Instrument 1992 No. 1315.
2. The Financial Services Act and the Press SIB Guidance Release No. 4/89 are available from the SIB Publications Office, price £5.

PART IV

Public policy and developments in Europe

TECs and the promotion of informal venture capital: the feasibility of an informal investor network in East Lancashire

Simon M. Shorter

Introduction

Ever since the identification of the equity gap by the MacMillan Committee some 60 years ago various official reports – one of the most recent being the ACOST (1990) report on *The Enterprise Challenge: Overcoming barriers to growth in small firms* – have periodically confirmed that there remains a need for the ready availability of smaller amounts of risk capital to be increased.

But from where is this risk capital likely to be obtained? One potential source which has recently been identified is informal venture capital. US research has established that 'business angels' – wealthy private individuals who invest in unquoted companies – are the largest source of risk capital for small firms (Wetzel, 1981). Recent research has also identified and examined the informal venture capital market in the UK (Mason and Harrison, 1991a, 1991b). The research in both the USA and the UK, however, has clearly identified the inefficiencies in the informal venture capital market, which raise serious questions about its ability to close the equity gap.

One of the key problems for the development of the informal investor market is the difficulty that investors and entrepreneurs have in looking for each other. Since investors wish to retain their anonymity, and are hence effectively invisible, the search by an entrepreneur for an investor is time consuming and often unsuccessful. The search by investors for investment opportunities is also difficult, since there is no readily identifiable list of businesses seeking outside investors. One method that has been developed to overcome these inefficiencies is the financial 'marriage bureau', which essentially acts as a matching agency, linking firms that are looking for finance with private individuals who are looking for investments.

There are three main methods of operating a marriage bureau:

- *Investment bulletin*: this represents the simplest method and involves the listing of investment opportunities in a publication which is distributed to investors on a regular basis. Typically, the bulletin only provides the essential details of businesses seeking finance, and the name of the company is not disclosed. Investors can obtain more detailed information on any investment opportunities that interest them from the service operator.

- *Computer matching*: this method was pioneered by Venture Capital Network in the USA (Chapter 3). It acts as a sifting mechanism for investors and businesses, using a computer program to match up the investment criteria of investors with the characteristics of investment opportunities. This ensures that investors only receive details of investment opportunities that may interest them.
- *Investors' meetings*: this method usually acts as an adjunct to the other two methods. Entrepreneurs make presentations to an audience of potential investors.

The concept of financial marriage bureaux is not new to the UK. For example, LINC (Chapter 7) operates through a number of local enterprise agencies and there are also a number of small, local match-making services. Some accountants (see Chapter 11 for an example) and solicitors also arrange matches on an *ad hoc* basis. However, questions have been raised concerning both their effectiveness and their feasibility in view of the difficulty of operating such services on a commercial basis (Chapter 2), leading Mason and Harrison (1992) to recommend that such services should be publicly funded.

This study focuses on one locality – East Lancashire or, more specifically, the operating area of ELTEC Ltd, the Training and Enterprise Council in the region, which is centred on Blackburn and Burnley in the North West of England. It has three objectives. First, it seeks to progress the understanding of the small firm equity gap from a subnational perspective. Specifically, do unquoted companies based and operating in East Lancashire have difficulties in raising risk finance in the range £10,000 to £150,000 due to the failure of the financial market in the region to meet their needs? The second aim is to establish whether there is potential for tackling the local equity gap by means of a local informal investor marriage bureau. Third, it seeks to develop a model for a local marriage bureau in East Lancashire.

Methodology

Rather than interview or send out questionnaires to a sample of small companies to gain an understanding of their experiences of raising finance, a series of interviews were conducted with financial intermediaries, including both providers of finance such as banks and venture capital companies and also business advisers and financial agents (e.g. accountants, solicitors, DTI business counsellors, enterprise agencies, local authorities) involved in helping companies raise finance. This approach is similar to that used by the West Midlands Enterprise Board (1988) in its equity gap study.

Entrepreneurs are often poor at judging the reasons why their project has not been funded, and may not accept the reasons given by the financier. Suppliers of finance and business advisers are able to provide a more objective account of the reasons why companies are unable to raise finance, with their views not clouded by emotion and personal feelings. There are a number of other advantages to focusing on suppliers of finance and business advisers:

- They meet a broad range of companies in the course of their business and are therefore ideally placed to judge the viability of a project.
- They are aware of the investment criteria used by the various finance providers.
- They are aware of the sources of finance that are available and also the most appropriate forms of finance to seek.

The disadvantage is that such organisations do not collect statistics on many of the issues explored in the survey. Thus the information obtained is heavily skewed towards impressionistic evidence.

Semi-structured interviews lasting approximately one-and-a-half hours were completed with 25 finance providers and business advisers. These advisers came from fourteen organisations providing financial advice, six banks, two venture capital companies, two legal firms and one other local organisation. The first part of the interview explored the existence of the equity gap in East Lancashire, while the second part looked at the potential for a local informal investor marriage bureau to close any gap that might be identified.

The equity gap in East Lancashire

The majority of interviewees believed that there was an equity gap in East Lancashire. However, the results of the questionnaire showed differences in the perception and nature of the gap. This is illustrated by the higher percentage (80 per cent) of respondents who thought an equity gap existed (Table 13.1) than believed that potentially viable businesses were unable to raise finance (60 per cent – Table 13.2). This variation reflects the more complex nature of the gap and the viability of the business, and takes into account not only the financial viability but also the credibility and quality of the business plan. The indications from the questionnaire are that the equity gap is more than simply a lack of suitable finance, but also includes gaps in information, management, presentation skills and professional assistance.

Of those interviewed, the banks and business advisers were the most likely to identify an equity gap, whereas accountants were least likely to agree that an equity gap existed. This is indicative of the fact that the accountants provide considerable information and professional advice to enhance the potential of their clients' businesses.

Table 13.1 Is there an equity gap in East Lancashire? Views of finance providers and business advisers

	Number of respondents	%
Agree	20	80
Disagree	2	8
Not sure	3	12

Table 13.2 Can viable business always obtain finance? Views of finance providers and business advisers

	Number of respondents	%
Agree	15	60
Disagree	7	28
Not sure	3	12

On average, each adviser/institution estimated that it had an average of one to two projects per week which it felt were potentially viable, but for which it was unable to raise finance. This is a conservative figure and excludes those entrepreneurs who are deterred from even approaching advisers/providers because of the perception that there is a lack of finance available. Trying to size the gap by extrapolating these figures to the Blackburn area, and making an allowance for multiple applications, suggests that the number of potentially viable businesses that are unable to raise finance exceeds 300 a year. This figure is likely to be even higher in times of economic prosperity.

The consensus of opinion among the interviewees was that the finance gap affects companies of all sizes and sectors and irrespective of the ethnic background of the entrepreneur. However, there was also an agreement among respondents that the manufacturing sector, technology-based businesses, businesses employing between 5 and 50 employees and two- or three-year-old businesses seeking expansion finance encountered particularly acute problems in raising finance.

Respondents identified a number of reasons why firms found it difficult to raise finance, the most common of which were lack of security, poor viability, lack of experience and poor management skills. When a slightly different question was posed regarding the main reasons why small business financing proposals were rejected, essentially the same factors were identified: level of risk; lack of security and poor management skills. Asked more generally about the reasons for the existence of an equity gap, respondents identified the strict and inflexible lending criteria of banks; the costs of making small investments relative to the potential risk/return ratio, and the lack of local sources of equity finance. Respondents also felt that the quality of investment proposals was often poor. This was attributed in many cases to the lack of support for businesses and the information gap affecting small growing companies.

Closer investigation of the quality of intermediaries indicated that there is a general awareness of the sources of finance within the area. However, access to this information is often difficult for companies to find, and in addition the information dispensed is often of variable quality. In particular, enterprise agencies provide an adequate information base for smaller companies and start-ups, but there is nothing equivalent for growing companies that have passed the start-up phase. It is these companies which experience the greatest gap in information provision.

Thus, the survey of financiers and business advisers has identified the existence of an equity gap in East Lancashire, although its nature and dimensions are complex. This complexity is a reflection of the diversity of causes, which include demand-side limitations, the insufficient supply of risk capital and the inflexibility of much of the finance and information that is available.

Turning to supply-side considerations, most respondents recognised that equity finance was an appropriate method of finance to meet the long-term financing needs of growing smaller companies. It was recognised that a stronger capital base gives companies more flexibility and creates greater credibility in the eyes of their creditors. These advantages, it was felt, were offset to some degree by the costs of raising equity finance and the need for careful structuring of equity investments.

Respondents agreed that sources of equity finance in East Lancashire were woefully inadequate. The efforts of Lancashire Enterprise and its various funds, including Rosebud, were acknowledged to be valuable but insufficient to meet demand. Similarly, the proposed Midland Enterprise Fund for North West England was seen to be limited in scope, as it was proposing to make only 15 investments per year across the region (McMeekin, 1991).

Respondents identified various sources of equity finance which could be developed in order to close the finance gap (Table 13.3). The diversity of opinion reflects the differing perspectives of respondents. The single most frequently cited solution was the promotion of informal venture capital, followed by the development of a local venture capital fund. A third suggestion was for a brokerage or information source to work with small firms to link them with

Table 13.3 Sources of equity finance to fill the equity gap: views of finance providers and business advisers

	Number of respondents	%
Informal investors	7	35
Venture capital funds	6	30
Brokers	3	15
Other	4	20

existing suppliers of finance, including venture capital funds, informal investors and government sources. There was little support for 'quasi-equity' in the form of soft loans and grants: these were seen as being open to abuse and involving little commitment by firms taking the grant.

Potential for an informal investor marriage bureau in East Lancashire

An informal investor marriage bureau is intended to link entrepreneurs looking for finance with private investors who are looking to make informal investments. The objective of the service is to provide a more efficient channel of communication between these two sets of actors, thereby improving the flow of information and overcoming the inefficiencies in the market.

Respondents were almost unanimous in their view that there would be a demand for an informal investor marriage bureau among entrepreneurs, both as an additional source of finance and also as an alternative to existing sources of finance (Table 13.4). The only reservations concerned whether investors would be attracted by the quality of the demand, and the willingness of small business owner-managers to sell equity. However, respondents did express strong views about the form that the marriage bureau should take. These views are discussed later in this chapter.

Most respondents also believed that there was a stock of informal investors in East Lancashire and that many would be interested in the service (Table 13.5).

Table 13.4 Do you believe that there is a potential demand by small firm owner–managers for an informal investor marriage bureau? Views of finance providers and business advisers

	Number of respondents	%
Yes	20	87
Possibly	2	9
No	1	4

Table 13.5 Do you believe that there are informal investors in East Lancashire who would be interested in an informal investor marriage bureau? Views of finance providers and business advisers

	Number of respondents	%
Yes	13	52
Possibly	9	36
No	3	12

Indeed, it was apparent from the interviews that many accountants and lawyers as well as one of the enterprise agencies already operated *ad hoc* informal investor networks. On the basis of their experiences, these respondents felt that a more organised service, but one which still maintained confidentiality and independence, could enhance informal investment activity. However, some respondents did express concern about the willingness of investors to make investments in recessionary conditions. Others suggested that investors would need positive encouragement to participate in the service. The need to create a local investor mentality was also highlighted as a potential barrier. It was also suggested that many investors would wish to make their investments through holding-type companies and that, in order to capitalise on corporate tax advantages, they would require a majority stake. This, it was felt, might conflict with the desire of most entrepreneurs, who only wish to make a minority stake available. To exclude such investors would risk significantly reducing the number of potential investors.

It was also suggested that, in order to overcome the possible limitations in the number of investors in the East Lancashire area, it might be appropriate to expand the catchment area to cover the whole of Lancashire. This increase in operating area would also increase the likelihood of potential matches. However, only business opportunities located in East Lancashire should be accepted.

Respondents identified likely investors as having a range of characteristics:

- Business background, usually with entrepreneurial experience.
- Active investors, playing a proactive role in business.
- Community oriented, with some measure of altruism in their investment patterns.
- Profit motivated: despite altruistic motives, investors are seeking capital returns.
- Moderately wealthy rather than super-rich.

These attributes closely conform to the profile of UK informal investors identified by Mason and Harrison (1991a, 1991b).

All of the interviewees stated that they would be willing to refer investors and business owners to the network. They identified a number of features that the service should have in order to attract their full support. First, it was essential that an experienced business person ran the service, both in order to advise small businesses approaching the service and also to undertake a quality review of companies which registered. Other desirable attributes that were highlighted included a speedy response time, a simple operating system, independence and confidentiality. Respondents also identified the need for the service to network extensively in East Lancashire to be successful. The preferred type of matching service was computer matching. There was some scepticism about investors' meetings on the grounds that informal investors would not wish to be identified. However, LINC has not experienced this difficulty (Chapter 7), and this comment may reflect a lack of experience with the format.

East Lancashire informal investor perspectives

Information was also collected from three informal investors in East Lancashire to ascertain their characteristics and investment behaviour, as well as their interest in participating in an informal investor marriage bureau.

All three investors were local businessmen, over 40 years old and with substantial businesses of their own. They currently rely on business associates and friends for identifying investment opportunities. Their most important criteria for evaluating investment opportunities, in rank order, were as follows:

- People: the quality and experience of the management and the compatibility between the investor and the investee.
- Product: the innovative nature of the product.
- Market: the competition within the market and the ability to obtain a small share of a large market.

These investors regarded business plans as an important factor in the appraisal process, providing an indication of whether the entrepreneur knew what he or she was doing. On average the investors considered about ten investment opportunities a year and invested in about three projects. They were seeking rates of return from their investments in the 20 to 25 per cent range.

All three investors tended to specialise in industries that they knew; two of the investors specialised in businesses at the leading edge of these industries. All three investors were particularly interested in new technology. Their investments ranged between £50,000 and £500,000. All of the investors were interested in early stage companies that had successfully negotiated the start-up stage. Each investor stressed the importance of the investment being local – within 40 or 50 miles – both to facilitate the close monitoring of the investment and to support their local community.

Only two investors were currently active, but neither of them perceived any shortage of good investment opportunities. None had used a business introduction service, but nevertheless all three investors agreed that there was potential for a marriage bureau. Since each of the investors currently had sufficient investment opportunities, they felt that they would need to be convinced to use the service. All three believed that there were sufficient currently less active investors who would be prepared to pay to use the service and benefit from it, as long as it was well managed and provided a flow of good investment opportunities. The biggest challenge these investors identified as facing the marriage bureau was convincing other investors to use it. The process of building investor confidence as well as educating them was felt to be a long-term process, perhaps taking over five years. In order to overcome these problems in the short term, it was suggested that a marriage bureau should provide a wider range of services than purely match-making. These services could range from educating and advising small businesses and investors on the equity process, to helping entrepreneurs to put their plans and ideas together.

Summary of questionnaire results

It is clear from the survey of financiers and business advisers that an equity gap does exist in East Lancashire. The equity gap takes a number of dimensions, as follows. First, there is a shortage of available and suitable sources of equity finance. Second, there is a shortage of information about the type and availability of different sources of finance. Third, there is a shortage of businesses with sufficiently well-developed ideas and business plans, as well as the skills to build these into an effective business proposal. Fourth, there is a shortage of appropriate consultancy and advisory services. Finally, there is a shortage of management skills in these businesses.

In trying to tackle the equity gap, consideration must be given to all the dimensions, and a unidimensional solution is unlikely to be successful. The implication of this is that a purely supply-side solution, such as the establishment of a simple introduction service, may be both costly and relatively ineffective. The research reveals that a more complex response is required.

In terms of the physical characteristics of the gap in East Lancashire, it is clear that the problem is most severe for manufacturing and manufacturing-related companies of between 5 and 100 employees, which are seeking to raise between £25,000 and £150,000 for expansion purposes. But as seen above, it is not just a finance barrier, since the lack of information and the absence of suitable professional assistance also act as barriers.

Finally, the survey established that there was the potential for an informal investor network in East Lancashire, and that it was felt that this would help to alleviate some of the problems. It also identified the local investment preferences of informal investors – small companies in manufacturing and in the early stages of growth – which surprisingly closely matched those of the local equity gap. The survey also revealed the hands-on nature of many informal investors, which in the majority of small companies is what is needed to close the people or management gap which they also face.

A financial marriage bureau for East Lancashire: a proposal

Lessons from the LINC approach

Before designing a marriage bureau from the research in East Lancashire, an analysis of the main UK bureau (LINC) was undertaken to establish what lessons could be learnt. Overall, LINC's performance has been very disappointing in terms of the number of matches. The main reason is that LINC has lacked publicity and so has a low profile and limited awareness. This is confirmed by the local survey of financiers and business advisers in East Lancashire: only 40 per cent were aware of LINC, and of these only 60 per cent really understood its function. Even the local branches of Lloyds Bank were not aware of LINC, even though Lloyds Bank is a national sponsor. LINC can also be criticised for its lack of follow-up of successful matches for promotional purposes. Moreover, prior to the work of Mason *et al.*, (1991) there had been little attempt to enquire into the nature of investor requirements or their behaviour. The cumulative effect has been that LINC has had difficulties in attracting sufficient investors – especially active investors. In addition, while the investee client base of many of the linked enterprise agencies is narrowly focused on start-ups and very early stage companies, these are of only limited interest to informal investors. A further factor which has perhaps contributed to the limited success of LINC is the limited amount of advice provided to investee companies or investors.

From this examination of LINC, in general, as well as its more successful member agencies, a number of criteria can be identified which can significantly improve the marriage bureau's potential for success.

Active marketing to generate and sustain a professional profile

The benefits of the network need to be promoted:

- The advantages of equity finance.
- The independence of the network and its position as an 'honest broker'.
- All industries and business types included.
- A simple operating system.
- Locally oriented investment.
- Educational vehicle.

Strong integration within the local community

The service will live or die on the power of the networks within the local finance and business communities.

Advisory centre

The investor network should operate as an adviser to businesses looking for finance, in terms not only of where to find finance, but of how to obtain it. Help should be provided on structuring and developing a business plan.

Accurate and fast matching

The matching service needs to be able to turn around proposals in a maximum of eight weeks. An active and accurate computer matching system and regular investment club meetings are required.

Quality investments

The network must maintain the quality and standard of its investments as well as looking for more interesting opportunities to generate attention from investors.

Local service

The service must operate within a region of between 50 and 100 miles. Investors may come from further afield, but investment patterns show that they tend to invest within this range rather than nationally. Investment opportunities should be generated from a tight geographical area to restrict the workload of the investment manager and ensure the maintenance of a local spirit of the bureau.

Management

The network must be run by a manager with strong business and financial skills and working on a full-time basis.

A marriage bureau for East Lancashire: a new model

Based on the preceding discussion, we are now in a position to propose an alternative model for an informal investor marriage bureau service in East Lancashire.

The aims of the service are as follows:

- To effect introductions of small businesses requiring risk capital for start-up or growth to investors prepared to invest equity capital and, potentially, other human resource skills.
- To ensure the maximum number of marriages within the geographical operating area.
- To increase the standard of business plans and enhance business development within the operating area.
- To improve the financial performance and skills of the small companies in the operating area in order to increase their chances of raising finance and raising their level of financial competence.
- To advise and provide information for companies looking to develop and expand.

These objectives sit comfortably with the business development strategy of ELTEC and complement its business review and mentor services which focus on the development and growth of small businesses with potential.

Geographical coverage

Previous research suggests that most informal investors make investments within a maximum range of 50 to 100 miles of home (Mason and Harrison, 1991a). The main reason is that they wish to play an active role in the companies in which they invest. It is also clear from the interviews conducted as part of this study that investors are often community oriented. The operating area of the bureau must therefore be capable of generating a critical mass of investors and investment opportunities, but still be small enough to allow close networking and a regional and community identity to be maintained. The area should therefore have some readily identifiable local characteristics, so that investors are able to invest in the 'local' area.

However, given the potentially limited number of active investors in an area the size of East Lancashire, as well as the need to broaden the number of attractive investment opportunities, a larger operating area will be necessary, although one which would still be small enough to allow close networking and provide a sense of locality.

The service should therefore be expanded beyond East Lancashire to include all of Lancashire and northern parts of Greater Manchester – Bolton, Bury, Rochdale – in effect, the 'West Pennines'. This larger geographical area retains sufficient regional characteristics to counteract any identity problems arising, and still enables investors to receive details of investments located within 50 to 100 miles of their home.

Operating the service beyond the ELTEC region will necessitate co-ordination with neighbouring TECs. One option is to form a joint bureau which, if funded by all of the TECs, could operate as a separate but related entity. An alternative approach is for one lead TEC to co-ordinate the bureau with contributions from other TECs in the form of resources, investors and investment opportunities.

Nature of organisation

The service should be co-ordinated through the TEC. In view of the size of the proposed operating area, the network will need to be operated by a regional or near-regional organisation. The organisation running the service will need to have experience of dealing with developing small businesses. The relevant organisation should also have a company client base. The only organisations currently with these characteristics are TECs. However, even their operating areas are too small. Thus, as discussed above, the service may need to be run by ELTEC in conjunction with neighbouring TECs, such as LAWTEC and the Bolton, Bury and Rochdale TECs.

Some marriage bureau services are already managed by a few of the local enterprise agencies, although the client base of a single enterprise agency is likely to be insufficient to sustain such a service. Moreover, both the client base and the experience of enterprise agencies tends to be focused on start-ups and very early stage businesses, which in many cases are less appropriate for a marriage bureau network. Nevertheless, it is imperative that the enterprise agencies are included as partners within the service as the local representatives on the ground, filtering propositions and helping to recruit investors.

Service for businesses

The market focus for the marriage bureau will be the businesses in East Lancashire that are most affected by the equity gap. The proposed service will therefore concentrate on the following areas:

- Companies looking for development/expansion finance.
- Companies in the technology and manufacturing sectors.
- Companies with between 5 and 100 employees.
- Companies looking for buyers.
- Companies in specialist circumstances looking for start-up finance.
- Companies looking for finance between £25,000 and £150,000.

Companies should be identified from a number of sources:

- Directly, through the current information service.
- Through wide-ranging publicity of the service.
- Through the marketing efforts of the business development manager to relevant 'gatekeepers' (e.g. banks, accountants, business counsellors).
- Through the network of local enterprise agencies.
- From the TEC's business development programme and on-going review services and mentor programme.

Businesses which approach the bureau will be asked to develop a business plan in a standardised format. The standardised format is necessary both for ease of access and to ensure conformity between the organisation's projects. The document will also need to be fairly rigorous to ensure the full commitment of the company and to reduce the level of human resources needed to assess the project while still maintaining quality assurance. The business plan must also be in a form that allows key information to be quickly loaded on to a database listing the most important details (e.g. industry, size, amount of finance required, market, etc.), to enable computer matching to be undertaken. The company will also be required to produce a one-page summary of its proposal. This synopsis will act as the initial marketing tool for the company.

It is proposed that three levels of service are offered to businesses to reflect the complexity of the gaps in information, business planning techniques and advisory services for growing businesses, as well as for finance.

Level 1: Basic service. This is a registration-only service. If a company is able to develop its own business plan and does not require any additional financial services, it will be asked to complete the standard business plan format. This will be checked by the business development manager and, if judged to be satisfactory, the business will be registered on the network. However, if the business is considered unsuitable for the service then various steps can be taken:

- The business can be turned away if it is thought that there is little likelihood that the proposal can be brought up to the necessary quality standard for the service.
- Advice can be offered by the business development manager, either to help the company put together a business plan or to suggest more appropriate sources of finance.

- Signposting to other programmes offered by ELTEC, such as the business review service and a mentor/non-executive director service.

Level 2: Financial audit service. This service will be offered to those businesses seeking financial advice and information on where, and how, to raise finance. Under this service, businesses will be advised on where to seek finance, provided with relevant contacts and advised on how to acquire this finance. The business will be helped with its business plans and supplied with the standard TEC format. The business will have full access to the TEC's information services. The service will comprise a half-day financial audit followed by recommendations on suitable sources of finance and help in obtaining these funds. If the most appropriate form of finance is equity finance, the business will be registered with the informal investor network following completion of the standard business format.

Level 3: Full service. If a business requires more detailed assistance – for example, because of the specialist nature of the company (e.g. a technology-based business) – then it can receive a more detailed review in addition to those in the Level 2 service.

Service for investors

Although there will be no geographical restriction on investors, strong encouragement of local involvement is necessary to create a community-oriented investor bureau. The main focus will be on individual investors, but this is not intended to exclude applications by companies. Investors will be attracted from the following sources:

- Direct publicity.
- Networking with local banks, accountants, solicitors and brokers.
- Networking with local enterprise agencies.
- Talks to chambers of commerce, business clubs, rotary clubs, etc.
- TECs.
- Local authorities.
- Lancashire Enterprise.
- Other regional organisations.

A one-page form will be devised for the investor to specify the nature, size and type of investment sought. The information obtained will parallel the information provided by the investee business for the standard business plan format. These details will be added to the database.

Matching and information system

The three main methods of matching – investment bulletin, computer matching and investor club – all have advantages and disadvantages. The research that has been undertaken for this study highlights speed of response and confidentiality as the primary business requirements of a marriage bureau. Investors emphasise the quality of proposals, clear role definition of the bureau, and the relevance of the investment proposals to their investment criteria. These two sets of requirements are best met by a computer matching system. This also keeps the personnel required to run the service to a minimum.

The database will allow businesses and investors to be matched on various criteria. The process should operate as follows:

- A business which seeks to register will develop a business plan in line with the standardised format.
- The plan will be assessed by the business development manager and if satisfactory, and if only the basic service is required, the details of the business will be added to the database.
- The computer matching programme will be run.
- The company's business plan summary will be sent to matched investors with a reply slip asking if further information is required.
- If the investor returns the reply slip, an executive summary of the business plan will be sent by return; however, if the investor does not wish further information, the reasons will be sought and added to the database.
- Investors who receive the business plan summary are again asked to return a reply sheet indicating their interest in the investment proposal; if they do not wish to pursue their interest, they are asked to indicate their reasons and this information is again stored on the database.
- Up to this stage the matching process has been undertaken on a no-names basis; if the investor remains interested in the investment, the bureau will introduce the two parties and will then withdraw.

Details of businesses registered with the bureau will be retained on the database for four months. At the end of this period, if a match has not been identified, the needs of the business will be reassessed in a meeting with the business development manager, and discussed particularly in the light of any responses from investors about their reasons for declining the investment opportunity.

Computer matching is relatively fast and is not constrained by publishing dates. The matching process ensures a large degree of confidentiality and, by enabling investors to target businesses meeting their investment preferences, significantly increases their interest in the service. The standard format ensures the quality of the service and makes the service cost-efficient to run.

However, while it is appropriate for computer matching to be the core component of the service, it is also necessary to devise an investment bulletin which contains very brief synopses of the businesses looking for finance as well as general articles of interest to businesses and investors. The bulletin will meet the needs of investors who have little or no restrictions on their investment criteria. In addition, once a critical mass of investors and businesses has been established, an investor club should also be established to meet the needs of those investors who would like a more personalised approach to matching. The businesses making presentations at these meetings will be selected by the business development manager on the basis of their potential.

Networking

It is vital for the bureau to obtain and maintain a high profile within its operating area. This profile is necessary not simply to make potential clients aware of the network, but also to raise general awareness and interest in investing in local businesses. The bureau should therefore build up networks with various local 'gatekeepers', such as the following:

- Banks at both local and regional levels – for example, by seminars and via enterprise agencies.
- Accountants, via the North West Society of Accountants, seminars and direct marketing.
- Solicitors, through direct marketing and via local groups.
- Chambers of commerce.
- Business clubs.
- TEC and enterprise agency board members.
- ELTEC members.
- Local business counsellors, Department of Trade and Industry counsellors, and the local society of business counsellors.
- Rotary clubs.

These networking processes should be supported by a full range of promotional literature and business development services, advertising in the local press and on local radio, and a high-profile launch event.

Management

A board of advisers should be established to oversee the operation of the network, assist in its development and help to establish the network in the local community. In order to fulfil these roles, board members should be prominent local business and professional people who can give the network credibility with investors.

Conclusion

This study has attempted to identify the nature and causes of the equity gap in one particular area of the UK. The findings have clearly established that an equity gap exists in East Lancashire, but that it has a number of components, which include not only the lack of finance normally associated with this gap, but also the shortage of information, the shortage of well-developed business plans, and ideas and the shortage of consultancy and advisory assistance. A solution to closing this more comprehensive gap has been examined in this study, with the focus on tapping the underutilised resources of informal investors through the establishment of a financial marriage bureau. The study has developed an operational model for such a service which is aimed at TECs.

In conclusion, it is important to emphasise two points. First, establishing a successful informal investor marriage bureau is a long-term project which is resource intensive, especially in its early years, and certainly prior to the establishment of a quality reputation. Some – but not all – of the costs can be recouped by offering a comprehensive fee-based service. However, tackling the investor supply shortage is the most expensive task facing a bureau, but is ultimately the smallest revenue earner. Second, an informal investor marriage bureau is only one element of the financial infrastructure of a local community. A variety of mechanisms are required to meet the financing and informational needs of businesses at various stages in their development. This can be illustrated as follows:

- Idea generation stage: the need is for creative clinics and workshops.
- Idea development stage: requires seed capital, either through specialist funds or informal investors.
- Start-up stage: requires sufficient funds to be available to allow businesses to be started, along with sufficient information and advisory services. These needs can be met through seed capital funds, informal investors and marriage bureaux.
- Development stage: needs finance to be available to meet the needs of growing firms that have exhausted the capability of internal cash generation. This is a key domain of the informal investor.
- Mid-development stage: financial needs are likely to be met by venture capital funds.
- Late development and maturity stage: financial needs are best met by a public stock market.

The implication is therefore that a marriage bureau cannot be seen in isolation from other elements in the local finance infrastructure, but must be viewed as one part of it. Tackling the problem of mobilising informal investors is one step to improving the situation of small business, but without other back-up the Department of Trade and Industry demonstration projects (see Chapter 14) will find life difficult in the longer term.

> **Implications for practice**
>
> - Local financial intermediaries believe that an equity gap exists and that potentially viable businesses are unable to raise finance.
> - Gaps in information are a major barrier for small firms seeking finance.
> - Many active business angels who have sufficient deal flow through their own personal networks will need to be convinced to join a business introduction service.
> - A locally based business introduction service needs to be larger than a single TEC area to be capable of generating a critical mass of investors and investment opportunities, but sufficiently small to allow close networking and retain regional and community identity.
> - A business introduction service should make additional business support services available to businesses seeking to join to enhance their quality.
> - Locally based business introduction services must achieve and maintain a high profile within their operational area to raise general awareness in informal venture capital and attract potential clients.

Postscript

A longer version of this chapter, which was submitted to ELTEC in August 1991, formed the basis of its bid to the Department of Employment for one of the informal investment demonstration projects (Chapter 14). This bid was successful and Investorlinks was launched in April 1992. ELTEC took the view that the demonstration project provided the opportunity to add to the range of business development services that it offers. Investorlinks is a service primarily for companies located in the ELTEC area. ELTEC has positioned Investorlinks as an integral element in its product offering, rather than as a separate, stand-alone project. By early 1995 it had recruited a total of 57 investors: 36 were currently registered and had an estimated total capital of £4 million available for investment, and a total of 90 companies had registered, most of which were established businesses seeking finance for expansion or diversification. Personal networking has proved to be the most effective method of recruiting investors; most businesses have been recruited through ELTEC activities. ELTEC has adopted a personalised and hands-on approach to matching, with the matches made on the basis of the personal knowledge of investor preferences and business characteristics and requirements. Thirty-three introductions had been made by early 1995 with five investments resulting.

Note

This chapter is based on a study undertaken on behalf of ELTEC in the summer of 1991. The work formed the basis of an MBA dissertation at Manchester Business School which was submitted in February 1992.

References

Advisory Council on Science and Technology (ACOST) (1990) *The Enterprise Challenge: Overcoming barriers to growth in small firms*, London: HMSO.

Mason, C. M. and R. T. Harrison (1991a) *Informal Investors*, CBI Smaller Firms' Economic Report, January, pp. 12–18.

Mason, C. M. and R. T. Harrison (1991b) 'A dating agency for "angels": a local approach to closing the equity gap', paper presented at the 1st Annual LEDIS Conference, Manchester Business School.

Mason, C. M. and R. T. Harrison (1992) 'The supply of equity finance in the UK: a strategy for closing the equity gap', *Entrepreneurship and Regional Development*, **4**, pp. 357–80.

Mason, C. M., R. T. Harrison and J. Chaloner (1991) *The Operation and Effectiveness of LINC. Part 2: Survey of Investors*, Southampton: Urban Policy Research Unit, University of Southampton.

McMeekin, D. (1991) 'Finance for enterprise: closing the equity gap', paper presented at the 14th Small Firms Policy and Research Conference, Lancashire Enterprise Ltd/Manchester Business School.

West Midlands Enterprise Board (Consultancy Services) Ltd (1988) *The Nature, Implications and Mitigation of the Equity Gap in Leicestershire*, Birmingham: West Midlands Enterprise Board.

Wetzel, W. E. Jr (1981) 'Informal risk capital in New England', in K. H. Vesper (ed.), *Frontiers of Entrepreneurship Research 1981*, Wellesley, MA: Babson College, pp. 217–45.

CHAPTER 14

The Department of Trade and Industry's informal investment demonstration projects: an interim assessment

Colin M. Mason and Richard T. Harrison

Introduction

In the UK, interest in the role and potential of the informal venture capital market has increased steadily since about 1990 as a result of two parallel developments. It is, first of all, a function of the growing concern about the decline in the supply of both loan finance and institutional sources of venture capital. Fears of a 'credit crunch' have been raised by the much more cautious attitude that the banks have adopted towards small business lending following the significant loan losses on their property and small business portfolios as they attempt to improve their capital/asset ratios. Banks are requiring firms to provide greater security and have more equity, and are giving more explicit recognition to risk in the pricing of loans. Indeed, as recent research has suggested (Vyakarnam and Jacobs, 1991), business size and the associated perception of security is an important determinant of bank attitudes in its own right, with bank managers regarding the bigger businesses as better than the smaller businesses.

A recent report by the Forum of Private Business (1992) has also identified problems in the small business–bank relationship concerning bank charges, interest rates and collateral, which represent real constraints on the ability of small firms to survive and grow. In all three categories, the smallest firms feel the constraints most keenly: they face higher interest rates on both loans and overdrafts, and are required to provide significantly higher levels of personal security. This suggests that the key issue is not whether banks have the funds available to finance small business development in the recovery, but whether such firms are in a position to meet the terms on which it would be provided when declining domestic and property values have reduced their borrowing capacity.

There has also been a decline in the availability of venture capital from institutional sources. Funds have moved even further away from making smaller investments in early stage ventures in favour of management buyouts (Mason

248

and Harrison, 1992), and have encountered difficulties in raising new finance from financial institutions (Murray, 1990).

The second factor that has generated interest in the informal venture capital market in the UK is the growing recognition of its role and potential in filling the small firm finance gap. The first UK study to draw attention to the importance of the informal venture capital market was the Advisory Committee on Science and Technology's (ACOST) report on *The Enterprise Challenge*, published in 1990. At about the same time, the major role played by the informal venture capital market in the USA in meeting the financing needs of smaller companies was highlighted by both academics and journalists (Mason and Harrison, 1990, 1993; Batchelor, 1990; Durr, 1991), and preliminary research findings (subsequently published in Mason *et al.*, 1991), disseminated through the media (e.g. Batchelor, 1991a; 1991b; Woodcock, 1991), highlighted the existence of a substantial informal venture capital market in the UK. It was also recognised that small businesses derive significant non-financial benefits from raising informal venture capital as a result of the hands-on characteristics of most informal investors (see Harrison and Mason, 1992).

Against this background, in October 1990 Eric Forth MP, the then Parliamentary Under-Secretary of State at the Department of Employment and Small Firms Minister, suggested as a 'very tentative idea' that the government might back the creation of a marriage-broking service for investors and entrepreneurs (*Financial Times*, 23 October 1990) in an attempt to stimulate informal investment in small businesses. Following his visit to the USA in the spring of 1991, where he examined some match-making organisations in detail, his department announced that it would provide pump-priming finance to stimulate a small number of locally or regionally based informal investment projects. The objective of the initiative was to test the proposition that bringing together informal investors and small businesses seeking finance by means of a business introduction service does satisfy a genuine market need, and offers a potentially worthwhile way of channelling new resources into the small firm sector. Although there were some existing networks and services which sought to fulfil this role, notably VCR (Venture Capital Report) (Chapter 8) and LINC (Local Investment Networking Company) (Chapter 7), it was recognised that their efforts had been handicapped by a lack of funding, making it difficult to assess adequately the impact and potential of these services as a mechanism for closing the equity gap. By funding these demonstration projects, the government's intention was to remove this constraint in order to test the proposition that properly funded business introduction services can be effective.

The government saw the Training and Enterprise Councils (TECs) – as key players in the local enterprise scene – playing a major role in creating further services of this type. However, the expectation was that in most cases the TECs would use other local organisations to deliver the service. Bids were therefore invited from the TECs in England and Wales to operate a small number of pilot business introduction services in partnership with other local organisations. Each demonstration project would receive funding of £20,000 per annum for two years to assist with start-up and administration costs. It was expected that this would be matched with a similar contribution (in cash or kind, or a combination of the two) from the TEC and/or its partner organisation(s). In early 1992 the Department of Trade and Industry, which had taken over responsibility for the initiative from the Employment Department, announced that five TECs had been selected from the 19 bids that had been received to run the demonstration projects: Bedfordshire, Calderdale and Kirklees, Devon and Cornwall, East Lancashire, and South and East Cheshire (Table 14.1). In mid-1993, following a favourable interim assessment, the DTI decided to allow each of the projects to bid for a third year of funding.

Each of the projects started at a different point on the learning curve. Trevint and Cheshire County Council had the most experience of small business financing issues. Trevint – the trading arm of Cornwall Council – manages a small investment fund and so was familiar with many of the issues involved in investment appraisal. Having identified local interest in informal venture capital, it proceeded to undertake some *ad hoc* matching. Some of these investments were made alongside its fund investments. Cheshire County Council's experience was derived from publishing *Cheshire Contacts* for many years. This is a business opportunities newsletter which includes, among other things, listings of businesses seeking finance and investors seeking investment opportunities. Resource constraints within the County Council had prevented a more intensive match-making service from being established. Discussions with South and East Cheshire TEC concerning the scope for collaboration were under way when the opportunity to tender arose.

In contrast, the East Lancashire Training and Enterprise Council (ELTEC) had no practical experience of informal venture capital. However, it had

Table 14.1 The five informal investment demonstration projects

TEC	Partner(s)	Proposed area of operation
East Lancashire (ELTEC)	–	East Lancashire (but will seek co-operation with TECs in adjacent areas)
Calderdale and Kirklees	Calderdale Business Advice Centre; Calderdale Partnership	Calderdale in West Yorkshire (but intends to extend operations to Kirklees at an early stage)
Bedfordshire	Grant Thornton	Bedfordshire (but possible future collaboration with neighbouring TECs)
Devon and Cornwall	Trevint (Cornwall Enterprise Board)	Devon and Cornwall
South and East Cheshire	Cheshire County Council; NORMID TEC; CEWTEC	Cheshire and the Wirral

commissioned an independent research survey on the role and potential of informal investment activity in the East Lancashire area (Chapter 13). Although no action was taken because of cost considerations, this exercise had given the TEC considerable understanding of the issues involved and provided the basis of their tender submission. Bedfordshire was nearer to the beginning of the learning curve. However, the partner in Grant Thornton who was involved with the service had been on secondment to a venture capital firm, and this was thought to represent valuable expertise. Calderdale and Kirklees had no prior experience of informal or formal venture capital, and so was close to the bottom of the learning curve.

Interim assessment

The interim review had five main objectives:

- To review the progress made by each of the projects.
- To make an initial assessment of the current and prospective value for money offered by the projects.
- To provide details of promotional activities undertaken by the projects.
- To provide details of the charging policies and fee structures which have been established to assist with the running costs of the projects.
- To examine outcomes in terms of the number of investors registered and the amount of finance that they have available for investment, the number of small businesses seeking investment, the number of introductions made, and the number of 'marriages' which have resulted from introductions.

The assessment was guided by two major principles. First, it was felt appropriate that in an interim evaluation the main emphasis should be devoted to operational considerations. While this was not intended to play down the importance of the outcomes of each project, it was considered premature to devote too much attention to this issue at this stage. In any case, most of the projects had only been operating for a few months (maximum of eight months) at the time of the review, and one had not even had its formal launch. An evaluation of outcomes was felt to be more appropriate for the final evaluation of the initiative.

Second, these projects were designed as experiments. A major consideration of the initiative was to select projects that provided a variety of models and approaches, and different types of partnership. The aim was to gain an understanding of which approaches work and which do not. Thus, the view was taken that the evaluation should adopt a non-judgemental approach, exploring what has been learned by each of the TECs, bearing in mind that each TEC was starting from a different level of knowledge and experience.

The evaluation was based on a visit to each demonstration project. Each visit included extended meetings with the TEC staff involved in running the service and, where appropriate, with staff in their partner organisations. Each TEC was also requested to provide appropriate documentary material on its activities.

Organisational characteristics

Format

The demonstration projects have a variety of formats. Four 'models' can be identified:

- In two cases the day-to-day operations have been devolved by the TEC to freestanding not-for-profit organisations. The Devon and Cornwall Business Angels Programme is operated by Trevint Ltd, the trading arm of Cornwall County Council, while IRIS, the Calderdale and Kirklees project, is managed by the Calderdale Business Advice Centre, a local enterprise agency. In both cases, the initiative to prepare a tender was taken by the partner organisation.
- One project involves a partnership with the private sector. The Bedfordshire Investment Exchange is managed by the TEC in partnership with the local office of chartered accountants Grant Thornton. The role of Grant Thornton is to assess applications from companies, to assist them in preparing a business plan and using information supplied by the companies, to prepare material for circulation to investors.
- TEChINVEST is managed by South and East Cheshire TEC, but involves collaboration with Cheshire County Council's Economic Development Service and two neighbouring TECs, whose operational areas cover the rest of Cheshire and the Wirral. TEChINVEST has also established partnership arrangements with VCR and LINC, enabling its entrepreneurs to reach far more investors than can be found in Cheshire alone, and providing its investors with a larger number of projects than are available locally.
- East Lancashire's Capital Connections (originally named Investorlinks) project is run totally within the TEC. No external organisations are involved. Indeed, Investorlinks is seen as an integral part of the TEC's product range, rather than as a separate project with its own brand name.

There is no doubt that the DTI initiative has played the role of catalyst in the launch of each of these demonstration projects. Four of the TECs or their partners had investigated the possibility of establishing a business introduction service, but in each case they had been deterred by the costs of operating such a service. It is therefore probable that none of the pilot projects would have got off the ground without the pump-priming funds provided by the initiative.

Operational area

The operational area for four of the five projects corresponds to that of the sponsoring TEC. Two projects – the Devon and Cornwall Business Angels Programme and TEChINVEST, which involves a partnership between South and East Cheshire TEC and two neighbouring TECs covering other parts of Cheshire and the Wirral – therefore operate at larger than the county scale. One project, Bedfordshire, operates at the county scale. Two projects – IRIS and Capital Connections – operate at below the county scale. Each of the projects is reluctant to accept businesses that are located outside its operating area because they see their role as serving local businesses. However, each project is willing to accept investors from any location.

In our view the present geographical scale of these projects is too small and limits the number of businesses and investors that can be recruited. One consequence is that it prevents the use of more sophisticated computer matching approaches, which are inappropriate until upwards of 100 investors and businesses are recruited. Larger numbers of clients also bring economies of scale in administration and reduce the gap between operating costs and fee income. These considerations have encouraged each of the projects to explore the possibility of collaborating with neighbouring TECs in order to expand the geographical scale of operations of the projects.

However, a larger operating area brings a different set of problems. First, investors may dismiss some of the investment opportunities that they receive on the grounds that they are located too far away. Second, it may be difficult to serve all parts of a large operating area adequately. A decentralised operating structure may overcome this difficulty, although there are potential problems if this necessitates the use of two or more independent organisations to deliver the service. Nevertheless, TEChINVEST demonstrates that it is possible for separate organisations to collaborate successfully in order to enable a business introduction service to serve a larger geographical area.

An alternative means of overcoming the limitations of a small operating area is to link up with a national business introduction service such as VCR or LINC, to provide businesses with a larger investor population and investors with a wider range of investment opportunities. VCR has been very keen to encourage such an arrangement (Chapter 8). Although most of the projects have considered such collaborative arrangements, TEChINVEST is the only project to have established formal links with VCR and LINC (although very recently a similar co-operative arrangement has been established between the Devon and Cornwall Business Angels Scheme and VCR). Businesses which register with TEChINVEST have the option, on payment of a higher fee, to have an article published in *Venture Capital Report* and their details listed in the LINC *Investment Bulletin*. Similarly, TEChINVEST's investors can select a membership option which includes subscription to VCR and membership of LINC, which enables them to receive a larger number of projects than are available in Cheshire alone.

Staffing

Each of the projects has a part-time project manager who is on the staff of either the TEC or its partner organisation, and 'field workers' who undertake business appraisals, counselling of businesses seeking to register with the service, preparation of business plan summaries of those businesses that do register for circulation to investors, and follow-up liaison with businesses and investors. In each case the staff who undertake the business counselling function do this as part of a wider job function which involves business counselling/advising either for the TEC or for its partner organisation. Administrative input is absorbed by the organisation that is managing the project.

Sources of finance

One of the requirements was that the projects should match the DTI's financial contribution with equivalent funding from other sources. Four of the five projects have been successful in raising additional finance. In aggregate, the pilot projects have almost matched the DTI contribution in terms of *cash* contributions (including fee income), raising £95 for every £100 of DTI money. However, a complete estimate of the value of the inputs from other sources must also take into account in-kind contributions. Although it is difficult to cost in-kind contributions accurately, we have conservatively estimated that their value is in the order of £40,000 to £50,000. Thus, taking both cash and in-kind contributions into account, the projects have raised approximately £140 for every £100 that the DTI has contributed. Moreover, it should be emphasised that fee income will increase over time as the projects expand their client base, thereby increasing the leverage even further. These contributions in cash and kind have been raised primarily from the TECs and, to a lesser extent, their partner organisations: the Bedfordshire Investment Exchange is the only project to have raised finance from private sector sponsors.

Fees

The five projects have adopted very different approaches to charging for the business introduction service (Table 14.2). Three of the projects charge registration fees to investors and businesses. The rationale is the same in each case: not only do fees provide an income stream, but they also serve as a useful filter to deter non-serious clients.

TEChINVEST has the highest charges. Investors pay between £100 and £400 depending upon which services they require. Businesses pay a registration fee, as a contribution towards the costs of preparing the investment proposal and circulating this to investors registered with its various networks, and a success fee payable when an investment is made. TEChINVEST is also the only project to adopt a differential pricing structure: corporate investors are charged between £25 and £75 more than private investors, depending upon which service they require, while businesses based outside Cheshire and the Wirral also pay higher registration and success fees. Devon and Cornwall has adopted a fee of £75 for investors and a fee of £250 for businesses (£50 for initial appraisal and £200 to

Table 14.2 Fees charged by the demonstration projects (VAT not included)

	Investors	Business	Success fees
Devon and Cornwall	£75	£50 + £200[a]	No[b]
Bedfordshire	£50	£50	No
TEChINVEST	£100–£400[c]	£200[d]	Yes[d]
Capital Connections	No charge	No charge	No
IRIS	£50[e]	No charge	No

[a] The fee of £50 is charged on all businesses wishing to join the service, to cover the cost of a business counsellor visiting the company to assess its suitability. Businesses which are considered suitable are charged a further fee of £200.
[b] A success fee is being considered.
[c] The fee varies according to whether the investor only joins TEChINVEST (£100) or also takes a subscription to LINC (£150), VCR (£350) or both (£400). Fees for corporate investors are higher.
[d] Companies outside Cheshire and the Wirral are charged a higher fee.
[e] Fee is waived for the first year of registration.

prepare and circulate their details to investors). It did consider adopting a success fee, but found investor resistance to this method of charging. Bedfordshire's fee structure is £50 for both investors and businesses. The two remaining projects do not charge a registration fee. Capital Connections has made the decision not to levy any charge on investors and businesses at this stage, in order to stimulate interest in the service. For similar reasons, IRIS does not charge businesses a registration fee and charges investors only if they wish to register for a second year.

It is interesting to note that the two projects which have waived fees in a deliberate attempt to attract clients have the smallest numbers of clients (see Table 14.4), whereas the relatively high fees charged by Devon and Cornwall and TEChINVEST have not deterred interest among investors or businesses. This inverse relationship between fee structure and level of interest would suggest that offering the service at no charge is not an effective method of building a client base. Indeed, it can be suggested that not charging a fee will actually result in a loss of clients in the longer term because the lack of fee income will affect the quality of the service, primarily by limiting the expenditure on marketing to expand the client base, which will, in turn, reduce its attractiveness to both investors and businesses.

Marketing strategies

The marketing of a business introduction service is critical to its success. There is sufficient evidence both from established business introduction services in the UK and overseas and from the five demonstration projects to conclude that there is a close relationship between marketing effort and size of client base.

There are two contrasting philosophies to the marketing of business introduction services. The 'mainstream' view states that, because of the hit-or-miss nature of matching investor preferences to business characteristics, it is necessary for business introduction services to maximise the number of businesses and investors which register with the service. This will maximise the chances that compatible investors and entrepreneurs will be included in the service. It therefore follows that marketing is high profile. The contrary view argues that the 'informal' in informal venture capital, with its connotations of low key, trust, confidentiality and so on, represents its key attraction, particularly to investors. This gives rise to the concern that these intrinsic advantages will be lost by high-profile marketing.

The marketing of a business introduction service must take account of the nature of the 'product'. A business introduction service is a 'low-perception product', thus the concept needs to be actively marketed to attract investors and businesses. However, a business introduction service is also a 'high-sophistication product', which means that only certain kinds of marketing strategy are appropriate. These characteristics have implications for the marketing strategy that is used to promote business introduction services. First, they need to be promoted initially by a high-profile launch event and then with on-going, targeted marketing to reinforce the message. Second, mailshots are likely to be ineffective in promoting the service, as they are inappropriate for a low-perception, high-sophistication product.

A wide variety of marketing activities have been used by the projects to attract investors and businesses to the services (Table 14.3), with each project using a different combination of strategies. Three projects organised high-profile launch events, targeted at potential investors and businesses in the case of Devon and Cornwall and TEChINVEST, and at professional intermediaries in the case of

Table 14.3 Marketing strategies used by the demonstration projects

	Devon and Cornwall	Bedford-shire	TEChINVEST	Capital Connections	IRIS
Leaflet		★	★	★	
Brochures/information pack	★		★		★
Launch event	★		★		★
TEC literature, seminars, etc.	★	★		★	
TEC business counsellors	★	★	★	★	★
Seminars	★		★		
Press releases/press and media coverage	★	★	★	★	★
Speaking engagements	★	★	★		
Press advertisings				★	
Mailshot	★	★	★	★	★
Presentations to professional intermediaries	★		★		★

IRIS. In contrast, both ELTEC and Bedfordshire adopted fairly low-key approaches. The Bedfordshire project did have a launch, but only as part of a business exhibition jointly organised by the County Council's economic development unit and the TEC. A major launch event is undoubtedly a very effective means of promoting awareness of a business introduction service, both directly and also indirectly through the press coverage that it attracts. For example, the three events that Devon and Cornwall hosted in different locations attracted a total of 500 people, and over 40 per cent of its investors became aware of the Business Angels Programme as a result of pre- and post-event publicity.

All of the projects have used mailshots to market the service. Devon and Cornwall undertook a mailshot of 10,000 'wealthy individuals' using rented mailing lists, both to invite people to the launch event and more generally to promote the service. Bedfordshire's approach was somewhat different: instead of renting mailing lists, it sought to mailshot wealthy individuals via professional intermediaries. However, this approach was not particularly successful on account of the reluctance of the majority of these intermediaries to co-operate, even though their costs would be reimbursed. Both ELTEC and IRIS have undertaken mailshots of local professional intermediaries. TEChINVEST used the mailing lists of *Cheshire Contacts*, LINC and VCR to promote its launch event.

All of the projects have obtained media coverage, some of it unsolicited and some achieved through press releases. The amount of media coverage has varied between projects, with Devon and Cornwall being the most successful in this respect. Two factors can help to explain this. First, it is a function of the nature and range of media in each area. Devon and Cornwall is a media-rich region, with a morning regional daily newspaper and regional BBC and ITV stations, as well as local newspapers and radio stations. Nevertheless, it is important to stress that the media's appetite for press releases on business introduction services is not infinite, even in regions with a range of media. Indeed, the Devon and Cornwall Business Angels Programme has found it harder to obtain press coverage over time. Second, as the project with the most matches, Devon and Cornwall has had the greatest scope for newsworthy press releases.

All of the projects have sought referrals from professional intermediaries (e.g. banks and accountants) by means of mailshots, presentations, seminars and informal face-to-face contacts. However, it appears that many of these intermediaries have been lukewarm about promoting the service to their clients, and so in most cases they have not been a particularly productive source of referrals. Moreover, the investment proposals that have been referred by these sources have often been of low quality.

Finally, all of the projects have utilised TEC-based channels of communication to promote their service. These include TEC publications and other publicity, and TEC staff involved in delivering other business programmes (notably business counsellors). Here again, the number of referrals from this source has often been lower than anticipated. One reason may be that many of the businesses that come into contact with the TECs – for example, on courses or through counselling – are inappropriate for referral to business introduction services on account of their small size, their 'lifestyle' orientation or because they are in financial difficulties. However, this cannot be a complete explanation because TECs also provide services that are targeted at growth-oriented businesses.

These marketing strategies have been supported by promotional literature. Devon and Cornwall, IRIS and TEChINVEST have each produced high-quality information packs containing brochures, registration forms, etc. The two other projects have relied on leaflets to promote the service.

Client base

The short time period in which the projects have been operating (less than six months in all but one case) must be borne in mind when considering the number of clients that they have recruited. The five projects had a total of 85 registered investors by January 1993, almost all of whom had joined in a personal capacity. The Devon and Cornwall Business Angels Programme, which has been active since April 1992, accounted for 40 per cent of this total, with 34 registered investors. The other projects, which had all been operating for a shorter time period (and in the case of TEChINVEST had not had its formal launch), had between 11 and 18 registered investors each (Table 14.4). The majority of investors were recruited within a few months of the launch, with enquiries declining quite sharply thereafter. This reflects the high level of marketing effort at the launch of the projects and the subsequent decline in promotional activities over time. The obvious implication is that efforts to promote business introduction services need to be on-going.

Registered investors had an estimated £13.4 million available for investment (£7 million of which was accounted for by just two investors). When compared with the amount of venture capital available from alternative sources (e.g. regionally based funds, public sector funds, Midland Bank Enterprise Funds), the amount of finance that has been mobilised by the projects is very considerable, particularly when the short period in which they have been operating is taken into account. What is not known is how liquid these funds are: however, information collected by Devon and Cornwall suggests that some investors will require to sell assets before they can make any investments.

It is impossible to assess how much of this money has become available directly as a result of the projects. The existence of the projects may have encouraged some business angels to make available a larger sum for informal investments than they would otherwise have committed because they expect to find more investment opportunities. For the same reasons the projects may have encouraged other individuals to become business angels. Indeed, a significant number of the investors who have registered with the projects are 'virgin' angels. Even if the conservative assumption is made that the projects have not influenced the amounts of money available for informal investment, they have nevertheless succeeded in making it much more visible and accessible for small businesses.

Table 14.4 Number of investors and businesses registered with the projects at
January 1993 and the amounts available for investment

	Investors registered	Amount available for investment	Total number of business registered (no. currently registered)
Devon and Cornwall	34	£2.4m[a]	32 (23)
Bedfordshire	10	£5.5m[b]	14 (11)
TEChINVEST[c]	11	£1.7m	11
Capital Connections	18	£2.5m[d]	21
IRIS	12	£1.3m[a]	23

[a] Estimated amount.
[b] Estimated amount; includes one investor who has £5 million available.
[c] These figures are prior to the launch event in February 1993.
[d] Includes one investor with £2 million available.

Interest in the projects is greater than the number of registered investors
implies. In each case considerable numbers of individuals have expressed an
interest in the service, yet relatively few have actually signed up. This is best
documented in the case of Devon and Cornwall, where 150 people expressed an
interest in joining but only about one-fifth of this total signed up. An urgent
research priority is therefore to understand the reasons why many potential
investors do not follow through their initial interest by registering so that
strategies can be devised to achieve a higher conversion rate.

Each of the projects has collected some personal information and details of
investment preferences from the registration forms that their investors were
required to complete on joining the service.

It is clear from this information that the investors who have registered with
the five projects exhibit similar characteristics to those identified in the national
studies of informal investors (Mason *et al.*, 1991). They are almost exclusively
male and have a business background which in many cases includes entrepreneurial experience. Indeed, some of the investors have recently sold businesses and
are looking to reinvest some of the proceeds in another venture. Investors include
both experienced angels and also 'virgin' angels, with the latter group probably
in a majority. The amount that investors are willing to commit to a single
investment ranges from less than £10,000 to over £100,000, although the majority
of investors are seeking investments of less than £50,000. Their sectoral and stage
of business preferences are very wide. Most are looking for a hands-on involvement. Some investors are seeking a full-time role. They tend to be managers who
have received a redundancy payment and are looking to use their investment as
a means to 'buy themselves a job'. There must be some concern that such individuals will not be value-added investors. While most of the investors registered
with the Devon and Cornwall Business Angels Programme are local, the other
projects have attracted a significant minority of non-local investors.

The caveat concerning the short time period in which the projects have been operating also applies to the number of business clients that have been recruited. A total of 101 businesses have registered with the five projects, of which 12 are no longer registered, in most cases because they have successfully raised finance either through introductions provided by the service or from other sources. The number of businesses registered with each project ranges from 11 to 32 (Table 14.4).

All of the projects have filtered the businesses wishing to register on two main criteria: (1) their suitability for equity investment, and (2) the presence of a suitable business plan. Hence, here again the number of businesses that have actually registered considerably understates the level of interest in the projects. A considerable number of businesses – exceeding 100 in some cases – have enquired about registering with the projects, but have been advised either that they are inappropriate or that further preparation of their business plan is required.

The types of business registering with the projects are varied in terms of stage of development and sector, although manufacturing firms are overrepresented when compared with their significance nationally. No attempt was made to assess formally the quality of the businesses that have registered with each of the projects. However, it is clear from a subjective review of the businesses that have registered that there is considerable variation between the projects. Two projects appear to have attracted a significant number of relatively low-quality businesses. This appears to be associated, at least in part, with the higher proportion of businesses that have been referred to these projects by banks, accountants and business advice centres and, in turn, points to the need for more proactive marketing in order to recruit better-quality businesses.

Matching processes

Four of the projects have sought to introduce investors to businesses and vice versa by means of the circulation of summary information on businesses seeking finance, either as separate documents or in the form of a newsletter, combined with more personalised matching undertaken by the project staff, acting as an 'honest broker', on the basis of their detailed knowledge of the businesses and the investment preferences of investors. ELTEC is the exception. To date it has relied exclusively on hands-on matching by the staff involved in Investorlinks, who have a detailed knowledge of the companies and investors registered with the scheme. TEChINVEST's matching process is the most extensive: company profiles are featured in the LINC newsletter, *Venture Capital Report* and *Cheshire Contacts* as well as included in TEChINVEST's own newsletter, which is circulated to all its registered investors. In addition, it hosts investor forums at which selected business owners can make presentations to an audience of potential investors. Devon and Cornwall has attempted to run investors' forums, but has found difficulties in attracting a sufficiently large audience to make this feasible on account of the lack of a critical mass of investors in any location within their operating area.

Three of the projects – Devon and Cornwall, Bedfordshire and TEChINVEST – have purchased custom-designed computer software to enable them to undertake computer matching, whereby the investment preferences of investors can be taken into account when circulating details of investment opportunities. However, none of the projects has sufficient numbers of investors or businesses to make computer matching appropriate at the present time.

Outcomes

The mission of business introduction services is to provide introductions. They do not get involved in the negotiations between investor and business, and indeed are legally precluded from doing so (Chapter 12). It is therefore inappropriate to assess their performance in terms of investments made. The basis for evaluating the performance of business introduction services should be in terms of the following three measures:

- The number of businesses and investors registered, and the amounts of finance that investors have available for investment.
- The number of introductions that result.
- The proportion of businesses and investors that have received introductions.

Of course, the ultimate objective of business introduction services is to enable businesses to raise finance. However, they have no control over the outcome of the introductions that they facilitate. Nevertheless, business introduction services can enhance the likelihood that introductions will lead to matches in various ways: notably, by strategies to attract quality investment opportunities, through their role as an 'honest broker' and by means of training workshops.

The projects have had limited success to date in achieving introductions and investments. In total, the projects have recorded just 38 introductions and 12 investments. Moreover, the Devon and Cornwall Business Angels Programme is responsible for a significant majority of these introductions and investments (Table 14.5). However, the limited operating period must again be remembered (indeed, TEChINVEST was only launched in February 1993). An interesting and unanticipated feature is that two matches have involved non-equity investments by other companies.

One of the most important conclusions from our review of the demonstration projects is that the economic impact of business introduction services extends beyond introductions and matches. Thus, the evaluation of business introduction services must seek to measure their overall value-added impact. This has a number of elements.

First, business introduction services have a much wider impact than simply facilitating introductions. They provide firms with *business advice and counselling*.

Table 14.5 Introductions and investments resulting from the demonstration projects[a]

	Number of introductions	% of clients receiving introductions		Number of investments	Amount invested (£)
		Investors	Businesses		
Devon and Cornwall	30	41	50	8	300,000
Capital Connections	4	22	19	3[b]	–
Bedfordshire	2	20	14	0	–
IRIS	2	17	6	1[c]	n.a.

[a] TEChINVEST is not included in this table as it had not been formally launched at the time of the survey.

[b] One firm raised an investment from a private investor and another attracted an investment from a company (in neither case were the amounts specified). The third deal was a non-equity arrangement in which the firm obtained expertise from another company.

[c] This was a non-equity investment: support and expertise have been provided by another firm.

A firm which contacts a business introduction service will initially receive some business counselling from the service's business advisers, who will assess the firm's business plan and general suitability for equity finance. Where appropriate, the firm may be assisted in preparing its business plan. A business introduction service also acts as a *signposting service*. Any firm which is considered inappropriate for equity finance, or not yet ready to raise external finance, will be directed to providers of advice, consultancy, training and other business support services.

Second, most informal investors are hands-on investors. Thus, businesses which are successful in raising finance from investors to whom they have been introduced through a business introduction service also benefit from a range of other inputs, including know-how, contacts, advice, trouble-shooting and consultancy. Benefits also arise for businesses which are introduced to investors who subsequently decide not to invest. These businesses benefit from feedback either directly from the investor or indirectly via the business introduction service. All of the projects explicitly provide such feedback to businesses.

Third, measuring the amount of finance that business introduction services have enabled firms to raise must also take into account the full range of secondary effects. In some circumstances, raising finance from a business angel will enable a firm to raise further finance from other investors or from their bank. For example, investors registered with the Devon and Cornwall Business Angels Programme have invested a total of £300,000 in eight businesses. However, on the strength of these investments the businesses have raised a total of £430,000 – a significant leverage.

Issues arising

This interim review of the demonstration projects has identified a number of key issues that are of relevance for their future development, but which also have more general relevance in the establishment and operation of business introduction services. These issues are considered in the remainder of this chapter.

Marketing issues

Based on their experience to date, the five demonstration projects have found the recruitment of investors to be much less of a challenge than attracting quality businesses. As a consequence, the marketing effort is being concentrated on identifying and attracting business clients. This seems appropriate as a short-term tactic. However, it should not be assumed that all of the investors that have registered with the services are equally active and interested in making investments, or that they have liquid funds. None of the projects has any objective measure of the commitment and seriousness of its registered investors (although the information collected by the Devon and Cornwall Business Angels Programme suggests that by no means all investors are in a position to react quickly to investment opportunities). Moreover, none of the projects has a sufficiently large or diverse panel of investors to ensure the possibility of matches with investment opportunities. Thus, in the longer term it is essential for each of the projects to give renewed and equal effort to marketing the service at investors because a mature business introduction service will require a sufficiently broad spread of investment preferences to maximise the chance of matches.

Quite correctly, the projects are seeking to generate increased demand for the service from quality businesses in order to improve the quality of their investment opportunities. The businesses that have approached each of the services have generally been of low quality and their business plans have been poor. It is clear that investors will not renew their subscriptions if they receive a constant flow of poor-quality investment proposals; nor will they be willing, under such circumstances, to recommend the service to their friends and business associates.

Recruitment of better-quality investment opportunities can be achieved by means of three related strategies. First, a business introduction service must filter investment opportunities. Many businesses which approach the service will not be appropriate for informal venture capital but they may have other support requirement needs. Businesses which are judged to be inappropriate, or not yet ready, for equity investment should be directed towards more appropriate business support services. Indeed, TEChINVEST currently puts forward to investors only one in every 12 businesses that approach the service.

Second, a business introduction service must give assistance to companies that it puts forward to investors: for example, by helping in preparing the information that is provided to potential investors, and coaching entrepreneurs who are to make presentations to investor forums. In order to perform both functions, it is clearly necessary for the business introduction service to work closely with companies, although the amount of 'handholding' that is given to businesses will inevitably vary according to the capabilities of organisations managing the service.

Third, growth-potential companies in the operating area of the service must be identified and targeted for the service. One way in which this can be achieved is by exploiting the TEC's own business support services to generate quality investment opportunities through programmes that are oriented towards 'fast-track' businesses: with appropriate training and counselling these businesses may be appropriate for referral to a business introduction service. For example, informal venture capital can be presented as part of a training package for growth-oriented businesses.

Another potential source of investment opportunities with growth potential is businesses which have been rejected by venture capital funds. Such businesses are often of good quality, but simply do not meet the fund's investment criteria in terms of amount sought, stage of development or sector. A further advantage of such businesses is that they are likely to have a business plan already and, having made the decision to sell equity, the owner-manager(s) will possess the appropriate psychological disposition. Business introduction services should therefore seek to establish long-term links with venture capital funds: this is desirable not only in order to get venture capital funds to pass on deals that do not meet their investment criteria, thereby improving the business introduction service's flow of quality investment proposals, but also as a source of second-round finance for businesses that outgrow the financial capabilities of their business angel investors.

Financing issues

There is general agreement that a business introduction service cannot meet all of its running costs from fee income alone. At present, the projects are, with the exception of the Bedfordshire Investment Exchange, entirely reliant on DTI and TEC funding to cover the gap between fee income and total running costs. Two questions therefore arise. First, how can fee income be maximised without deterring clients? Second, how likely is it that sponsorship can be obtained from the private sector to fill the gap between fee income and running costs, and, if so, what is the best strategy for raising such funds?

Fee structure

Charging a fee to investors and businesses is desirable on three grounds: first, it creates credibility for the service; second, participants will value the service and so put in the effort to maximise their benefit from it; and third, it reduces the amount of finance that must be raised through sponsorship or from the public sector.

Nevertheless, there are some reservations about charging fees. First, the experience of the five projects indicates that the income generated from fees is marginal to the finances of a business introduction service. However, this is likely to be only a temporary phenomenon: fee income is likely to increase as the services expand their client base.

A second reservation concerns the effectiveness of fees as a filter. It can be argued that more effective non-monetary filters could be employed. In particular, the use of rigorous quality control procedures for businesses seeking to register is likely to be a better approach.

A much more fundamental reservation is that to charge a fee goes against the free service culture of many public service organisations. Moreover, any fee would have to be compatible with the policies of TECs towards charging for their business development and advice services.

A final reservation concerns whether investors and, in particular, businesses feel that they get value for money from a fee. It is difficult to assemble supporting evidence for this reservation in view of the considerable advice and counselling which businesses receive when they join a service over and above circulating their details to prospective investors. Indeed, TEChINVEST argues that the help and advice which its business clients receive in either bringing them to the necessary standard to be presented to investors or, alternatively, referring them to more appropriate TEC programmes is well worth the fee. Furthermore, the concern that good-quality companies may be deterred by a fee can be removed if fees are administered flexibly. There is also no evidence that fees deter serious investors.

The merit of a success fee approach to income generation remains unresolved. There is little support for a success fee among the TEC projects except where there is a need to achieve financial self-sufficiency, or where links with other introduction services (e.g. *Venture Capital Report*) require it. It can be argued that a success fee sends out the wrong signals and is unlikely to be acceptable to potential clients, at least before a service develops a track record of successful matches. There are also practical problems in operating a success fee system. Because the deal is done by other people, it is necessary to devote considerable resources to following up the outcomes of introductions in order to find out whether investments have occurred. Further potential problems arise in valuing the investment and in extracting the fee. However, these problems can be minimised by the development of a close relationship between the staff of the business introduction service and the businesses that register with the service. Thus, there is a need to expand our knowledge base in order to reach a conclusion regarding the merits or otherwise of success fees. Specifically, we require the answers to the following questions. First, do success fees deter investors and businesses, as some anecdotal evidence suggests? Second, what proportion of fee income is derived from success fees? Third, are there any difficulties obtaining success fees from companies that have raised finance through introductions?

Fourth, how much time elapses following registration before there is an income stream from success fees?

Corporate sponsorship

There are contrasting views about the willingness of the corporate sector to sponsor business introduction services. On the one hand, it can be argued that a combination of recession and 'compassion fatigue' have encouraged potential sponsors to reduce their community involvement budgets. Furthermore, most sponsorship income is likely to be a one-off donation, so that the same sponsors could not be approached year after year. The implication is that reliance on sponsorship to finance a business introduction service will result in a precarious hand-to-mouth existence, with the energies of the management diverted to on-going fundraising rather than operating the service. In short, a convincing case can be made for suggesting that reliance on sponsorship does not provide a firm long-term basis for operating a business introduction service.

The contrary view is that large privatised utilities (e.g. telephone, electricity, gas, water) are willing to sponsor local economic development initiatives if approached through the 'commercial' rather than the 'charity' route. Such companies are concerned to demonstrate that they are contributing to the community. Furthermore, the profits of these businesses are linked to the health of the local business community.

Bedfordshire TEC's experience indicates that it is possible to raise sponsorship income. However, this was very much due to the efforts of a particular individual who is a partner in an accountancy practice and sits on the TEC board. As well as contributing from his own firm, he also utilised his business contacts to secure contributions from other financial companies. Bedfordshire's success in raising sponsorship income may therefore be of only limited relevance to the other projects.

It therefore seems unlikely that the financial needs of business introduction services will be met by corporate sponsorship. Moreover, it can be argued that it is undesirable for a business introduction service to be dependent upon corporate sponsorship because of the danger that this might be perceived as compromising the impartiality of the service, particularly if financial services companies were sponsors. It may be feasible, and less objectionable, to link sponsorship to specific events and activities such as training and development seminars and workshops. However, this does not remove the need for long-term core funding if business introduction services are to be viable. The only realistic source of this funding is the public sector – either direct from central government or else via an intermediary organisation such as a TEC or, in the future, Business Links.

Appropriate size of client base

A major issue concerns the appropriate size of a business introduction service.

How large does a business introduction service need to be in order to be effective? There is an argument for small networks on the grounds that local flavour is attractive to investors and businesses alike and personalised matching may bring a higher conversion rate. However, this approach is likely to be untenable because many investors are likely to have narrow or idiosyncratic investment preferences, have illiquid funds, or be 'just looking' or otherwise inactive. Under such circumstances, investment opportunities will need to be circulated among a large number of investors, and investors will need to see a large and varied range of investment opportunities for successful matches to occur. These considerations underpin the argument for seeking to build up a large client base of both investors and businesses. Indeed, it has been suggested that business introduction services must aim to generate eight to ten new proposals per month to meet the reasonable expectations of their investors.

Exchanging investment opportunities between introduction services could improve the chances of achieving matches. However, this seems unlikely to occur in the absence of common and transparent quality control systems. It is clear that those demonstration projects that already have a rigorous process of filtering and supporting businesses in order to maintain a high quality control will be reluctant to accept investment opportunities from other business introduction services which have fewer or lower quality control standards, or where the application of quality controls is inconsistent.

Matching mechanisms

At present the small numbers of businesses and investors recruited by each of the services has meant that the greatest reliance has been placed on personalised matching processes. Where the operators know the investors and businesses personally, this approach has proved to be quite effective. However, personalised approaches to matching are expensive in terms of staff time and will become less feasible as the number of clients increases beyond a client base of about 50 investors.

Investors' forums, at which entrepreneurs make presentations to a group of investors, are widely regarded as both an effective matching mechanism and also a means of marketing the service and generating credibility. TEChINVEST is the only project which has run an investor forum to date. Its experience has been very favourable: investors have been positive in their reactions and most of the companies that made presentations subsequently received offers of funding. A key factor in running successful investors' forums is that the businesses making presentations should be carefully selected and coached in order to avoid the danger that investors will be turned off by poor presentations.

However, one problem with investors' forums is that by no means every investor registered with a business introduction service will be able to attend such events. Attendance is likely to be biased towards local investors rather than those located in other parts of the country and to investors living close to the venue rather than those located in more distant parts of the operating area of the service. Some thought should therefore be given to the potential of alternative technologies – such as videos and tele-conferencing – which overcome the friction of distance in order to enable investment opportunities to be presented to a larger number of investors than would normally attend an investors' forum.

Role of the TECs

TECs are particularly appropriate organisations to operate a business introduction service, and arguably more advantageous than alternative local economic development organisations, which are not as well resourced as TECs. Business introduction services benefit from the pro-active marketing that TECs undertake. Specifically, TECs are looking to assist growth-oriented and growth-potential businesses, precisely the segment of the small firm population at which business introduction services are oriented.

There are also benefits from integrating the business introduction service alongside other TEC activities. This enables businesses which approach the service to be made aware of and, in appropriate circumstances, be offered other TEC services. Businesses which are inappropriate for the business introduction service are therefore not sent away empty-handed. Similarly, businesses which approach the TEC in connection with any of its other services can also be offered the business introduction service if it is appropriate. However, some TECs could probably do more to link their business introduction services more formally into their growth and innovation programmes. From a TEC perspective, business introduction services are also an important part of the overall TEC 'product', not least by emphasising that they are not simply a last refuge for companies in difficulties, but are also able to assist growth-potential businesses.

Business introduction services that operate at arm's length from their sponsoring TEC are at a disadvantage in generally not having a range of additional services. However, this disadvantage is offset by the fact that the existing profile of such organisations may enable them to attract businesses that would not otherwise contact the TEC. The clear implication is therefore for better cross-referral between TECs and their subcontract organisations.

The major disadvantage of the TEC connection is that it ties the business introduction service to a specific geographical area. Most TECs are simply too small to operate a viable service. As noted earlier, investors need a flow of investment opportunities to keep them interested in the service. The ability of a business introduction service to generate a sufficient flow of quality investment opportunities is likely to be a function of the size of geographical operating area, although the same does not apply to attracting investors, as all of the projects accept investors from anywhere. The implication is therefore that small groups of neighbouring TECs should collaborate in the running of business introduction services.

A further reason for advocating collaboration between neighbouring TECs is to avoid the danger that the market for investors will be fragmented if too many TECs – encouraged by the success of the demonstration projects – decide to set up their own business introduction services. Collaboration will also minimise the 'boundary effect' problems that arise if too many small business introduction services are established. However, the creation of a larger geographically viable operating area for a business introduction service should not be at the expense of losing the local identity of the service. This risk can be minimised by ensuring that the service has a local presence in each of the constituent parts of its operating area.

Conclusions

Reaching definitive conclusions on the outcome of the five informal investment demonstration projects is clearly premature in view of the short period of time in which they have been operational and the different levels of progress that, for a variety of reasons, each has made. Nevertheless, even at this early stage there are clear signs that the initiative is proving to be a worthwhile and beneficial experiment with positive outcomes in a number of areas:

- Additionality: it is most unlikely that any of the five business introduction services would have been created in the absence of the DTI's pump-priming funds. Moreover, the Department of Trade and Industry's financial contribution has been more than matched by cash and in-kind contributions from the sponsoring TECs, partner organisations, sponsors and fees.
- Activity, in terms of investor and business registrations, the amount of finance that has been mobilised and made more accessible for small businesses, introductions and deals made.
- Spin-off benefits, notably in terms of the number of businesses that have received advice, counselling and signposting to other support services from the staff of the business introduction service.
- Wider awareness of informal venture capital issues, among investors, businesses and professional and support networks, which is, in part, associated with increased media coverage of informal venture capital in general and the demonstration projects in particular.
- Interest among other TECs in establishing business introduction services. The five demonstration projects are playing an important role in disseminating information on best practice based on their experience.

Nevertheless, the full potential of the projects is still some way from being achieved, and they will require on-going funding in order to achieve this potential. Experience elsewhere, which the demonstration projects seem likely to confirm, indicates that there is a close association between the financial resources of the business introduction service and its success in terms of introductions and investments. Indeed, the two attributes are mutually reinforcing (Figure 14.1). A well-resourced service can devote a significant amount of expenditure to marketing. This enables the development of a large client base of investors and businesses, which increases the probability of successful matches and, ultimately, investments. This in turn adds to the reputation of the service, which feeds back to the further enlargement of the client base. A large client base also increases the amount of registration fee income that is generated and produces significant economies of scale. Fee income also increases as investments are made from the levying of success fees (where applied). Well-resourced business introduction services are also able to hire professional staff to implement quality control measures which filter out poor-quality investment opportunities and provide assistance to those businesses which are accepted. The effect of this is both to increase the probability of matches (and hence investments) and to enhance the reputation of the service among investors and entrepreneurs, helping to attract new clients and retain existing ones. Thus, the fundamental issue which needs to be resolved is how the projects are to be resourced after the DTI's pump-priming ends, in order to ensure that this virtuous circle is maintained and enhanced.

While the TECs and their partners demonstrate a high level of commitment to the projects and a willingness to make further financial and in-kind contributions, there must be some concern whether these sources alone are able to make good the financial shortfall which will arise with the ending of the DTI's

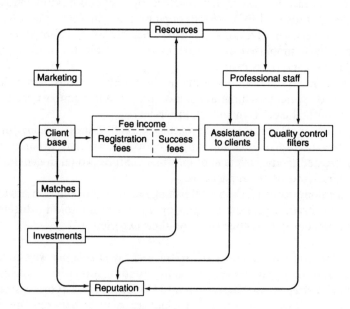

Figure 14.1 The link between resources, reputation and success.

pump-priming funding. There is also considerable doubt about whether alternative sources of income generation such as corporate sponsorship can provide a solid funding base for a business introduction service. Indeed, the only realistic source of long-term core funding for business introduction services is the public sector. The DTI made it clear at the outset that its funding was for developmental purposes only; it does not see the on-going funding of the projects as its responsibility. However, if the operation of a business introduction service were to be regarded as a core activity of the TECs and hence written into their contracts with the Secretary of State for Employment – and the experience of the demonstration projects to date provides a convincing argument that they should – this would enable them to receive funding as part of the overall TEC budget, with specific funding earmarked for this purpose.

Implications for practice

- Interest and enquiries drop off quickly following launch – marketing effort must therefore be on-going.
- Launch events attract considerable interest among potential investors; however, converting this interest into signed-up investors is a major challenge.
- Local/regional business introduction services can mobilise significant amounts of hitherto invisible risk finance.
- Business introduction services attract both active and virgin angels.
- Local/regional business introduction services attract both local and non-local investors.
- Investment opportunities must be of a high quality to attract and retain investors.
- A large client base of investors and investment opportunities is essential for successful matches to occur.
- Investors' forums are an effective matching mechanism: however, because not all investors are able to attend, they should be used in conjunction with other mechanisms. The use of alternative technologies such as tele-conferencing, CD-ROM and videos should also be considered.
- TEC areas are too small to operate a business introduction service successfully; moreover, there are dangers of fragmentation if too many TECs set up their own business introduction services. The implication is that TECs should consider collaborating.
- Charging success fees raises both image problems and practical difficulties.
- Evaluation of business introduction services should consider the wider benefits to businesses: advice and counselling; the hands-on involvement of investors; feedback from investors who decided not to invest; and the leverage effect on other sources of finance.

Note

This chapter is based on material from the *Interim Review of Five Informal Demonstration Projects* (Small Firms Policy Branch, Department of Trade and Industry, February 1993).

We are grateful to the Small Firms Policy Branch and the Controller of HMSO for permission to publish the chapter. The views expressed are those of the authors and do not necessarily represent those of the Department of Trade and Industry, Her Majesty's Stationery Office or any other government department.

References

Advisory Council on Science and Technology (ACOST) (1990) *The Enterprise Challenge: Overcoming barriers to growth in small firms*, London: HMSO.

Batchelor, C. (1990) 'Angels form the majority in the US', *Financial Times*, 2 October, p. 18.

Batchelor, C. (1991a) 'Angels give a helping hand to small firms', *Financial Times*, 1 October, p. 17.

Batchelor, C. (1991b) 'Flights of pin-striped angels', *Financial Times: Venture Capital Survey*, 6 November, p. II.

Durr, B. (1991) 'Angels rush in where bankers fear to tread', *Financial Times*, 23 July, p. 9.

Forum of Private Business (1992) *Small Businesses and Their Banks*, Forum of Private Business Report, December.

Harrison, R. T. and C. M. Mason (1992) 'The roles of investors in entrepreneurial companies: a comparison of informal investors and venture capitalists', Venture Finance Research Project, Working Paper No. 5, Southampton: Urban Policy Research Unit, University of Southampton.

Mason, C. M. and R. T. Harrison (1990) 'Informal risk capital: a review and research agenda', Venture Finance Research Project, Working Paper No. 1, Southampton: Urban Policy Research Unit, University of Southampton.

Mason, C. M. and R. T. Harrison (1992) 'The supply of equity finance in the UK: a strategy for closing the equity gap', *Entrepreneurship and Regional Development*, **4**, pp. 357–80.

Mason, C. M. and R. T. Harrison (1993) 'Informal risk capital: a review of US and UK Evidence', in R. Atkins, E. Chell and C. Mason (eds.), *New Directions in Small Business Research*, Aldershot: Avebury, pp. 155–76.

Mason, C. M., R. T. Harrison and J. Chaloner (1991) 'Informal risk capital in the United Kingdom: a study of investor characteristics, investment preferences and decision-making', Venture Finance Research Project, Working Paper No. 2, Southampton: Urban Policy Research Unit, University of Southampton.

Murray, G. (1990) *Change and Maturity in the UK Venture Capital Industry 1990–95*, Coventry: Warwick Business School.

Vyakarnam, S. and R. Jacobs (1991) 'How bank managers construe high technology entrepreneurs', paper presented at the National Small Firms Policy and Research Conference, Lancashire Enterprises Ltd/Manchester Business School.

Woodcock, C. (1991) 'Angels are waiting in the wings', *Guardian*, 18 November, p. 17.

CHAPTER 15

Informal venture capital in Sweden

Hans Landström and Christer Olofsson

Background: the risk capital gap in Sweden

Over the last 20 years the problem faced by the small business sector in gaining access to capital for development has been an important policy issue in Sweden. Most importantly, the problem has been seen to be undercapitalization in terms of too little equity, not permitting the firms to take the risks associated with expected business development. In particular, the need for initiatives to increase the availability of equity capital has been based on the perceived needs of the young, innovative businesses seen as important to industrial development in Sweden.

The problem has been a twofold one: on the one hand, the tax system of Sweden over a long period has made it difficult for owner-entrepreneurs to increase the equity by reinvestment of after-tax income from the firm; on the other hand, the lack of wealth accumulation in Sweden at large has not produced the wealthy individuals needed for the provision of external, informal equity capital. Furthermore, for a long time, there was also a lack of formal venture capital funds oriented towards the provision of equity to small businesses on a minority (temporary) basis.

The problem faced by the small firm sector has also arisen from the cautious attitude towards the small firms on the part of the banks, accentuating the difficulty in finding external financing. The equity gap and the loan capital gap facing the small firms have made them a recurring theme of political debate in Sweden.

The introduction of formal venture capital

In the first part of the 1980s the situation changed through the introduction of formal venture capital on a large scale (Olofsson and Wahlbin, 1985). From 1982 to 1985 about 20 new venture capital funds were created with the stated purpose to fill the need for finance of growth-oriented companies and with a special interest among many of them for new, technology-based firms. Over this period many expectations were formed of the role of the venture capital industry. It was supposed to provide not only capital but also professional management support, not least to young innovative companies.

At about the same time, in 1982, an over-the-counter market was created in Sweden in order to provide one of the exit mechanisms needed for an effective venture capital market.

The early experiences from the operations of the venture capital firms led to a shake-out in the industry in 1985–6, leaving only a few actors which have a more cautious attitude towards new, technology-based firms (Fredriksen *et al.*, 1990). This again led to a perceived shortage of risk capital for ventures in need of external financing.

The situation during the late 1980s was to a great extent characterised by the deregulation of the banking sector. This meant, for example, that the competition among banks became more intensive, thereby leading to loan capital being substituted for equity capital. However, the finance gap for young, innovative companies remained a real constraint. This was intensified towards the end of the 1980s as the banking sector met with heavy financial problems, again leaving the SME sector with fewer opportunities to get the finance for business investment and development.

The continued problem of access to finance facing small and newly formed companies, especially those with a new technology base, in the early 1990s led to the proposal for new, regionally operating venture capital companies with the stated purpose of showing a special interest in young companies with a technology angle. After the change of government and with the banking crisis as a backdrop, the new venture capital companies became part of a new structure with a total of eight actors with a joint capital of 6,800m SEK, largely privatized at the beginning of 1993. This new structure is expected to solve many of the financial problems being faced by small and medium-sized businesses, not least by changing the scale of the equity gap. In so doing, it continues a Swedish tradition of seeking formal, institutional solutions.

It should be mentioned that there are a few other actors in Sweden providing high-risk capital close to equity. In early phases of technical development where seed capital is required, the National Swedish Board for Technical and Industrial Development is providing loan capital with conditional repayment clauses. The Swedish Industry Development Fund, created in 1978, has also lent money to start-up and development projects in industry, and has shared risks in technical and/or market risk situations with firms of all sizes.

From the beginning of 1993, the Swedish Industry Development Fund has been remodelled into a new fund with the specific task of supporting the SME sector. It is also responsible for the Swedish version of a German system for 'equity support', *Eigenkapitalhilfe*: this is supposed to provide capital that is formally loan capital but on terms that make it part of the risk-bearing capital.

There are also regional development funds with the role of giving professional advice and finance to the SMEs. The role of the regional development funds is, however, under scrutiny at the moment, and in recent years part of their financial resources has been transferred to the newly created risk capital companies.

The role of informal venture capital

Against this background, to what extent is informal venture capital of interest in a Swedish context? As already stated above, the Swedish tax system by and large has not been supportive of the accumulation of wealth by private individuals, one of the exceptions being gains from gambling. Over recent years, however, there has been a growing interest in the potential role of private investors in the business development process and, as we will show below, there is an informal venture capital market in Sweden even if we do not know very much about it so far. The hypothesis must be, however, that it is not abundant, for the reasons given above.

The new (political) interest in the role of informal venture capital has been stimulated in part by research on the role of informal venture capital in the USA, and to some extent in the UK, from which we have learned that informal venture capital has a very important role in the business development process, and in particular for the seed and start-up stages of development (Harrison and Mason, 1991). The estimates by Wetzel (1986) and Gaston (1989) that informal venture capitalists finance 20 times as many ventures and invest twice as much as the formal venture capital sector give some perspective on the potential.

The present Swedish liberal–conservative coalition government that came into power in the autumn of 1991 also represents a change in perspective as to the importance of private capital in business development. Representatives of the new government have advocated measures to make private investments in small firms more profitable, and to make it less costly for owner-managers to increase the equity in on-going businesses. The first of these should be realised by allowing tax deductions from income, and the second by exemption from wealth tax for all capital remaining within the firm.

A few changes in taxation rules have so far been implemented, one of which lessens the tax burden on capital put to work in a firm: the part of private wealth that is put in as equity by the owner-manager is exempted from wealth tax. And company taxes have been reduced from 50 per cent to 30 per cent.

Other propositions have come from the industry organisations and from public bodies. The Swedish Federation of Industry, for example, has suggested a system for mainly science-based or technology-based firms where individuals could deduct capital put in special investment funds from their salaries, and the National Swedish Board for Technical and Industrial Development has suggested a closer look at the Business Expansion Scheme in the UK.

However, most ideas for change focusing on tax incentives will probably have to wait until the present economic crisis has been handled. In the meantime, the government points to the new capital being put into the risk capital market through venture capital companies and other measures to make it easier for the small business sector to lessen the capital gap.

Apart from the solutions created by the political system, there have been some local/regional attempts to investigate the interest from private investors, or business angels, in becoming part of a match-making system to put technology ventures in contact with professional business angels. One of those attempts, Chalmers Venture Capital Network, is discussed later in this chapter.

It thus seems that there are forces working in Sweden to make the private investor more important and informal venture capital a better-used resource. However, in the short run it also seems that Sweden will continue being dominated by formal institutions, to a large extent created by the political system.

We will now turn to two studies of the informal venture capital market in Sweden as it seems to be operating. The studies have been conducted in order to shed some light on the characteristics of informal investors in Sweden, one with focus on business angels' interest in match-making services (Olofsson, 1992), the other a broader study of the characteristics of informal investors in Sweden (Landström, 1992). These provide a context within which to consider the role and potential of informal venture capital business introduction services in expanding the Swedish informal venture capital market.

Business angels in Östergötland

A county in Sweden (Östergötland) was picked in order to investigate the need for and the interest in match-making services among potential business angels, entrepreneurs and other actors, such as banks and chartered accountants. Some 16 business angels were identified and asked to describe not only their investment interests, but also their opinions about being part of a match-making arrangement with the University of Linköping, and what kind of services they would be interested in. The same kind of questions were put to the other actors. The survey was undertaken in the period from autumn 1991 to spring 1992.

The business angels, mostly being experienced businessmen (and one woman) who had developed at least one business, were still active but had during the last three-year period sold a business from which they had raised investment capital. Apart from their role as chief executive, the respondents had most of their expertise in marketing, economic control and finance. Several of them were now acting as consultants and professional board members. As in other studies in the United States, Canada and the United Kingdom, their reasons for acting as informal investors were economic, even if they also felt that it was a more personally rewarding way to get value added than other, more passive investments.

The investments being made and preferred were in a field known to the investor. With some exceptions they wanted to feel knowledgeable about the business field in which they were going to invest, thereby minimising the product and market risks of the investment. They also wanted to take an active role in companies in which they invested, mostly as board members, but also to some extent as professional advisers in their fields of expertise, ranging from strategic aspects of marketing to financial expertise.

Most of the investors expressed an interest in becoming part of a match-making system, provided they could keep a low profile and that the services were provided by an organisation with a neutral and professional standing. They did not want a matchmaker to have too many vested interests in the deals being made. At the same time they did not seem to feel too much in need of active assistance to find business opportunities. Through different channels, banks, chartered accountants, business associates, they did get proposals from time to time. Most of the angels interviewed also had a rather high visibility in their local communities, having official roles in the local business organisations. In this reliance on personal and business networks for investment opportunity identification, Swedish business angels are similar to those researched elsewhere.

Other actors in the study expressed very much the same attitudes to a match-making service in the region. They all agreed on the importance of having a neutral body running such a service and maintained that the confidentiality of the parties involved must be guaranteed. It should be added that among the entrepreneurs the main interest was to get finance with as few demands as possible from an outside investor. This was stated in a way that led to the conclusion that, in many projects, differences of view in the pricing of equity and in the conditions attached to that equity would become a major problem in finding a basis for agreement.

The conclusion from the study was that there was a need for and an interest in some match-making services being offered, but that a region was much too small to carry such services. Accordingly, it was decided not to proceed with a locally based match-making service: instead the business angels contacted during the study were informed about the match-making services to be provided by Chalmers Venture Capital Network.

Informal investors in Sweden

In the second study, 124 informal investors were identified through contacts with banks, regional developments funds, formal venture capitalists, and individuals who were known to make informal investments. A questionnaire was sent out to the informal investors during the autumn of 1992. Of the 124 informal investors who received the questionnaire, 52 investors sent back questionnaires that were completely filled in. Thus, the response rate is 42 per cent. The questionnaire consisted of 45 questions organized within the general headings of investor characteristics, investment activity, investment portfolios, investment decision-making processes, and investor involvement in the firms in which they invest.

Demographic characteristics

Informal investors in Sweden are mainly in middle age, with 38 per cent in the 45–54 age range, and 35 per cent in the 55–64 age range. Relatively few are under 45 years old (15 per cent). The results may reflect the effects of high tax rates in Sweden on the rate of capital and wealth accumulation.

One main characteristic of the informal investors in Sweden is that they are very experienced entrepreneurs. Nearly all of them have started at least one business, and 45 per cent of them have started more than five businesses. The impression of very experienced entrepreneurs is strengthened by the fact that 69 per cent of investors in the study stated that they had been business managers in small or medium-sized firms. Furthermore, 69 per cent classified their present occupation as business owner or business manager.

In terms of income and wealth, the informal investors are well off. In total, 60 per cent of the informal investors had an annual income of 500,000 SEK or more, and 27 per cent had incomes in excess of 1m SEK. Likewise, in terms of wealth (excluding their principal residence), the informal investors in Sweden are rather rich: 85 per cent are millionaires in SEK, and 57 per cent have a net worth of 5m SEK or more.

The study gives no information on how the informal investors obtained their wealth, but in view of the high proportion of informal investors who have started businesses, and in many cases sold one or more businesses, it can be assumed that the majority of informal investors are financially self-made through a cash-in of their businesses.

Investment activity

The motives to make informal investments show a rather comprehensive picture of the informal investors: they had a combination of financial motives (e.g. for high capital appreciation, and for current or future income), entrepreneurial motives (e.g. to play a role in the entrepreneurial process, and to have influence over an investment), and other non-financial motives (e.g. for the fun of investing).

The study also gives a picture of a relatively professional investor. The typical informal investor in Sweden came across ten investment opportunities during the previous three years (on an aggregate level, the sample of informal investors reported that they had come across 733 investment opportunities). Out of ten investment opportunities they had seriously considered five opportunities, and actually made three investments (i.e. an average of about one investment a year), equivalent to 30 per cent of all investment opportunities received, which is a very high acceptance rate (see Table 15.1).

Table 15.1 Investment activities among Swedish informal investors

Number of investment opportunities received	10
Number of investment opportunities seriously considered	5
Number of investments made	3
Median amount invested per investor	1.2m SEK
Equity–debt ratio	3:1
Median amount available for investment	1.5m SEK

It is also interesting to note that informal investors in Sweden are relatively frequent investors. The average portfolio was 3.8 investments, and 35 per cent of the investors had made four or more investments during the previous three years. Three out of four reported that they would have invested more in the last three years if they had come across a greater number of suitable investment opportunities.

The average amount invested per investor in the past three years was 1.2m SEK. The investments were made not only as equity, but also as loans. For every three Swedish crowns invested in equity, another crown was lent. The average informal investor had an additional 1.5m SEK available for investment.

The study shows that informal investors in Sweden are careful in their evaluation of new investment opportunities. They spend a relatively long time on a serious evaluation. Nearly 50 per cent of the informal investors spend 20 hours or more in evaluating an investment opportunity. At the other extreme, only 10 per cent devote less than 20 hours. The vast majority of informal investors (53 per cent) rely on their own evaluation, reflecting their entrepreneurial/ business background.

Portfolio characteristics

Informal investors in Sweden seem to invest in all industry sectors, but there seems to be a particular concentration on the industrial product sector, and the finance/insurance/real estate sector. The industrial product sector accounts for 31 per cent of the investments made, and the finance/insurance/real estate sector for 32 per cent.

In a similar way, informal investors make investments in all stages of business development. However, the most popular investments are in established firms, which account for 30 per cent of all investments. Pre-start-ups are the least popular investment, accounting for 7 per cent, and start-up firms account for 20 per cent of investments.

There is also a rather wide distribution of amounts invested. In 51 per cent of the investments, the informal investor has invested less than 500,000 SEK. At the same time, 28 per cent of investments exceeded 1m SEK.

As mentioned earlier, in Sweden there seems to exist a finance gap for small firms in terms of a shortage of equity capital to young and technology-based firms.

However, the results of the study indicate that informal investors seem to play only a partial role in filling this finance gap. The informal investors in Sweden seem to invest in more established firms, and in more low-tech industry sectors.

Relationship between informal investors and portfolio firms

The majority of informal investors in Sweden are minority shareholders in the firms in which they invest. Only 15 per cent of the deals involve a majority share, and in a further 20 per cent the informal investor took 50 per cent of the equity. However, the survey gives no information regarding the total share of the syndicate investments.

The informal investors' relationship to their portfolio firms can be characterised as active but not involved in daily operations. According to the informal investors, they devote an average of 12 hours per month to each portfolio firm. The frequency of contacts is rather high. The informal investor typically indicated contacts every day (35 per cent) or every week (43 per cent).

The most common way of organising the relationship between the informal investor and the portfolio firm is by the investor working actively on the board, and providing consulting help when needed (see Table 15.2). Involvement in daily operations is seldom found.

Besides the investment of capital, different kinds of expertise are transferred. These are primarily in the form of 'management expertise', 'wider range of contacts' and 'acting as a sounding board' (see Table 15.3). On the other hand, functional expertise is not transferred to the same extent.

The informal investors' exit horizon and way of exit reflect one of the main problems for informal investors in Sweden: namely, the lack of adequate exit routes. Some 41 per cent of informal investors expect to liquidate their investments in three to five years. But many respondents indicated that they did not know the holding period, or did not regard it as important. Furthermore, informal investors in Sweden seldom sell their shares to company insiders (e.g. sell back to the entrepreneur or inside investors). The most frequently cited exit route was a sale to, or merger with, another company (22 per cent of informal

Table 15.2 Investors' relationship to investments

Participation in the firm's operation	Number	%
None, other than reviewing periodic reports and attending stockholders' meetings	17	7
Being a member of the board of directors	128	56
Providing consulting help as needed	65	28
Working part time with the firm	12	5
Working full time with the firm	4	2
Other	3	1

Table 15.3 Investors' contributions of resources (% of respondents answering)

Provision of resources	Limited extent	Medium extent	Large extent
Acting as a sounding board	2	12	86
Wider range of contacts	7	18	75
Management expertise	7	14	79
Professionalising of the firm	9	18	73
Formulating a business idea and strategic planning	11	16	73
Expertise in negotiating and contract making	14	14	72
Obtaining capital from outside sources	14	14	72
Facilitating contacts with third parties	9	30	61
Financial expertise	16	16	68
Marketing expertise	16	16	68
Administrative expertise	34	27	39
Financial security	36	24	40
Co-operation with other portfolio firms	48	17	35
Technological expertise	57	20	23
Production expertise	72	21	7

investors). However, there seems to be a high level of uncertainty about exit routes among Swedish informal investors. To some extent this is reflected in the fact that many respondents cited that they had not decided their likely exit route.

Finally, informal investors in Sweden are dissatisfied with the performance of their informal investments. Only one-quarter of the informal investors surveyed felt that their investments were performing moderately or substantially above expectations. This can be explained by the fact that Sweden has experienced a deteriorating economic climate and a rising number of company liquidations in recent years.

Business introduction services

Mason and Harrison (1990, 1992) have emphasised that the informal venture capital market in the UK is inefficient in terms of the communication channels between entrepreneurs seeking risk capital and investors seeking investment opportunities. Against this background, different kinds of business introduction service have been established, such as the Local Investment Network Company (LINC) and *Venture Capital Report* (VCR).

What about the situation in Sweden? Surprisingly, this study shows that very few informal investors in Sweden regarded the search for new investment opportunities as a problem. One possible explanation is that there are other problems that seem to have a more restraining influence on the operation than the search for new investment opportunities. Another explanation may be that the informal investor's entrepreneurial experience makes him or her known in the business network.

The study shows that business associates, friends and entrepreneurs are important sources of information about new investment opportunities. Informal investors in Sweden are also very active in making personal searches for new investment opportunities. Through these information channels, informal investors receive investment opportunities in proportion to their chance to evaluate them seriously.

On the question of which type of information about a new investment opportunity the informal investor would prefer to receive first, nearly half of the respondents indicated that 'a personal meeting with the entrepreneur' would be preferred, and one-quarter indicated that they would prefer a short description on two pages about the firm or project. Some informal investors point out that it could be an advantage to get information about new investment opportunities through a third party because of the possibility of making a more independent evaluation. The conclusion is, as in the study in Östergötland county discussed earlier in this chapter, that there seems to be some interest, from the informal investor's point of view, in a databased match-making service. One such match-making service has been established in Sweden to facilitate the communication between informal investors and entrepreneurs in need of money.

The Chalmers Venture Capital Network (CVCN) was established during the spring of 1992 and is administrated by the Chalmers Innovation Centre at Chalmers University of Technology. One main reason for the establishment of CVCN was to facilitate the financing of the spin-off companies which have been growing up around Chalmers University of Technology. CVCN has been modelled after and in co-operation with the Venture Capital Network (VCN) at the University of New Hampshire in the United States (see Chapter 3).

Both the investors and entrepreneurs complete a short registration questionnaire in which the investors provide information on the investment opportunities that they consider to be of greatest interest, and the entrepreneurs provide information on the characteristics of their business and a business plan summary. The computerised matching process is then made in a two-stage process.

In the first stage, the investor receives information about the business seeking finance but the identity of the business is withheld. If the investor wants to go deeper into the project, the second stage means that direct contacts are arranged between the investor and the entrepreneur. The role of CVCN ends at this point. CVCN makes no evaluations of the investment opportunities and gives no recommendations to investors.

The lowest amount of money CVCN is interested to mediate is 50,000 SEK. The investor pays 1,200 SEK for one year's subscription to information about projects that meet the investor's 'profile', while the projects or entrepreneurs pay 500 SEK for six months' registration. One year after the introduction of CVCN, there are very few members of the match-making service, and only very occasional deals have been made so far.

The experiences from the first year of operations can be summarised as follows:

- CVCN is not very well known among informal investors. Furthermore, CVCN operates mainly on a regional basis around Gothenburg. This means that the database is insufficient in terms of the number of investors and entrepreneurs registered, and the possibility of getting a positive match is therefore rather small.
- There is no evaluation service involved in the CVCN, which means that bad proposals ('lemons') are not excluded from the spectrum of investment opportunities: this is likely to lead to investor dissatisfaction over time and will reduce the impact of the network.

Policy for the future

To most participants in the Swedish debate, a system built on informal risk capital seems preferable and more efficient than a total dependence on the formal institutions so well established in Sweden. Many of the changes planned in Sweden are part of such thinking. It is problematic, though, to change a well-established structure and attitudes and behaviour in the short run.

Not only does the present system have consequences for the supply of risk capital, it also reinforces existing attitudes among the small business owners. The overall impression from different studies on small business owner-managers in Sweden is that their interest in taking partners, including equity partners, is rather low. They ordinarily want to develop their own business without any interference from 'outsiders'. Thus, the size of the group with growth ambitions beyond what they feel is possible to manage on their own is somewhat limited.

Business owners with a limited interest in partner solutions seem to favour loan capital when they need external financing. Even if this is more expensive, they feel that it leaves the power and control where it should be. This also means that some of the solutions introduced by the politicians to reduce the capital gap felt by the small business sector seem to be aimed at a rather small group of firms, leaving the bulk of businesses to find other solutions.

It should be noted that not only might there be a lack of enthusiasm for a new capital partner on the part of the small businessperson looking for finance, but also the interest from the capital supplier would be on the same level given the lack of growth interest from the bulk of small businesses. The problem on the demand side itself, therefore, can be considered partly responsible for the problems on the supply side.

What should be done in order to promote the development of well-functioning capital markets, and what different strategies are needed for different types of business looking for capital for business development?

In the short as well as the long run, (tax) incentives making it attractive for the external investor to invest in growth businesses in need of risk capital are of the greatest importance. Investment must take place for capital reasons as well as for management reasons; the contributions of active business angels should be promoted, especially in early stages of development. As part of such an orientation, the Swedish government has announced its intention to introduce a scheme based on the UK Business Expansion Scheme.

Even if success from new channels for communication between investors and potential investees, such as business introduction services, is in no way guaranteed, the potential value of such channels makes them of interest. One possibility would be to cover the initial costs of the operations of match-making services and also to make them part of an on-going evaluation. A second and related initiative would be to extend the operation of the service to cover a wider area, and thereby develop a critical mass of investors and businesses on which to build a successful matching operation.

For the ordinary business with need for finance but without the need for an external capital partner, changes making it less costly to generate new capital in the business could be implemented. But it might also be important to improve the visibility of role models, providing examples of the kind of advantages that could come from partnerships with external investors. In Sweden, as elsewhere, development of the informal venture capital market is only one element in the provision of a full range of options for the financing of new and small business ventures.

Implications for practice

- A business introduction service should be run by an organisation with a neutral and professional standing without vested interests.
- Differences between entrepreneurs and investors in the pricing of equity and in the conditions attached to that equity are major difficulties.
- It is important to have a large enough operating area for a service to ensure that a viable number of investor and entrepreneur registrations are obtained.
- Personal meetings between the entrepreneur and investor are the preferred first stage among investors.
- Evaluation and screening of investment opportunities is necessary to prevent investor dissatisfaction.

References

Fredriksen, Ö., M. Klofsten, H. Landström, C. Olofsson and C. Wahlbin (1990) 'Entrepreneur–venture capitalist relations: the entrepreneur's view', in N. C.

Churchill, W. D. Bygrave, J. A. Hornaday, D. F. Muzyka and W. E. Wetzel Jr (eds.), *Frontiers of Entrepreneurship Research, 1990,* Wellesley, MA: Babson College, pp. 251–65.

Gaston, R. J. (1989) *Finding Private Venture Capital for Your Firm: A complete guide,* New York: Wiley.

Harrison, R. T. and C. M. Mason (1991) 'Informal venture capital in the UK and the USA: a comparison of investor characteristics, investment preferences and decision-making', in N. C. Churchill, W. D. Bygrave, J. A. Hornaday, D. F. Muzyka and W. E. Wetzel Jr (eds.), *Frontiers of Entrepreneurship 1991,* Wellesley, MA: Babson College, pp. 469–91.

Landström, H. (1992) *Informellt riskkapital i Sverige,* Ekonomicentrum, Högskolan i Halmstad.

Mason, C. M. and R. T. Harrison (1990) 'Informal risk capital: a review and research agenda', Venture Finance Research Project, Working Paper No. 1, Southampton: Urban Policy Research Unit, University of Southampton.

Mason, C. M. and R. T. Harrison (1992) 'The supply of equity finance in the UK: a strategy for closing the equity gap', *Entrepreneurship and Regional Development,* **4,** pp. 357–80.

Olofsson, C. (1992) *Änglar–finns dom? En studie i Östergötland av förutsättningarna för en informall riskkapitalmarknad,* Linköping: IMIT.

Olofsson, C. and C. Wahlbin (1985) 'The Swedish venture capital market – an early appraisal', in N. C. Churchill, W. D. Bygrave, J. A. Hornaday, D. F. Muzyka and W. E. Wetzel Jr (eds.), *Frontiers of Entrepreneurship Research 1985,* Wellesley, MA: pp. 191–210.

Wetzel, W. E. Jr (1986) 'Entreprenuers, angels, and economic renaissance', in R. D. Hisrich (ed.), *Entrepreneurship, Intrapreneurship and Venture Capital,* Lexington, MA: Lexington Books, pp. 119–39.

CHAPTER 16

Equity finance and the role of a business introduction service in Denmark

Peter Koppel

Introduction

The lack of equity capital for entrepreneurs and small and medium-sized enterprises (SMEs) seems to be a major barrier to industrial development in western Europe – Denmark is no exception. In discussing equity financing, the key potential institutional players are the banks, institutional investors and venture capital firms. In the 1990s, however, experience shows that the actors in the equity-financing field are not the banks, they are not the pension funds, and they are not the venture capital firms. They all tried it in the early 1980s with substantial losses. Thus, to meet the entrepreneur's demands for equity financing, the only available sources are the entrepreneur's assets, private individuals' fortunes and the possibility of investment by private companies. Although it is still possible for growth-potential SMEs to raise venture capital, severe conditions normally have to be met. Additionally, for development activities in general, the Danish government has several support schemes to provide financial help at the start of the development process. From a planning point of view, these schemes represent the provision of quasi-equity capital.

This chapter summarises the Danish financial environment for entrepreneurs and SMEs. There will be no separation of the two target groups, as they both experience the same possibilities and restraints. Following this introduction, the chapter concentrates on summarising the work carried out at the Danish Technological Institute concerning the matching of entrepreneurs and private wealthy individuals.

The financial environment in Denmark

Entrepreneurs

In 1992 the Danish Statistical Bureau published data on the number of entrepreneurs and the characteristics of their businesses for the period 1985–90. Based on these statistics, a number of key conclusions can be drawn:

- The number of new companies formed annually has dropped over the period, but it is now back at a level of 15,000 per year.
- 50 per cent of the new companies are still in business after five years.
- Only 9–10 per cent of the entrepreneurs establish companies in the production sector.
- The technology level is estimated to be low for 85 per cent of the new companies in the production sector.

As in other economies, therefore, the majority of new companies being established are unlikely to desire or require access to development capital in the form of external equity investment. However, the characteristics of these companies, as generally low-technology, service sector businesses with a relatively high likely failure rate, do condition the attitudes of the financial institutions to the financing of small and new businesses.

Banks

The main role of the banks in the Danish economy lies in the provision of liquidity for the financing of debtors, stocks and other day-to-day working capital. In some very special cases, the bank will make an equity investment in a private company, but these occasions are few and play no significant role in closing the equity gap for the entrepreneur. Nevertheless, the first place an entrepreneur will seek equity capital is in the banks, as part of the overall search for start-up capital. However, the banks are not comfortable when face to face with an entrepreneur. The reason for this is that the bank sees the entrepreneur as a risk, with unprocessed or relatively undeveloped ideas, and often few assets against which to secure a loan. Accordingly, the banks find it difficult to provide the service demanded by the entrepreneur in terms of either equity finance (where the risks are not compensated for by an expected return to the bank) or extended loan finance.

Venture capital firms

For those new and small businesses which do have capital requirements outside the range normally considered by the banks, the venture capital industry provides a possible source of funds. The Danish venture industry emerged at the beginning of the 1980s as a result of a general discussion about the special need for financial services to new companies. Many of the venture capital firms were spin-offs from banks, pension funds and labour movement activities – in contrast to the American way, where the venture capital firms often had their origin in universities and independent private firms. The number of venture capital firms decreased during the second half of the 1980s and today numbers nine. During the 1980s several of these firms were subject to mergers, and a great number of them have simply left the industry due to economic failure. One result of this restructuring of the Danish venture capital industry is that entrepreneurs have little chance of finding equity with the surviving venture capital firms, as almost all of them invest only in established companies to reduce their risk exposure as far as possible.

For the last five years, however, one firm – Danish Development Finance Ltd – has been operating as a venture capital fund oriented towards new and innovative companies. The firm has been established as a joint venture between the government and private pension funds, insurance companies and others. Originally, it was meant to be a purely state-owned company, but for ideological reasons it became an ordinary limited company based on funds from the national bank and from the private sector. Danish Development Finance Ltd has made around 40 investments in new high-tech companies, and represents a key exception to the investment preferences and practices of the rest of the Danish venture capital industry.

Government

In the absence of a full meeting of the needs of entrepreneurs for development capital from the financial institutions, the government has chosen to support the entrepreneurs through both the Ministry of Labour and the Ministry of Industry. The support from the Ministry of Industry is allocated to the end-users through the National Agency of Industry and Trade.

The Ministry of Labour is in charge of the Enterprise Allowance Scheme, which provides support to any applicant who fulfils two conditions: intending entrepreneurs have to be unemployed; and they have to be a member of an unemployment insurance fund for at least 12 months. The allowance is around 750 ecu per month, equal to half the amount of the unemployment benefit otherwise receivable.

The National Agency of Industry and Trade offers support to entrepreneurs mainly through three schemes. First, it provides grants for working up high-potential product ideas: an entrepreneur or an SME will have the opportunity to seek financial support for development programmes. This support is in the form of loans or grants up to 50 per cent of the expenses. This scheme is run by the agency itself. Second, under the Scholarship Scheme, high-tech entrepreneurs are offered government scholarships in order for them to test, over a period of one or two years, the feasibility of their business ideas. The annual scholarship is worth around 37,500 ecu before tax. The scheme is administered by the Danish Innovation Centre, a department of the Danish Technological Institute (DTI). Third, through the Business Introduction Service, prospective business developers are provided with consultancy services relating to technical appraisal and to the preparation of business plans for their activities. The scheme is administered by DTI/Danish Innovation Centre.

Additionally, at the end of 1992 the government decided on a new scheme, to be launched in mid-1993, very similar to the loan guarantee scheme in the UK, but with a much smaller support ratio, specifically to address the shortfall in financing available from institutional sources.

Business Introduction Service

The Business Innovation Centre (BIC) runs the Business Introduction Service for entrepreneurs. BIC is located in both Aarhus and Copenhagen and employs ten consultants and several subcontractors. During each of the last five years, BIC has been approached by 500–600 entrepreneurs: that is, people who are thinking of becoming entrepreneurs, or people who have recently started a firm. Prior to the entrepreneur approaching BIC, he or she will often have been visiting the bank, an accountant or another SME consultant. Based on experience to date, the entrepreneur's main problem is lack of capital. Furthermore, the entrepreneur will often be experiencing problems with the formulation of a business plan.

The overall purpose behind the Business Introduction Service is to create an incentive for entrepreneurs and small companies to make use of experienced external counsellors, either from the DIC or from other professional business advisers, as many young companies tend to invest an excessive amount of time and resources in overcoming standard start-up barriers. The support comes in two steps: a 100 per cent funded evaluation and action planning phase, and a subsequent documentation and implementation phase in which the entrepreneur contributes 25 per cent of the costs. Once the outline of the new company has been established, BIC will accompany the entrepreneur to various sources of financing, such as banks, to make sure that no misunderstandings will prevent an agreement for a loan.

Finance for entrepreneurs

These government and government-supported initiatives have gone some way to supporting the development of new business ventures in Denmark. However, it remains the case that throughout the last ten years it has become more and more difficult to obtain loans from banks and similar sources due both to a general recession and to insufficient security for the loans provided.

Given the defensive attitude of the banks and the venture capital firms, therefore, it has been necessary to look in other directions for financing entrepreneurs and SMEs with development potential. One key element in this was a growing recognition of the role played by the informal market for investment capital: for example, the fortunes of private companies and private individuals. In particular, it was decided that, in the absence of a clearly defined or easily identified market for informal venture capital, an initiative should be taken to place the Business Innovation Centre in the position of a marketplace for informal investments, in which entrepreneurs could meet with 'business angels' on a proper basis. However, one major obstacle had to be overcome for this process to start, and this was BIC's relatively modest knowledge of business angels and their significance and potential in Denmark. Accordingly, the first stage of this new initiative was to identify a sample population of actual or potential business angels.

Stimulating the informal investment market

The pilot study

In June 1991 the Business Introduction Service, with support from the Danish Agency of Industry and Trade, undertook a pilot study into the provision of private capital for new companies and projects considered to have outstandingly high potential. The objective of the study (Action 1) was to define and examine the obstacles which exist to the expansion of private capital in small companies and to the application of such capital for feasible innovative projects. This objective was to be achieved through the arrangement of information meetings for potential investors, conclusions being drawn on the basis of the resulting dialogues and meeting reports.

A further objective of the study (Action 2) was to match two projects to private investors; in one case, an attempt would also be made to assign an experienced senior executive. For this phase a brief description of the cycle of events was to be formulated, with the focus on successful matching criteria based on the established model. As a subsidiary objective, the study would provide the basis for an evaluation of the most appropriate approach to the stimulation of communication between the capital investors and the project entrepreneurs. This objective was realised in the form of a questionnaire survey conducted among the investors who had responded to the marketing.

In the following discussion, the specialist terms 'Investor', 'Project' and 'Entrepreneur' have been assigned the following simplified definitions:

Investor: A person able to provide a project with financial support in the form of equity capital; a business angel.

Project: An innovative and/or otherwise high-potential production project.

Entrepreneur: The person masterminding the project, either as the originator or as the initiator of a planned development process culminating in commercial realisation.

To distinguish the present concept from ordinary stock exchange investment, the constellation of investor and project (enterprise) in this study is termed 'informal investment'. In the remainder of this chapter, the various activities included in the pilot study are reviewed, and a subsequent assessment of the results of the individual activities is summarised.

Contact establishment activities (Action 1)

The activities undertaken in Action 1 took the form of three information meetings arranged on a regional basis. This regional approach was the result of initial contact experiences with private investors, where it was discovered that group meetings of potential informal investors would be considerably easier to organise in western Denmark than in Copenhagen in eastern Denmark. Accordingly, although informal investors may be found on a widespread basis (Mason *et al.*, 1991), their willingness to participate in business introduction services and other similar informal investment mechanisms may vary by location. This has implications for the success of any initiative organised on a multi-regional basis (see Chapters 7 and 14).

In the Danish pilot study, a variety of methods were tested to persuade potential investors to come forward. In north-western Denmark an advertisement was placed in the newspapers *Jyllandsposten* and *Aalborg Stiftstidende* on Sunday, 20 October 1991, and repeated in the latter medium on the subsequent Thursday (Figure 16.1). This advertisement produced the results shown in Table 16.1: of

INVESTORS

SEEKING INNOVATIVE PROJECTS FOR ACTIVE PARTICIPATION

are invited to attend a meeting at Hotel Scheelsminde, Aalborg, on October 29 starting 15.30 and lasting approx. 2 hours.

The purpose of the meeting is to exchange views and experiences on private capital investment in new enterprises and projects.

As an increasingly important role is forecast for private investors in the financing of development-based projects, there is a need for a frank discussion of the economic perspectives and risk profile associated with innovative projects.

We shall also be presenting an example of a project which might be suitable for private financing.

DTI will also provide information on international initiatives and results in this field, and on the current situation in the informal investment market.

DTI will therefore be pleased to meet persons with a specific interest in investing in innovative projects, whether within a private or corporate framework.

Interested parties may enrol for admission by contacting:

DTI Innovation, Tasastrup
Tel. no. 42 99 66 11

Figure 16.1 Initial informal investor recruitment.

Table 16.1 Response to advertising in north-western Denmark

Replies to advertisement	38
Investors from other regions	4
Non-relevant replies	12
Potential participants at meeting	22
Of which banks and others in non-target group	4
Notified cancellations	3
Investors present at meeting	15

38 replies to the advertisement, 22 potential participants at the meeting were identified, of which 15 actually were present.

In south-western/central Denmark, participants for the information meeting were to be enrolled through a series of approaches to contacts in this area, which in practice meant the Danish Technical Information Centres (TICs). The results of this initiative were at the same time both very disappointing and extremely positive. The disappointment concerned the number of specific participants obtained by the TICs. Despite ample time and considerable publicity, only one participant was found through TIC channels. The positive aspect was that, due to the existence of excellent contact between one specific TIC and local solicitors and accountants, sufficient interest was aroused to provide the basis for an additional information meeting.

In order to do everything possible to ensure that an information meeting could be held as planned, the same advertisement (Figure 16.1) was repeated in *Jyllandposten* on 18 November, but with Hotel Munkebjerg, Vejle as the venue. The results are shown in Table 16.2. A total of 20 replies were received, including contacts made by TIC: to the 11 identified participants were added three more potential investors from earlier marketing, giving a total of 14 investors present at the meeting. An additional information meeting was held at a minor Danish bank, Varde Bank in Esbjerg. The bank provided accommodation and refreshments for the meeting and made efforts to attract participants. Of the ten persons who attended, three were potential investors and the rest consultants. Two investors cancelled prior to the meeting.

Table 16.2 Response to advertising in south-western/central Denmark

Replies to advertisement, including TIC	20
Investors from other regions	4
Non-relevant replies	5
Potential participants at meeting	11
Investors from earlier marketing	3
Notified cancellations	0
Investors present at meeting	14

Table 16.3 Response to advertising in eastern Denmark

Replies to advertisement	10
Investors from other regions	0
Non-relevant replies	4
Potential interviewees	6
Investors from earlier marketing	5
Notified cancellations	1
Investors present at meeting	10

In eastern Denmark a similar advertisement to that already described was placed in the commercial daily, *Børsen*, the only difference being that interested parties were requested to contact BIC directly with a view to a personal meeting. The results of advertising in eastern Denmark are shown in Table 16.3: after allowing for investors identified from previous marketing, ten responses to the advertising were converted into ten investors present at the meeting.

Form and content of information meetings

The group meetings were organised on the following plan:

- Introduction, including the presentation of DTI/Innovation and other parties involved.
- Background and purpose of the project 'Provision of Private Capital for High-Potential Projects'.
- Summary of international experience from similar investment projects.
- Brief presentation of a project in which private venture capital might be – or already had been – invested.
- Introduction to risk and evaluation of projects with a view to feasibility, earnings capacity and organisation.
- Discussion and expression of opinions.
- Conclusion – how to proceed?

The meetings were generally successful and the atmosphere positive. The participants praised the initiative, recognising it as an attempt to overcome the paradox whereby large numbers of investors are unable to find sufficient projects, while large numbers of entrepreneurs are unable to find sufficient investors. The North Jutland Science Park (NOVI) assisted at all the meetings held.

The reports of the meetings revealed the following common features:

- A Danish investor is a 35–55-year old male who has either sold or is currently running a small, successful production enterprise.
- Most of the participants had never previously invested capital in a small firm or high-potential production project.

- Most of these inexperienced investors were uncertain as to how to establish project contact. Should they simply place an advertisement in the newspaper?
- The prevailing attitude among the experienced investors was that projects presented to investors who expressed their interest openly were purely fanciful in nature, and did not represent viable or realistic investment opportunities.
- The experienced investors said that conventional advisers did not support investors searching for high-potential projects.
- The role of DTI/Danish Innovation Centre as a project mediator between universities/research environments and potential investors aroused particular interest.
- Both the experienced and inexperienced investors considered a certain degree of restraint and discretion appropriate with regard to matters relating to their personal capital.
- The role of DTI/Danish Innovation Centre as an intermediary or facilitator was considered by the participants to be an important factor in their decision to participate in informal investment.
- Tax issues were touched on only superficially at the meetings and personal interviews.

The advertisement in eastern Denmark produced only one person with previous experience of informal investment, but attitudes to the problems involved otherwise corresponded to the reports from the group meetings. The origins of the potential investors are summarised in Table 16.4.

Table 16.4 Origins of potential investors

Investors from north-western Denmark	15
Investors from south-western/central Denmark	14
Investors from eastern Denmark	10
Investors from additional meeting	5
Investors known in advance	15
Total investors	59

Now that positive contact has been established with a relatively large number of potential investors the pilot study was ready to proceed to the next stage.

Questionnaire survey

In January 1992 a questionnaire survey was conducted based on the contacts listed in Table 16.4. The purpose of this survey was to spotlight more distinctive characteristics of investors and investors' behaviour, and to determine the most suitable means of communication. The questionnaire was partly based on international surveys, principally the work of Mason *et al.* (1991), which thereby facilitated international comparisons.

A total of 59 forms were distributed and 30 replies received. Four respondents reported that their interest had waned in the interim due to changed job circumstances and related reasons. The geographical distribution of the remaining 26 replies between the three regions is shown in Table 16.5.

Table 16.5 Origin and distribution of questionnaire respondents

North-western Denmark	4
South-western/central Denmark	11
Eastern Denmark	11
Total	26

The questionnaire was subdivided into nine sections, each covering aspects pertaining to investors. The key results from this survey will be presented below.

Section A

Section A of the questionnaire was concerned with the respondents' experience of informal investment in small enterprises. Thirteen respondents reported having undertaken such investment in the past three years, and the remainder were potential investors: examination of the replies showed that a further two of these respondents had previous investment experience, albeit dating back more than three years. The investment group thus comprises 15 experienced investors and 11 potential investors.

Section B

This section dealt with the scale of potential and previous investment. The questions in this section were formulated to facilitate comparison with the UK survey. In Table 16.6 the 'Maximum' column contains the maximum value stated by the respondent. The 'Mean' column contains either an arithmetic mean or a

Table 16.6 Number and scale of previous and potential investments

	Maximum	Mean	Mean X
How many investment offers have you been presented with in the past three years?	40	9	7
How many of these offers have you seriously considered?	9	3	3
How many investments have you made?	6	2	1
What is your total investment – in ecu '000 – in equity capital?	2,500	342	188
What is your total investment – in ecu '000 – in loan capital?	5,625	908	233
What is your potential future investment in ecu '000?	938	178	148

weighted mean of the actual replies. The values in the 'Mean X' column were calculated after the exclusion of extreme values. It will be seen from the table that investors had been presented with an average of nine potential investments in the past three years. However, there was also a considerable variation and the mean figure after elimination of extreme values was therefore seven.

There are indications to suggest that somewhere between one-half and one-third of investment possibilities receive serious consideration. It should be noted that the level of previous investment is relatively high, both before and after elimination of extremes, in both investment categories. Compared to expectations and to a UK study, Danish investors appear to make relatively large but fewer investments. (This is similar to recent evidence from Sweden – see Chapter 15.) The smallest equity capital investment recorded in the questionnaire was 3,750 ecu.

Potential future investment averaged around 150,000 ecu, corresponding to a total investment of more than 3.75 million ecu by this small group alone. One investor wished to maintain his future investment at 6,250 ecu, which is below the level generally reported and which investors considered realistic.

Section C

This section dealt with communication channels previously used by investors to establish contact with investment projects. The study showed that information was typically obtained through friends and business contacts, and by active personal effort. A less frequent basis for informal investment was information obtained from conventional advisers: banks, solicitors, accountants, company brokers and newspaper articles. Communication with venture companies, stockbrokers, investment companies and other entrepreneurs rarely leads to consideration of a project with a view to investment. The UK study also found that – as in Denmark – contact with investment projects is typically established through friends and business acquaintances, and not least through considerable personal effort.

Section D

This section was concerned with time – the amount of time spent on studying and analysing an investment project once contact is established. The respondents varied widely in their replies, but for the majority the figure – and the weighted average – exceeded 30 hours, which was the maximum recordable figure on the form. This represents a time involvement which, relative to the size of the investments being considered, cannot be contemplated on cost grounds, by the venture capital fund or other institutional providers. In this respect, informal investors make a significant potential contribution to overcoming some of the factors which give rise to the equity gap experienced by small firms.

Section E

In this section, the investors themselves were asked to indicate which type of behaviour most closely resembled their own. The four categories listed were based on those used in the UK survey (Mason *et al.*, 1991) and there is some degree of overlap between the individual type descriptions.

A   I search actively for investment opportunities, take investment decisions independently, and pass on good tips to other investors.

B   I accept tips from others, but carry out my own analysis and decide on that basis whether to invest. Other investors do not influence me.

C   I ask questions and study documentation on specific investments, but for me professional recommendation is important.

D   I only invest in partnership with others, and only if the group is unanimous on investment. I do not allow myself to be driven by others.

The majority of respondents identified positively with the descriptions in D and C above, while there was wide variation in the extent of identification with statements A and D. This means that the 'average' investor acts independently after conducting his or her own studies and conferring with sector specialists. By the same token it may cautiously be concluded that the investors do not act independently and do not seek a more anonymous role in a large group of investors, but instead assign major importance to their own judgement and efforts. The *a priori* hypothesis, which is that many Danish investors would prefer to invest in syndicates, cannot therefore be verified at this juncture. International studies show roughly the same pattern, although with a more pronounced emphasis on the B-type than in the Danish case.

Section F

Section F was concerned with investors' views on the physical form and content of information provided, particularly with regard to *initial* information on investment opportunities (Table 16.7).

A relatively large number of respondents consider a business plan – which may run to many pages – to be useful as initial information. This is surprising, given the time necessary to read and assess such plans, which suggests that the question may be too weakly formulated. A 50-word description such as that provided by the Local Investment Network Company (see Chapter 7) in the UK is considered irrelevant by the majority of these investors. Respondents voted a two-page description necessary for the purpose of initial information, and fewer described it as irrelevant than in the case of the full business plan; indeed, based on these responses, it may be concluded that the two-page project description is the preferred alternative with investors either strongly committed to or strongly averse to receiving the full business plan.

Responses to the idea of a short video and the establishment of a project

Table 16.7 Investor preferences concerning the form and content of initial information

	Irrelevant	Necessary	Good idea
Complete business plan	9	5	12
50-word description	16	6	4
Two-page description	3	17	6
Five-minute video	11	1	14
Personal meeting with the entrepreneur	5	13	8
Meeting at which several entrepreneurs present their ideas	4	5	17
On-line access to database containing investment projects	13	0	13

database were highly polarised, which makes a valid conclusion difficult. Closer examination reveals that around one quarter of respondents considered both ideas good.

Some respondents consider a meeting with the entrepreneur at an early juncture to be a necessary measure, which underlines the importance of the interpersonal aspect in capital funding and project mediation. Further, the idea of a meeting at which a number of entrepreneurs would present ('sell') their ideas quite clearly aroused enthusiasm: only four respondents considered this option uninteresting. Arrangements of this type have been conducted twice by DTI/ Innovation in partnership with Aarhus City Council. The arrangements in question consisted of between three and ten projects in varying stages of development, each project being 'sold' independently to 20 to 30 investors or investors' representatives. The events were very positively received by all parties and will be repeated.

Section G

Investors often find themselves in the situation of having to base an investment decision on documentation produced by the entrepreneur personally. This means that the investor is compelled to verify personally the accuracy of various technical and market details to evaluate the merits of a given project. This phase is extremely time consuming, as well as fraught with difficulty when a technical specialist has to be consulted. The role of screening the project merits is one which might very well be played by, for example, BIC at DTI/Danish Innovation Centre. There is no doubt about whether investors prefer to receive information in 'raw' or screened form. The vast majority prefer the latter option.

Section H

If this screening process is to be performed in a systematic manner, several alternatives may be envisaged. The preferences of the respondents are shown in Table 16.8. In this case the respondents were clearly polarised into two distinct

Table 16.8 Investor preferences concerning type of project mediator

Private commercial company	1
Private fee-based organisation	3
Organisation financed by public and/or private contribution	10
Centralised mediation body	2
Irrelevant	10

groups – those who considered the matter irrelevant, and those who supported the establishment of a body funded by a mixture of public and private contributions. From the viewpoint of most investors, the precise nature of this organisation is thus of little interest.

Section I

In this section the respondents were asked to state whether they would be willing to pay such an institution to provide information, irrespective of whether or not a contact obtained in this way resulted in investment (Table 16.9). The replies showed that many respondents would be willing to pay for information which had been screened. However, this probably also reflects the respondents' awareness that such a system would reduce the number of projects reaching the investment stage to a minimum, which at the same time would increase the likelihood of investment. In other words, they would be paying for the work of producing a successful match. However, the largest category excluded any possibility of payment for screening work. They held the view that this task should be regarded as an integral part of project realisation, and should therefore be funded by the project as a financing charge.

Table 16.9 Investor preferences concerning payment for project information

Would only pay for unscreened information	2
Would only pay for screened information	9
Willing to pay to a subscription scheme	4
Unwilling to pay for information	11

Specific matching attempts (Action 2)

Action 2 was intended to implement various specific activities designed to match certain projects to some of the potential investment candidates with whom a contact had been established as part of the first stage of the process.

In the preliminary plan for Action 2, a method which was to form the basis for this process had been devised. This method was structured as set out in Figure 16.2. The relevant activities proceeded largely as described, with the result that as yet none of the attempts have produced the desired objective.

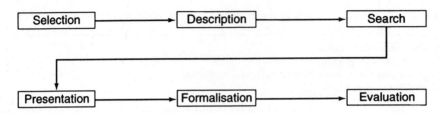

Figure 16.2 Structure of the matching process.

Reasons for lack of success

As an extension of the method described here, which was to form the basis for the specific capital investment procedures, the following general four-phase method in which the project mediator is active has been developed:

1. *Analysis phase.* Formulation of descriptive documentation and adoption of financial action plan.
2. *Project mediation phase.* An investor is located and introduced to the entrepreneur. Discussion is limited to the business plan, business concept and personal aspects.
3. *Agreement phase.* Providing agreement is reached on the areas mentioned in phase 2, the legal and tax aspects will be discussed and settled in phase 3.
4. *Implementation phase.* Assuming successful resolution of the aspects in phase 3, the agreements formulated will be implemented in phase 4.

The project mediator's role is central both in phase 1 and at the start of phase 2, after which the initiative is temporarily transferred to the parties involved. If a problem arises, however, the mediator is at hand with the necessary resources to resolve the difficulty.

During phase 3, expert advisers, such as accountants and solicitors, are called in to assist. During phase 4, the mediator may again assume a central role in response to the requests or needs of the parties. For the purpose of this model, and as an element in the efforts to ascertain the cause of the negative results obtained, the hypothetical reasons may be classified thus:

Phase 1   Project documentation
          Entrepreneur's personality
          Role of mediator
Phase 2   Quality of search
          Role of mediator
          Communication problems
Phase 3   Technical obstacles
Phase 4   Changed preconditions

As none of the specific mediation attempts has progressed beyond phases 1 and 2, the reasons for lack of success must be sought within these phases. In phase 1, BIC has in several cases performed the task of documentation establishment by preparing a summary of a business plan formulated by the entrepreneur, using information supplied by him, subject to the screening of central data such as market figures. In discussions with investors, it has been shown to be extremely important that the documentation presented should be produced in accordance with the BIC model and printed on DTI/DIC paper. This is not because the presence of the DTI name guarantees elimination of all risks, but because it demonstrates to investors that systematic processing has taken place. This means that maintaining the integrity of the documentation establishment process is crucially important.

The entrepreneur's personality is to some extent a dark horse in a project mediation process of the type described. There is no guarantee that a given entrepreneur will be able to relinquish project sovereignty etc. to a total stranger. Furthermore, the negotiating flexibility of the entrepreneur is a second crucial factor. Theoretically, the same should also be true of investors, but the distinct impression has been gained that investors are in possession of this flexibility. The role of the project mediator to predict the development and growth of potential problems is a further crucial factor. The cases mentioned included situations which could have been handled differently. By way of example, there were vague reports of problems affecting both parties which were never followed up and resolved, and factors such as physical distance to project location suddenly assumed immense importance.

From a closer examination of the search process which took place, it is immediately apparent that the geographical element is of major significance. At the time when the specific search for investors was being conducted, there were around 30 candidates on file, all concentrated either in north-western Denmark or in Copenhagen. As two of the projects were far removed from these areas, a barrier to successful capital investment was in these cases created at the outset.

The next criterion for linking an investor to a project is that the prospective investor must have a fundamental interest in the business area concerned. Formulating a project description which is both broad enough to meet the wishes of the potential investor, and yet narrow enough to reflect the true nature of a given project, is clearly a matter of very fine judgement. It is considered that the failure to resolve this dilemma has been responsible for two of the abortive matching attempts.

The problem may be summarised thus: the more detailed the description of an investor's interest, the smaller the likelihood of finding a matching project, or the greater the number of projects required to obtain a successful match. It is therefore believed that one of the main reasons for the lack of success in the match-making process was the fact that the portfolio of potential investors was not large enough for the four projects selected.

Conclusion

The implementation of this pilot study showed that, given the necessary resources, it is possible to find individuals interested in undertaking informal investment. Furthermore, the study showed that, among the investors contacted, considerable resources are available for potential investment provided suitable projects can be obtained and documented.

Considerable uncertainty exists on the part of investors as to how to establish contact with high-potential projects, and there would appear to be a need for an organisation to mediate such contacts. However, investors were not interested in bearing the full cost of the work performed by such an organisation. BIC's role as mediator and adviser in the projects mentioned was rated as extremely important by the investors.

The tax aspect would appear to be of only minor significance, as the subject was rarely raised by the participants at the information meetings, despite the fact that the opportunity for such discussion was provided. However, there is probably a link between the number of potential investors and the fiscal treatment of profits and losses in companies.

The specific task of matching investors and entrepreneurs has not in the first instance yielded the desired result. The work involved is lengthy and heavily dependent on the personal characteristics of both parties. Formulating business plans, screening central data and coaching entrepreneurs are resource-intensive activities.

The distance between the investor's home and the project location is of considerable importance to the majority of investors.

Although this cannot be substantiated from the questionnaire survey, several investors remarked that they attached importance to participating in syndicates with other investors.

Successful matching demands positive declarations from a relatively large number of investors in order to expose the relevant project to a wide range of investment alternatives. This means that the pool of potential investors must be increased in number, and that the projects registered must be more evenly distributed nationwide.

Perspectives

From the results of this pilot study and from other activities performed by BIC, it seems realistic to believe that it will be possible to remedy the paradox referred to earlier. The remedy lies in increased interaction between the participating players.

The central issue in the debate on the lack of venture capital stems from the common misapprehension that it is the task of the banks to provide investment capital, and that this is something which they used to do in the past. Generally speaking, they did not; but now to demand 50 per cent capital adequacy (the proportion of total financing requirement represented by equity capital) at least opens the way for discussion as to how the banks can assume a role in the financing of more complicated production projects. It is therefore necessary to help promote a more flexible attitude among the banks towards venture capital. To do this, contacts must be established with the banks so that the 'package' – the entrepreneur with project, the private investor with equity capital, and the bank – becomes the key element in solving the relevant financing problems.

In order to make use of the experience and add more potential investors to the pool, there is a need for continued publicity to be given to the problem of financing and its solution at events like those arranged in Aalborg and Vejle.

Implications for practice

- The importance of the 'local' aspect as a spur to investment is vital, and should be translated into the establishment of local investment associations, networks or syndicates.
- There exists a need to publicise and support the formation of local investor groups in which a small number of local investors (say, between two and four) act as a financing company for local projects.
- In order to increase the incentive to potential investors to help finance high-potential projects, the introduction of the following types of measure should be considered:
  - a facility for long-term financing of the entrepreneur's personal capital investment (*Eigenkapitalhilfe*);
  - the creation of marketplaces (investors' forums) in which investors can meet entrepreneurs;
  - a facility for tax relief on investment in limited liability companies (along the lines of the Business Expansion Scheme, now the Enterprise Investment Scheme, in the UK);
  - the monitoring of foreign experiences and implementation of best practice.

References

Mason, C. M., R. T. Harrison and J. Chaloner (1991) 'Informal risk capital in the UK: a study of investor characteristics, investment preferences and decision-making', Venture Finance Research Project, Southampton: Urban Policy Research Unit, University of Southampton, Working Paper No. 2.

Index